LEARNING IN MOROCCO

PUBLIC CULTURES OF THE MIDDLE EAST AND NORTH AFRICA
Paul A. Silverstein, Susan Slyomovics, and Ted Swedenburg, editors

LEARNING

in

MOROCCO

LANGUAGE POLITICS

and

THE ABANDONED

EDUCATIONAL DREAM

CHARIS BOUTIERI

INDIANA UNIVERSITY PRESS

Bloomington & Indianapolis

This book is a publication of

Indiana University Press
Office of Scholarly Publishing
Herman B Wells Library 350
1320 East 10th Street
Bloomington, Indiana 47405 USA

iupress.indiana.edu

Manufactured in the United States of
America

Cataloging information is available from
the Library of Congress.

ISBN 978-0-253-02051-2 (cloth)
ISBN 978-0-253-02049-9 (paperback)
ISBN 978-0-253-02050-5 (ebook)

1 2 3 4 5   21 20 19 18 17 16

To my father Thanos and sister Elina

CONTENTS

ACKNOWLEDGMENTS

THIS BOOK effectively began more than a decade ago. It has escorted me across three continents and compelled me as much as helped me negotiate a number of life experiences and relationships—academic and not—including my relationship to the discipline of anthropology, my research, and myself.

I carried my curiosity, passion, and ruminations around language, identity, and education in North Africa to a formidable department of anthropology at Princeton. Abdellah Hammoudi and Lawrence Rosen gave me the truly special opportunity to relate to them as academic mentors and fieldworkers; my memories of both of them in the field form the foundation on which I built my conviction in the intellectual and ethical commitment that anthropology can show toward a subject and toward people. Carol Greenhouse and Carolyn Rouse were more generous with their time than I ever felt I deserved and continue to astound me with their friendship and willingness to engage with my work many years later. The entire anthropology department with its staff, its students, and its most hospitable administrative team—whose iconic figure for generations of students has been the always encouraging Carol Zanca—made graduate school a space of true personal growth. Dimitris Gondicas kindly included me in the active intellectual life of the Princeton Hellenic Institute and has been a steady and comforting presence throughout my scholarly trajectory. Colleagues from a range of graduate cohorts remain to this day trusted interlocutors and scholarly companions; they include Erica Weiss,

Suad Abdul Khabeer, Sami Hermez, Jamie Sherman, Claire Nicholas, Nikos Michailidis, Joel Rozen, and Dimitris Antoniou. Michelle Coghlan and Briallen Hopper are dear friends, excellent scholars, and keen proofreaders of the earliest versions of this book.

Fieldwork in Morocco over the years has been a powerful experience that pushed me to connect the dots between my own background and my intellectual pursuits, as well as to shape and consolidate my understanding of education and of the era in which we live. It would not have been so powerful without the mentoring of the late and deeply missed Mustafa Benyakhlef, an admirable thinker and dedicated educator whose voice echoes in my head every time I reflect on the scenes that feature in this book. I am immensely appreciative of the assistance of Mohamed Zernine, Mohammed Amelal, and Rachida Guelzim who facilitated the untangling of numerous practical and conceptual knots that came my way. The directors of the Regional Academies for Secondary Education of Gharb-Chrarda-Beni Hsenn and Rabat-Salé-Zemmour-Zaer were both kind and daring in granting me official permission to conduct research inside public high schools. My warm thanks go to the school principals, inspectors, and teachers who hosted me everyday in their schools, their meetings, and their classrooms, as well as their homes; their tolerance and support have been invaluable to this research project. For the Moroccan high school students I had the pleasure and honor to meet, I have no words to express my gratitude. Their curiosity and warmth turned this project into a life-changing process. One unflinching objective of this book has been my resolve to communicate as vividly as possible the creativity with which these students handle the localized versions of the global dramas of socialization in the neoliberal era.

The Laamouri family made me part of their lives by sharing their time, joys, and dilemmas with me to the extent that they became relatives undistinguishable from my original ones. Barbara Götsch, Kristin Pfeifer, Claire Nicholas, Cortney Hughes Rinker, and Elizabeth Buckner—fellow researchers of Morocco—offered me the rare opportunity to share my fondness of the country with fellow researchers while in the field. Omama Masrour, Yassine Amelal, Halima Benjelloun, Leslie Coghlan and Amina Coghan, Nia Eustathiou and Makis Melissaratos, and Polina Chotzoglou became close friends, turning the field into a place where I not only worked but also lived and had fun.

Over the years, new intellectual companions emerged and exciting friendships materialized: Youssef el Kaidi and Youssef el Kaissy offered precious advice with incredible speed and precision and constitute sources of inspiration regarding the future of the teaching profession in Morocco. Martin Rose shared my interest in the systemic intricacies and experiential complexities of multilingualism in education and encouraged me to trust the urgency I felt in disseminating my work. Youssef Amine Elalamy, my favorite Moroccan novelist, was a catalyst for pushing this project forward at a difficult juncture when, over dinner, he divulged in his truly captivating way that he wrote his francophone novels by "hearing voices in his head" and his short stories in *dārija* by "feeling the rumblings of his gut." Marouane Laouina, Baudouin Dupret, and Catherine Miller from the Centre Jacques Berques in Rabat and Ibtissame Berrado from the British Council in Morocco gave me the chance to discuss, publish, and enhance with illustrations parts of this book. Most recently, Nabil Belkabir and Simo Alami injected my work with fresh energy through their neat critique of education in Morocco and their impressive activist work to reshape it.

I have shared my fieldwork experience and theoretical propositions with academic audiences of various disciplines at the Institute of Social Anthropology in Vienna, the Middle East Centre at St. Antony's at the University of Oxford, the Ethnography and History of Southwest Asia and North Africa Seminar Series at the Department of Anthropology at the London School of Economics, the Near and Middle East History Seminar at the School of Oriental and African Studies, the Middle East and Islamic Studies Department at New York University, the Center for International and Regional Studies at the Georgetown University School of Foreign Service, the Department of Anthropology and Sociology at George Mason University, and the Centre d'Etudes Maghrébines in Tunisia. Fellow panelists, discussants, and the audience at numerous meetings of the American Anthropological Association, the Middle Eastern Studies Association, and the British Society for Middle Eastern Studies asked pertinent questions that blocked and unblocked this project just enough to keep propelling it forward. I have benefited tremendously from all these interactions, though I insist that the opinions and errors in the pages that follow are mine alone.

A number of prominent scholars who have written on North Africa and/or on education whom I deeply admire gave parts of this manuscript their careful attention and constructive feedback: they include Shana Cohen, Linda Herrera, Rachel Newcomb, Aomar Boum, Paul Silverstein, Fida Adely, Michael Willis, , and Veronique Bénéï. I sincerely thank them for their encouragement. The brilliant Erica Weiss and Su'ad Abdul Khabeer suffered through innumerable versions of the entire manuscript that they nonetheless kept reading with meticulousness, imagination, and some much-needed humor. I can only hope to have returned some of the favor in the completion of their own monographs. Hania Sobhy, Roozbeh Shirazi, Zeena Zakharia, Rehenuma Asmi, Elizabeth Buckner, and Rebecca McLain Hodges—the new and impressive generation of researchers of public education in the region—work tirelessly to thoughtfully address our joint concerns over the predicament of public schools and to disseminate the insights of our specific inquiries on academia and beyond. They have enriched my perspective and inspired me to continue working for what truly feels our common cause. My colleagues at King's College London, especially Carool Kersten, Madawi al-Rasheed, Marat Shterin, and Martin Stokes, urged me to highlight the broader implications of my work for the study of contemporary Muslim societies. Students in all my classes pushed every inch of my thinking further and brought my formulations of public schooling, the neoliberal state, and youth experience in Morocco back home, thus tempting me into stimulating comparisons.

I am indebted to Susan Slyomovics, Paul Silverstein and Ted Swedenburg for accepting this book in the series that I most longed to see it placed and to Rebecca Tolen from Indiana University Press who encouraged me to recalibrate my work in ways that made it more consequential and more far-reaching than I had originally imagined.

Research for this book was financially supported by the Princeton Graduate School, the Princeton Institute for Transregional Studies, the Princeton Center for Migration and Development, the J. F. Coustopoulos Foundation, the A. G. Leventis Foundation, and two King's College London Arts and Humanities Grants. The writing of this book was logistically and emotionally supported by Elina Boutieri, Vasilis Larentzakis, Sophia Krigou, Fanis Sklinos, and Katerina Gemidopoulou in Athens; Elina Korkontzila, Menel Methni, and Souhir Zekri in Tunis; and Monica Michalopoulou, Brett Migdal, Emmanuela Bakola, and Saeed Zeydabadi Nejad in London. Members of my family and my—mercifully—patient friends across the globe tolerated my occasional feelings of anxiety and my frequent and long absences in a number of countries and an even greater number of libraries.

I can only but dedicate the end product to my father, Thanos Boutieris, a courageous parent, a role model, and the reason behind my insatiable appetite for learning new things.

WRITING ABOUT LANGUAGE:
TERMINOLOGY AND TRANSLITERATION

THE INTERROGATION of the politics of language and knowledge in contemporary Morocco required a number of terminological choices that are inescapably loaded and necessitate qualification. The nationalist language policy of Arabization, which is the scaffold of my investigation of Morocco's post-independence trajectory, hinged on the standardization and generalization of a modern Arabic language. However neither of these processes, standardization and generalization, nor the concept of "Modern Arabic" are transparent and straightforward. In fact, a more accurate description of Arabization ties in well with Sumathi Ramaswamy's evaluation of *tamilparru* (that is, Tamil language nationalism): "neither a wholly homogeneous nor an entirely consensual activity, because the principal entity at its center is itself not conceived in a singular manner" (1997, 78). In the same vein, I contend that the Arabic language that Moroccan public schools teach, despite being officially differentiated from Moroccan Arabic and endorsed as the heir of Classical Arabic, is a multifaceted entity. The affinity between Arabization and *tamilparru* signals that the linguistic and political processes this book delves into are not unique. Yet this book argues that the terminological indeterminacy around the Arabic language in Morocco lies at the center of a series of dilemmas around education, cultural identity, governance, and the economy that are products of a particular history, which in turn engenders specific experiences of living and learning in the current moment.

With the purpose of probing this indeterminacy, I decided to name the Arabic of educational Arabization "*fuṣḥā.*" On the rare occasions when I wish to underscore the political visions that informed the transformation of the language into the register of an indigenous modernity, I add the adjective "modern." In English, it is common to refer to this version of Arabic as "Modern Standard Arabic" or MSA. The problem is that in Morocco the distinction between MSA and Classical Arabic—the language of the Qur'an and of knowledge production since the classical Islamic period—is not commonly made. In fact, the term *fuṣḥā*, which means "eloquent," can refer to either register. Hence instead of relying on preexisting theoretical categories, my investigation of the meaning and function of language ideology on the ground critically engages with the classifications speakers make and the links they draw between language and society (on this point, see Armbrust 1996; Caton 2006).

The book shows that there is considerable fluidity as well as ambivalence in the way Moroccan school participants (students, teachers, parents) designate and use different versions of Arabic or Berber at school and beyond. Outside of class, students extend the inconclusiveness over Morocco's languages and innovate with it. This way, the public school becomes one of the many spaces where the broader dynamics of the neoliberal commodification of language, Arabo-Islamic nationalism, and minority activism play out. It is important to bear in mind, however, that the public school is the place where the complexities of Arabization and its competition occur most dramatically. After all, the public school was the main instrument of the policy of Arabization and, given the thriving multilingualism of everyday life in Morocco, one of the truly few institutions whose mandate was to promote *fuṣḥā.*

The linguistic behavior and attitude of my interlocutors suggested to me that the equally politicized term "mother tongue" is analytically impractical. My interlocutors designated Moroccan Arabic, which I call *dārija*, as the lingua franca of the country even if it was not their family's first language. *Dārija* has an intimate and intricate relationship to *fuṣḥā*, as well as to regional, gender, and generational divisions. *Dārija* equally indicates someone's social background: *dārija* can be *rasmiyya* (official, refined) or just *lughat al-shāriʿ* (street slang, vulgar). The book gestures at some of these complexities, but does not do justice to them. Terminologi-

cal negotiation is central to the status of the Berber languages and becomes integral to the activism of the multifaceted Moroccan Amazigh
movement. My labeling choices regarding this group of non-Arabic languages hinge on my decision to follow the labeling trend on the ground;
that is, in and around the urban arabophone high schools where I worked.
I am very conscious that this context is not representative of Berber experience everywhere in the country, but it does constitute a key setting
where labeling with all its ramifications takes place.

In the context of these urban public high schools, Moroccans of non-
Arab background largely identified as "Berber." Those who deployed the
term "Amazigh" simultaneously disclosed their activist stance for historical reasons that the book explores in some detail. I respect my interlocutors' choices by referring to them as "Berber" unless I discuss activism and
activists. Some students, teachers, and parents used the regional classifications Shleuḥ (speaker of *tashelḥit*), Riffi (speaker of *tarifit*), or Amazigh
(speaker of *tamazight*). As expected, these regional classifications sub-
sume further local difference. To make this book accessible to a non-
specialist audience, I usually avoid these regional classifications and group
the Berber languages under the umbrella term "Berber." However, I complicate this over-simplification on two occasions: I inform the reader that
this umbrella term can also appear as *amazighiyya*; for instance, in the
latest Moroccan Constitution (*al-dustūr* 2011). In chapter 5, I single out
the standardized version that the Royal Institute of Amazigh Culture
(IRCAM) has developed as *Tamazight* (with a capital T).

Terminological choices are inevitably unsatisfying because they are both
laden with the power struggles they index and are unable to fully capture
lived experience. The act of writing a book about language training and
use holds analogous challenges. In an effort to disentangle the ideological
premises that undergird language policy at school through the exploration
of certain arenas of pedagogy, I risk a certain misreading of the issues at
hand. For instance, by singling out the competition between Arabic and
French in some chapters, I temporarily circumscribe the linguistic richness of the school and misrepresent *dārija*, which is the language of classroom communication and schoolyard conversations, and Berber. Outside
the school curriculum, French is especially prominent among youth who
color their exchanges with French slang. They may greet each other by

saying, "*Salām, ça va ʿlīk?*" (Hi, how are you) or call a good-looking girl a *beaugossa* (a feminization of the French expression *un beau gosse*). I invite the reader to visualize that the plethora of experiences taking place in each chapter may well add up to one single day in these Moroccan students' lives.

ON TRANSLITERATION AND TRANSLATION

Fuṣḥā (Classical and Modern Arabic) transliteration broadly follows the IJMES system. I italicize and fully transliterate all Arabic words that appear in the text (*tarbiya islāmiyya, khuṭba*). To facilitate comprehension by readers who are unfamiliar with Arabic, I do not make any exceptions to this rule apart from proper names for people and places. I simplify those by shedding diacritics as well as the letters *ʿayn* and *hamza* (Allal al-Fassi, Fes). Proper names for people and places also appear in roman throughout the book. I have modified the IJMES system in the following three ways. First, I italicize but do not apply IJMES transliteration to Berber words as a reminder that these words are non-Arabic. Second, the names of Moroccan interlocutors, public figures, and intellectuals, as well as places, appear in the Latin alphabet as they would in the Moroccan context (Mohammed V, Khaïr-Eddine, Jemaa al-Fna, al-Qaraouine). This mode of transliteration is the product of a long history of francophone scholarship in North Africa (see Wagner 1993). For non-Moroccan Arab proper nouns, I respect IJMES recommendations (Muhammad Tawfiq al-Bakri, Yusuf al-Qaradawi). Third, I fully vocalize the titles of articles, official reports, essays, extracts of poetry, and quotations from the Qurʾan.

Because *dārija* (Moroccan Arabic) shares words, sounds, and syntax with *fuṣḥā*, I do not always mark it as distinctive. Whenever I want to emphasize that a pronunciation is more specific to *dārija*, I signal it with [dar.]. As with other not officially transcribed languages, *dārija* transcription has varied greatly. My transcription largely follows other anglophone works on Morocco, with one exception: in chapter 6, when discussing online communication, I use an entirely different codification in order to render what online writing techniques look like on the screen (hence instead of *kanḥamaq ʿlīh*, I give the transcription *kanʒamaʒ 3lih*).

Translations from *fuṣḥā*, *dārija*, and French into English are mine unless otherwise stated. For literary and scholarly works in Arabic or French that exist in English translation, I have privileged the translation—except for a few instances—for the benefit of readers who are unfamiliar with these two languages. For some key foreign texts, I provide references for both the original work and its translation in the bibliography.

LEARNING IN MOROCCO

1

Schools in Crisis

A s we walked toward a bookshop in Kenitra, a medium-sized city on the Atlantic coast, Lahiane, a high school student in his senior year, and I passed a gathering of several hundred unemployed demonstrators. This buzzing crowd made up of both sexes and a variety of ages, anger and boredom imprinted on their faces, had gathered outside the town's city hall to organize yet another rally demanding more jobs that were both secure and more highly paid (see Figure 1.1). Lahiane, his somber gaze fixed on the crowd, smiled bitterly and asked me, "What do you say? Shall I join them?" He had not yet graduated high school.

The pessimism Lahiane voiced has informed the actions of large numbers of unemployed school and university graduates, known by the term *diplomés chômeurs*. Approximately 27 percent of all educated young Moroccans are unemployed, and more work on an irregular basis or have insecure jobs (African Development Bank 2013, 12). For the last two decades, many of these graduates have spent their days frequenting the offices of labor unions syndicates and demonstrating outside government buildings. Seeking access to white-collar jobs in the new service sector that has superseded Morocco's mainly agricultural and small industrial economy, these lower-middle and middle class youth have seen their job prospects systematically dwindle. As a consequence, these youth move between advocating forcefully for a chance at social integration and economic prosperity based on the meritocratic evaluation of their educational skills and expressing deep cynicism about the material and ideological

FIGURE 1.1

Unemployed graduates demonstrating in downtown Rabat, July 2011.
Photograph by author.

value of these skills. It is hardly surprising then that both students and
graduates took to the streets during the tumultuous Arab Uprisings (2011–
2012). They protested not only the current set-up of political institutions
and their own economic marginalization but also that the failure of educational experiences to give them the possibility of pursuing a "decent
life." They staged sit-ins, confronted the security forces, and engaged in
highly symbolic acts of self-immolation across the kingdom.[1]

What went wrong? The post-independence state that founded the Moroccan public school system deemed it as the counterweight to the socioeconomic and cultural domination of France and the main mechanism
for scientific and technological progress; hence public schools were a crucial arena for the remaking of the country along modern(ist) nation-state
lines. Yet not more than sixty years later, international donors, the state,
and school participants acknowledge that the public schools are in serious

trouble. In his address to the nation on August 20, 2013, the sixtieth anniversary of the nationalist struggle against French colonization, King Mohammed VI addressed the persistent, prolonged, and widely acknowledged educational crisis in the country, asking, "Why is it that so many of our young people cannot fulfill their legitimate professional, material, and social aspirations?" Despite considerable advancements, he deplored the current conditions in which the "path" to the pivotal transformation of the educational system "is still arduous and long" (Mohammed al-Sadis al-Alawi 2013). His phrasing echoed an earlier World Bank report that relegated Morocco to the bottom of the Middle East and North Africa (MENA) region's educational ranking, a region that the same organization assessed as performing worse than the rest of the developing world. The report bore the emblematic title, "The Road Not Traveled: Educational Reform in the Middle East and North Africa" (IBRD and World Bank 2008). In a more recent evaluation, the World Bank, which funded Morocco's latest educational reform with two USD100 million loans, bemoaned the fact that, despite relative progress in expanding access to education, increasing gender parity, and raising literacy rates, the Moroccan public educational system had "a long way to go on quality" (World Bank 2013). The use of spatial metaphors, such as "still arduous and long" paths ahead and "untraveled roads," implied the frustration of both multilateral donors and governments in the region over the unachieved goals of modern public schools.

The international consensus that both national and transnational initiatives since the mid-twentieth century have failed to improve substantially the educational experience of the developing world—which in large part is the postcolonial world—has recently led to a flurry of development activity. The UN Global Education First initiative in July 2013 recognized these problems and renewed the UN's commitment to educational provision, replacing another global campaign that had run out of steam: UNESCO's Education for All campaign launched in 1990. The repetitive character and labeling of the Moroccan government's initiatives to improve the educational system—from the National Charter for Education 1999–2009 to the Emergency Plan 2009–2012 and the Action Plan 2013–2016—hint at the state's alarm over the demise of the post-independence educational dream.

A largely untold story that illuminates both the frustration and alarmism pervading the Moroccan public, as well as national and international official spheres, is that of the nationalist policy of educational Arabization. Its aim was to translate public school curricula into *fuṣḥā* (Classical Arabic) with the objective of creating a homogeneous, literate, arabophone society. The post-independence school was the structural heir of French Protectorate schooling, which was divisive along linguistic, racial, and economic lines. Despite these foundations, the post-independence school became the scaffold on which was built a Moroccan nationalism expressed in Arabo-Muslim terms and dependent on the expansive use of the Arabic language. Not only would the Arabic language replace French as the language of instruction but it would also unite a multilingual population versed in varieties of *dārija* (Moroccan Arabic) and Berber. Given political tensions and the complexities of the multilingual experience of learning, the incorporation of Arabization inside the public schools has been tenuous and incomplete. Moroccan students are educated in Arabic until they graduate high school, but most have to shift to French for higher education and then have to manage a predominantly francophone and increasingly anglophone job market. Given this linguistic split and their late entry into francophone instruction, the job market treats them, in their own words, as "multilingual illiterates" and hence unemployable.

The material implications of this language policy have brought graduates into ideological tension with previous generations that fought for and invested in cultural decolonization through *fuṣḥā*. Arabization, which has promoted a single unifying national language at the expense of the spoken registers, appears to young people to exclude and marginalize the substantial number of uneducated Moroccans and the sizable Berber (non-arabophone) population. The ambivalent implementation of this policy through an ambiguous mix of theocratic, monarchical, and avowedly modernizing mechanisms has limited the prospects of educated Moroccans and alienated them from the state. Filtered down to their younger siblings still in school, Lahiane being a prime example, this alienation has turned into a broader disengagement from public education, the key arena for the implementation of Arabization. Shockingly low retention rates— only 23 percent of all incoming primary school students graduate high school (Rose 2014, 38)—are one concrete indicator of Lahiane's and his peers' disappointment with public school education and the state.

Drawing on long-term fieldwork in and around public high schools, this book traces the origins and facets of Morocco's educational crisis, explores its impact on the lives and aspirations of students, and narrates the multiple ways in which students take learning into their own hands. Privileging the voices of these students as well as those of their teachers and parents, I show the critical role that linguistic tensions play in their efforts at integration, participation, and creativity. These linguistic tensions and their inventive handling by students shed light on the country's fundamental struggles around nominal versus actual decolonization from France, the negotiation of ethnolinguistic difference, the trials of political transformation, and the management of the national economy and consequently of the labor market. These struggles are complex and multilayered; what adds to their intricacy is that they currently play out on the bigger stage of global neoliberalism. By neoliberalism, I refer to the current period of global consolidation of a fifty-year U.S.-led market strategy of penetrating national economies and to a matching ideology of self-reliance and self-management in an imagined arena of unfettered competition. Neoliberal policies deregulate the labor market, reduce state funding of social provisions such as education, and encourage private sector growth. In its turn, neoliberal rhetoric naturalizes the adjustment of social and cultural practice to the logic of the market, placing communication skills at the altar of global competitiveness. Moroccan youth at school grapple with the uncertainties of both state-promoted identities and globally oriented market identities in their quest for economic survival and social integration. This quest takes place in putatively accessible but in essence very uneven platforms (Heller 2003; Ong 2006).[2]

In investigating Moroccan youth's experience in the Arabized public schools, I probe the linguistic tensions that have tripped up students since decolonization and, through these tensions, show how the definition of "valuable knowledge and skills" is being rearticulated in the period of neoliberalism (see Figure 1.2). Arguing that linguistic resources are central to the meaning and management of both political institutions and the economy, this book merges the cultural consequences of educational language policy with its material ramifications. In doing so it makes the broader claim that the cultural dilemmas of post-colonial societies are

FIGURE 1.2

Urban high school. Photograph by author.

inseparable from the mode of insertion of these societies into world capitalist markets. The robust debate over language and knowledge that takes place inside Moroccan high schools becomes my entry point to rethinking the role of the public school in the contemporary state. This new formulation not only has urgent implications for the future of young Moroccans and other youth in the region but also resonates with the larger predicament of formal schooling across the globe.

"Education is the future!" is the mantra of colonialism, nationalism, and neoliberal modernity. Endorsed by policy makers, pundits, and a general public made up of members of most political persuasions, this mantra extends into a series of arguments about the inherent value of formal mass-based education: education should promote, if not ensure, individual empowerment, erase gaps between sociocultural divides, encourage economic growth on a large scale, and support the cultivation of the values of democracy. In the field of international development, a sense of urgency in bringing educational systems across the globe up to contemporary Euro-American standards has imbued the missions of multilateral agencies and the advocacy of developing states for decades. Since the 1980s— the period of expansive market liberalization—a strategic push for global uniformity has justified the inculcation of new skills for both labor and citizenship. These skills hinge on the principles of entrepreneurship and flexible accumulation (Harvey 1990). Predominantly Muslim societies have faced particular pressure to conform to these objectives within the post-9/11 landscape, in which foreign policy has located religious fundamentalism and "the clash of civilizations" in traditional spaces of pedagogy—essentially reformulating the War on Terror as a pedagogical matter.[3] There is little doubt that public education undergirds geopolitical rhetoric and policy on a global scale. Moroccan public education is both a good example of this multifaceted emphasis and the case study that throws the modernist paradigm of education into turmoil. Frustration, cynicism, and alarm over public education in Morocco reveal significant fissures in the broader teleological and hegemonic narrative of the modern school.

THE WORD IS A LUXURY

In February 2008, the World Bank report on public education mentioned earlier was disseminated by the country's mass media and sparked a series of public conversations that trickled into the urban high schools where I was conducting fieldwork. The report ranked Morocco particularly low among the MENA countries, placing it at number eleven of the fourteen countries in the region, above only Iraq, Yemen, and Djibouti. The gist of the World Bank's diagnosis was that "education systems do not produce the skills needed in an increasingly competitive world" (IBRD and World Bank 2008, 1). The report went on to address the "tenuous relationship" in the MENA region between education and development, defining the latter primarily as economic growth and secondarily as the redress of social inequality. The quality of instruction in the region was "too low for schooling to contribute to growth and productivity," especially in view of the emerging predominance of "the knowledge economy"

(2008, 5–8). Predictably, the solutions the report advocated required further liberalization of the job market and increasing privatization of educational institutions. In reality, such solutions were well underway in Morocco as in Egypt, India, and elsewhere under the auspices of the same international organizations that produced the report in question (Cohen 2004; Bayat and Herrera 2010, Lukose 2009; Jeffrey 2010; Mazawi 2010).[4]

The release of the report caused a great stir among Moroccan institutional and social spheres. Confirming the report's validity, the Moroccan press denounced the state's educational failures (Mokhlis and Zainabi 2008; Qattab 2008). Finally in April 2008 the state responded: per the king's recommendation, the *Majlis al-ʿAlā li-l-Taʿlīm* (High Council for Education) announced the Emergency Reform 2009–2012 plan. Its objectives were to build new schools for the increased population of children and youth, improve the monitoring of student progress, ensure teacher accountability, and accelerate privatization that would reduce the government's financial and administrative responsibility for providing formal education (Ministry of National Education and Professional Training 2008).[5] Tellingly, the reforms also shifted the educational emphasis to technology, science, and foreign languages. Thus the cluster of concepts that the World Bank and the Moroccan government used as a basis for problem diagnosis and the development of solutions—population increase, financial limitations, innovation, accountability, technology, science, and languages—captured the neoliberal reading of education through the instrumentalization of population size, budget, and selves. What is interesting is that, even though the report did not specify the "skills necessary for productivity and growth" or "the knowledge economy," these skills emerged as the measurable and inevitable outcomes of improved educational engineering (Hall 2005; Urcuioli 2008). What the report at best overlooked and at worst purposefully sidelined were the historical and political circumstances in which Moroccan public schools introduced and valued the subjects—technology, science, and foreign languages—that produced the skills in question. These historical and political circumstances and how they were changing in the present moment were the explicit focus of discussion among Moroccan school participants. Their diagnosis of the situation, which long preceded the World Bank's assessment, shifted the focus from interventions such as upgraded infrastructure and pedagogical planning into another sphere: the sphere of deliberation on the meaning of valuable skills and knowledge.

The following scene at a teachers' assembly exemplifies this process of deliberation. In October 2007 at the regional offices of Gharb-Chrarda-Béni Hssen, the local inspector for the French-language course, Ahmed Zirari, joined the regional inspector-coordinator, Abdellah Azizi, to discuss curriculum design and administrative arrangements with forty secondary school teachers.[6] All the participants seemed to know each other well as they exchanged news in *dārija* interspersed with French words and sentences. Their nearly constant code switching was an indication of their professional niche and of their status as urban civil servants. Inspector Zirari interrupted the chit-chat to welcome everyone with this sentence: "*bismillāh al-raḥmān al-raḥīm, marḥaba bikum fī hadhā al-ijtimā*" (In the name of God, the Beneficent, the Merciful, I welcome you to this gathering), before switching to French to conduct most of the meeting. After his welcome, the inspector launched into a plea that went straight to the crux of public education dilemmas in Morocco:

> Students come to us with great gaps despite the importance of this language. Sometimes they arrive at middle school without knowing how to read or write in French. Remember, this is not just knowledge that we pass on, it is a skill that cannot be obtained outside the classroom due to the sociocultural level of our students. The French language in the Moroccan context is the key to professional and social success. What will our students do after the Baccalaureate [the state-sanctioned national exam, equivalent of high school diploma)? As Moroccan citizens, we cannot ignore this reality. *The word is a luxury*, so I ask you to give everyone their part of the word. [emphasis added]

Mr. Zirari's entire speech and his final message in particular, "the word is a luxury," are remarkable for positing the politics of language as central to the instability of the educational system. This does not mean that he did not acknowledge that Moroccan public schools also face a number of structural impediments: overcrowded classrooms, inadequate facilities, an outdated curriculum and method of instruction, and differential access to education in relation to location, class and gender. Rather, he maintained, that even if these inhibiting factors were somehow surgically removed from the system, doing so would not eradicate the deep-seated linguistic discrepancies that undercut student efforts at academic and professional advancement and, concomitantly, their aspirations for empowerment and creativity. The inspector thus openly claimed that instruction in the French language could ensure the academic and professional success of students in an ostensibly fully Arabized public school system.

The policy of Arabization was a project of sociocultural engineering driven by the replacement of the French language with Arabic in educational, administrative, and economic domains.[7] Morocco implemented the policy in the mid-twentieth century as a response to the colonial experience and the rise of regional nationalism in the MENA region. The alliance of the emerging nationalist party *al-Istiqlāl* (The Independence) with King Mohammed V planted the seeds of Arabization during the French Protectorate (1912–1956) and set in motion implementation of this policy in the aftermath of independence. Reacting against the Protectorate's judicial, pedagogical, and social separation between Arabs and Berbers and the equally divisive francophone education for the elites, the alliance crystallized an Arabo-Muslim narrative as the foundation of Moroccan nationalism. Mohammed al-Fassi, the first minister of education in independent Morocco, concretized this vision through jumpstarting the Arabization of public education in 1957. Arabization crucially depended on the expansive use of modernized Classical Arabic and its eventual taking up of a central position in Moroccan society.[8]

Nevertheless, despite its popular appeal and vigorous political backing, the organization of various royal commissions, and the recruitment of Egyptian and Syrian educators to assist with the transition to Arabic, the Arabization process in primary schools from 1957 to 1960 suffered from hasty implementation and incessant disputes. Subsequent ministers of education, Omar Abdeljalil (1958), Abdelkrim Ben Jelloun (1958–1961), and Yousef Belabbès (1961–1965), continued to negotiate with various government bodies such as the *Bureau Permanent du Congrès pour la Coordination de l'Arabisation* (Permanent Bureau of the Committee for the Coordination of Arabization) about the mode and speed of Arabization (Segalla 2009, 253–254). They tried out several options from creating pilot arabophone branches in selected schools to proceeding with general

Arabization grade by grade. Nonetheless, already by 1966, and despite the initial vision of Arabization as a decolonizing and socially equalizing initiative encoded in the slogan "Unification, Arabization, Generalization, Moroccanization," there was already concern about its pedagogical consequences, given declining educational standards and a marked lack of qualified teachers to teach modernized Classical Arabic. Responding to this crisis, Minister of Education Mohammed Benhima (1965–1967) halted Arabization that year and ordered the return of French as the language of instruction in secondary education, especially in the scientific track. In 1980, Minister Azzedine Laraki completed the Arabization of primary education, but kept secondary and higher education bilingual. In 1989 the sciences were the last high school subject to be translated into Arabic. Yet indications of the ambivalent reception of Arabization abounded by the 1980s, even as its implementation was being completed. Minister Laraki himself admitted his serious reservations in an interview for the magazine *Jeune Afrique*: *"Nous arabisons parce que ous sommes condamnés à arabiser"* (We arabize because we are condemned to do so; Grandguillaume 1983, 86). More than thirty years after his statement, the policy remains profoundly contested.

After Inspector Zirari's short speech, he shared information on evaluation and examination arrangements before opening the floor to questions. Hesitating for a moment, a young teacher eventually raised her hand and responded to the speech in a noticeably defensive tone: "You have to think about the reality of our classes! How could we make students read novels when they can't pronounce single words? Public schools are very different from private schools or the schools of *La Mission*!" (The mission schools are elite private institutions under the control of the French Ministry of Education.) A middle-aged teacher next took the floor: he pointed out that even though in the past a delegation from the Institut Français (the French Cultural Institute attached to the French Embassy in Morocco) would make the rounds at public high schools in the area to distribute books to students and teachers, they no longer did so. The inspector acknowledged this, saying, "It is true; nothing is free from France anymore." The young teacher's indignation over the structural inconsistency and unrealistic demands of the curriculum and the middle-aged teacher's complaint about the absence of French patronage from formal schooling invite us to pay heed to the way linguistic resources tie in with political and economic conditions.

Clearly, Inspector Zirari's recognition that "nothing is free from France anymore" did not imply that the French Protectorate, in contrast, had a charitable character. Rather, it signaled the changing role of France inside Morocco from colonial patron, in which education was a Protectorate responsibility as part of its *mission civilisatrice* (civilizing mission), to serving as Morocco's main economic and commercial partner, investor, and donor. The French presence, noticeable in the educational field with its network of thirty-seven elite mission schools, extends to infrastructure— for example, major projects such as the new *train à grande vitesse* (high-speed train, TGV) between Tangiers and Casablanca—and to manufacturing, with the construction of a Renault car factory in Tangiers. In addition, France dominates the more fluid banking sector and the service sector in Morocco, in which telecommunications and tourism hire a significant proportion of the young labor force (Zejly and Achehbar 2014). What the teachers' debate tells us is that learning French is important to academic and professional success not only because of the Protectorate legacy alone but also because it is key to contemporary opportunities for development and global market integration. The continuing economic importance of French has modified the meaning of French and that of Morocco's other languages as linguistic resources: more so than being a feature of group identity, language increasingly functions as a measurable work skill. Because access to linguistic skills remains highly unequal, it is not surprising that there is unequal access to well-paid employment beyond the insecure positions in foreign outsourced businesses.

The evolving relationship between the central role played by language in shaping national identity and the set-up of political institutions, and what Monica Heller calls the "skilling of talk" (2003, 481) has been the subject of ideological disputes that have undercut the policy of Arabization since its inception. Early on in my fieldwork, I found myself in the animated living room of Hanane Tazi and her siblings. Hanane was a studious and very energetic senior-year student in her neighborhood high school and the second oldest of four siblings whose ages at the time ranged from 11 to 22. As a boarder at the Tazi house for more than a year, I spent most of my afternoons observing the children of the family as they studied, helping out with bits and pieces of homework, and listening to highly entertaining school gossip. During one such afternoon, while idly leafing through Hanane's textbooks, I paused to read more closely the textbook of Arabic literature that instructs students in prose and poetry written in *fuṣḥā*. Not knowing a great deal about high school curricula at the time, I mistakenly assumed that students in the scientific track, Hanane's high school option, did not take any literature classes during their final year. So I asked her, "Why do you study Arabic literature?" Misinterpreting my question, Hanane responded in *dārija*:"Because I'm an Arab! I'm Muslim and Arab! I study my country's language and literature; isn't this normal?" I clarified my statement: "I thought that, being a student of the scientific track, you would only study equations." Her mother, who happened to overhear our conversation while bringing us coffee and cookies, turned to me and said, "I'll give you an equation: *taʿrīb = takhrīb*" (Arabization = Devastation). We all laughed heartily at her wittiness.

Yet, it was rather surprising as well as highly revealing that Hanane's mother, a lover of Classical Arabic literature, coined this equation. In addition to speaking often in support of Arabic in a patriotic sense, she was a pious woman who promoted a deeper knowledge of religion based on textual mastery of the Qurʾan. This textual mastery necessitated knowledge of older versions of Classical Arabic. What she cynically alluded to in her equation and rhyme was the inconsistency between the implementation of Arabization at school and that in the wider society, as well as the disastrous effects of this inconsistency for the current generation of students. Hanane's response, "Because I'm an Arab! I'm Muslim and an Arab," is as informative as her mother's. A number of high school students have embraced the nationalist project that equates Moroccan-ness with Arabic. That such conflation is meaningful to Hanane is worthy of our attention, but so is the fact that there are other definitions of Moroccan culture that have been purposefully demoted by Arabization. Furthermore, Hanane's sense of national pride is unable to alleviate her own frustration and that of her family members about how this cultural narrative is playing out in the contemporary public sphere and job market.

This living room exchange becomes all the more poignant if we consider that post-colonial Arabization was a foundational element of the religious legitimation of the Moroccan state under a monarch who claims prophetic lineage. The intrinsic sacredness with which this facet of the state has imbued Arabic leads to an emphasis on its ancient and fixed character over its historical evolution and consequently its deployment in various other domains of communication. As far as students are concerned, the predominant connotations of this language are highly problematic for them as job seekers in the current labor market. The complementarity between Islam and Arabic, which became the two pillars of Moroccan nationalism, has had further ramifications: it has caused the linguistic and economic segregation of the Muslim but non-arabophone Berbers, potentially around 40 percent of the country's population, within the education sphere and the wider Moroccan society. Berber activists, who use the name "Imazighen" (sing. Amazigh, free man), have persistently advocated for an agenda of multilingualism as a harbinger of pluralism and democratization. Although recent state initiatives have offered Berber languages a degree of visibility as "minority" languages, these efforts have not placated the demands of berberophone students. The liberalizing state—which has prioritized economic over social liberalization—has pushed for recognition of linguistic and ethnic difference without addressing the disparities of class, region, and gender that make certain students less capable of succeeding in the Arabized school and the francophone job market than others. This policy explains, at least in part, the staggering difference in the enrollment of student-aged youth in urban versus rural high schools, the latter hosting the majority of Berber students in the country. This state move of offering official recognition of ethnic difference without providing tangible solutions to structural inequalities reveals a great deal about the neoliberal handling of cultural difference. Taking their cue from their linguistic and cultural struggles to navigate the educational system, some students have formulated trenchant critiques of the appropriation of the Arabo-Muslim cultural paradigm by what they see as an unjust and corrupt state. They deem Arabization an abortive attempt to redress socioeconomic disparities from the time of the Protectorate to the current period of advanced neoliberalism.

OF LANGUAGES AND MYTHS

As evident from the above, my approach to considering the language of instruction politicizes language and maps it onto the running of society, governance, and the market. Language is inherently ideological, whether we understand ideology more neutrally as the fact of formulating speech "as purposive activity in the sphere of interested human social action" or, more critically, as a process of mystification, that is, as attempts at social control (Woolard and Schieffelin 1994, 57).[9] The latter view maintains that ideas around specific languages and the policing of language use overlap with the set up of key social and political institutions. It is worth noting that, in both definitions of ideology, the attempt to figure out the features and boundaries of any language is metalinguistic and therefore mediated through culturally intelligible scripts. In this light, Arabization and its competitors, such as French modernity, Berber minority advocacy, or *dārija* as the Moroccan lingua franca, are all ideologies produced and sustained through specific discourses and actions. The concept of language ideology ties linguistic practice to social theory, opening up a dialogue between practices of communication, both structured and unstructured, and power relations. These ideologies, which aspire to influence the usage and perception of language in Morocco, help us discover dimensions of learning that instrumentalist evaluations of educational organization have systematically discounted. At the same time, these language ideologies push us to notice the constructedness of national culture, which often depends on the concept of one shared national language. If we revise our understanding of national culture based on a common language, it follows that we need to rethink what constitutes a region, either in the pan-national sense of the "Arab World" (Navaro-Yashin 2002) or in the intra-national sense of the Arab-speaking versus Berber-speaking regions of Morocco (Hoffman 2008b).

Language has been a central concern for historical research, sociolinguistics, post-colonial studies, and literary explorations of the Maghrib. These fields have addressed the geopolitical and symbolic motivations that historically defined, classified, and disseminated various linguistic registers. The attention that scholars have paid to language policy and practice in the Maghrib is significantly greater and more sustained than

to that in the Mashriq—this term generally refers to arabophone countries east of Egypt—and in Gulf societies. This stronger focus most likely
derived from the particular incentives of the French colonial mission: its
desire to map language onto racial differentiation (Lorcin, 1995; Silverstein
2004); its deployment of language difference for military, judicial, and
economic purposes (Hoffman 2008b); the distinctly pedagogical attitude
of its imperialism (Vermeren 2002; Segalla 2009); and its deep cultural
and material involvement in post-independence Maghribian societies
(Taleb Ibrahimi 1995; Ibaaquil 1996; Dakhlia 2004; McDougall 2006;
Benrabah 2007; Daoud 2011). Historical research on language ideologies
across the geographical spectrum has made significant contributions to
our understanding of nationalist imaginations (Ramaswamy 1997). These
imaginations implicated languages in statements of cultural essentialism
on which states laid claims for recognition. Anthropological research on
nationalism has consistently taken up the question of the investment and
risk involved in everyday life, as national citizens, as well as those excluded
from that category, engage with the politics of learning and speaking a
language (Jaffé 1999; Bryant 2004; Bénéï 2008).

Scholars who endorse the insights of sociolinguistics, practice theory,
and critical theory have unhinged language from claims to nature and
authenticity and delved systematically into the social and political under-
pinnings of linguistic practice (Haeri 2000; Suleiman 1994; 1996). Literary production in the Maghrib during the second half of the twentieth
century foregrounded both the desire and the impossibility of charting
any language onto identity—itself a highly elusive concept.[10] In a way,
this literature coincided with or even prefigured the analyses of recent
sociological and anthropological research on Moroccan and Maghribian
speakers more broadly (Goodman 2002; Hoffman 2008a; Boutieri 2012,
2013). As for Moroccan linguists and sociolinguists, they have persistently argued, sometimes despite credible fears of censorship and other
forms of persecution, that the various articulations of what Arabic is or is
not conceal the vested interests of actors who determine the "language-
ness" of a language (Bentahila 1983; Chami 1992; al-Fassi al-Fihri 2005;
Benyaklef 1980; 1996; 1997; Ennaji 2005).

French philosopher Roland Barthes (1993) understands this form of
articulation as myths. Myths are ideological constructs that depend on

the ability of linguistic forms to incorporate a range of meanings that, despite being influenced by historical circumstances, posit as neutral and eternal. In the book, I push this Barthean proposition into a largely unexplored domain of language ideology, that of scientific translation. I show that inside science classes and translation classes for scientific track students, school participants struggle with the myth of the scientific superiority of the French language over Arabic. In their desire to combat this myth, which relegates Arabic to a less capable register for scientific and technological advancement, school participants endorse other myths, such as the myth that there is a unified trajectory of arabophone knowledge or that science is free from the politics of world languages. In fact, throughout the book, students, teachers, and textbook authors continually grapple with the intricacies of translation. Translation emerges as a central practice, both ideological and affective, of calibrating knowledge and identity in relation to state and transnational demands.

Language ideologies operate in the orbit of various institutions, both local and translocal. In our case, these institutions are the *Makhzan* (the Palace), the Ministry of Education, language academies across the arabophone region, multilateral development agencies, mass media, transnational Islamic movements, and the global networks of Berber activism. They produce diverse narratives that in turn attempt to fix the meaning of knowledge, sanctioning legitimate modes of creativity as they do so. Along these lines, the nationalist project of Arabization, which serves as the scaffolding of Morocco's post-independence trajectory, and of Algeria and Tunisia as well, was contingent on the modernization and generalization of Classical Arabic.[11] Yet neither the modernization nor generalization of that language has been transparent and straightforward; nor is there a straightforward definition of Classical Arabic itself. What is worse, terminology and labels used to refer to the language often fail to provide clarity. In English, the Arabic promoted through Arabization in North Africa and the Middle East is referred to as "Modern Standard Arabic" or MSA. As Niloofar Haeri points out, MSA is an unhelpful term for three reasons: it suggests that language modernization is a transparent process of linguistic transformation that follows a clear trajectory from old to new; it implies that the process of modernization has been completed and therefore prevents engagement with the tensions, compromises, and failures involved in Arabization as a linguistic and political enterprise; and it risks conveying the message that speakers separate Classical Arabic from Modern Arabic conceptually and practically (2000, 63–64). In reality, both formal and informal linguistic interactions shift constantly between these registers.[12]

This linguistic flexibility also includes Morocco's other languages, the mother tongues often called "vernaculars." For some students, their mother tongue is *fuṣḥā*, for others it is *dārija*, and for some it is Berber or any combination of the above. In addition, everyday speaking offers the opportunity for infinite code switching. The Arabic of the Qur'an imbues every day speech in *dārija* across the generations. Young people and middle-class professionals in urban centers tend to code switch between versions of Arabic and French. Therefore, although I argue that learning *fuṣḥā* as a Moroccan student constitutes a long-term investment, one that may help us view Arabization as a political project, I avoid designating any language spoken outside the school curriculum as a "mother tongue." The concept of "mother tongue" is multi-referential and indeterminate; it is the product of debate as much as socialization. The term itself is problematic on other grounds: it naturalizes the historical features of modern nationalism by equating certain languages with the physical, archetypal figure of the mother. This negotiation between what one labels a language and how one uses it is equally central to the Berber languages and becomes integral to the multifaceted Moroccan Berber activist movement, which in fact contests the term "Berber" and replaces it with "Amazigh." In this multilayered linguistic scene, English lurks in the wings as the language of the global market and, ironically, as the most likely candidate to shake the socioeconomic supremacy of French. However, despite making significant strides, English is not yet firmly ensconced in political and economic institutions. Hence the Moroccan youth who do not emigrate to anglophone countries still hope for local participation in the global market through francophonie.[13]

This interdisciplinary conversation about ideas and usages of language shares the conviction of the inescapably social and, by consequence, political nature of speaking and thinking about language. It is surprising, but hardly coincidental, how little these insights have informed the analysis of two focal areas of social experience in Morocco: public education and global market integration. Today's silencing of language ideologies in these two spaces of engagement seems especially conducive to the naturalization of language skills as "aspects of personhood with exchange value on the labor market" (Urcuioli 2008, 212); this silence allows the market to appear more pragmatic, more neutral, and more efficient than collectivities such as states or ethnic groups. It is precisely this silence that this book attempts to break by providing insight into the experience of learning in Morocco. Using this experience to discuss the most urgent politico-economic issues that Morocco currently faces, the book shows that language ideologies and the strategies for their promotion are sites for the study of society and politics tout court, and for the multidimensional power struggles between those who attempt to dominate and those who respond, comply with, or resist such attempts.

Insofar as ideology is a multifaceted, evolving, and contradictory process, it is imperative to examine how diverse decision makers, pundits, and speakers endlessly reconfigure languages. Researchers of Morocco and the Maghrib may ask what is distinctive in my unpacking of the friction produced by earlier mappings of language onto unequal demarcations of modernity and tradition; class, gender, and regional hierarchies; and generational tensions—demarcations that have already deeply affected Moroccan society. Yet there is as much novelty here as legacy. In other words, language struggles today reify previous hierarchies by recasting certain languages as those of modernity, opportunity, and progress in the realities of global market capitalism. Simultaneously, these language struggles intersect new state projects on shaping personhood and sociality, as well as individual agendas for handling inequality, longing, and aspiration. A fine-tuned analysis of these shifting understandings of language exposes the current modes of orientalism and other forms of discrimination that determine who is left out of national and global circulation (Tsing 2000).

LEARNING AS A PROCESS

Attention to language use and language training invites us to rethink the juncture of literacy and individual endeavors of self-fashioning. In this book, the interface between linguistic education and other processes of becoming—a scientist, a Muslim, a modern young man and woman—suggests that formal schooling involves multifaceted and simultaneous negotiations over meaning, authority, and resources. For instance, when students grapple with the ideas of modernity, creativity, and success embodied by their high school track choices, examination results, and academic pathways, they evaluate *fuṣḥā* in relation to professional opportunities. *Fuṣḥā*, however, is not just their devalorized national language in social and economic terms. It is also an essential feature of their religious identity. The synergy between Arabic literacy and Islam is certainly not new, but has become especially useful to the modern Moroccan state's formulation and control of legitimate belief and practice. Its instrumentalization reveals another dimension of educational Arabization: the language policy was the prerequisite to widespread Islamization in accordance with state agendas. What is interesting is that some students who become well versed in Arabic then turn away from the regime's religious interpretation and make their own decisions about what constitutes morality and who holds moral authority (Starrett 1998; Eickelman 2000). In this case, the school becomes not just the stage for the breakdown of socioeconomic reproduction, as we saw before, but equally the site of a vehement moral and political critique. It is precisely the gap between goal and accomplishment—a gap that language training foregrounds—that unsettles more mechanistic theories of subjectivation that scholars, pundits, and state officials have applied to Muslims.

The view of learning I put forward is dialectical and open ended, positing that it leads to more than inculcation or reproduction. In fact, it would be more appropriate to think of learning as an approximation of an ideal, as the opportunity for a diversity of opinion, and as numerous practices that depend on the passing of time. To incorporate this awareness into an interpretive toolkit that escapes teleology requires focusing the analysis on acts of "bargaining for reality" (Rosen 1984; 2004; 2008) and the concept of "practical articulation" (Hammoudi 1997; 2006; 2009a), both of which entail examining pedagogical intentions in and out of the classroom as they affect and are affected by individual desires. A methodological and heuristic device based on the concept of "practical articulation" is to follow people in action and analyze their practices in motion. While in motion, the intentions and meaning of these practices are both set and indefinitely deferred to future experiences that may well bring about their drastic re-definition. This stance differs from the totalizing vision of Foucauldian governmentality or the reverberations of this vision in studies of religious subjectivity and piety.

A concern with learning as process, in all its ambiguity and contin-gency, not only builds on but also complicates existing research on pious Muslims. This research has privileged certain sites and formulations of subjectivity through which to explore contemporary Islam, which I wish to rework. Examining traditional Islamic institutions such as mosques and *madrasas* (religious schools) with the aims of unpacking the process of religious pedagogy and enriching public argument around this process was the imperative of empirical research in the post-9/11 world (Boyle 2002; Hefner and Zaman 2007). Nevertheless, at a time when education up to age 15 has become mandatory and state-controlled religious pedagogy imbues school life, the public school is a key space, despite being con-tested, for students to explore their positions on religion, morality, and collective identity (for excellent studies of public schools in Turkey and Jordan, see Kaplan 2006 and Adely 2012, respectively). In addition, an examination of the public school can add nuance to a portrayal of subjec-tivation developed in analyses of the phenomenon of Islamic Revival. Based on Talal Asad's formulation of Islam as a discursive tradition (1986a), treatments of moral cultivation among pious Muslims have cen-tered on the embodiment of sacred texts as being the precondition for deliberation and action (Mahmood 2005; Hirschkind 2006). Though this model of subjectivation offers a robust and much-needed critique to En-lightenment ideas around agency, freedom, and empowerment, it skews analysis in two ways: it risks suggesting that the experience of different religions is not comparable, and it underestimates the complex intercon-nections of morality with other spheres of life that test, compromise, or use morality to achieve diverse goals (Schielke 2009).

The insights of post-colonial literature and critical theory on how lan-guage learning affects an individual's self-perception and relation to others, be it other Moroccans, youth around the world, and so forth, are equally inspiring and limiting. The views and practices of students in this book strongly indicate that issues of cultural identification remain crucial in the post-independence period, a fact that seriously undermines the periodization of colonialism, nationalism, and neoliberalism and calls into question the validity of a distinction between post-colonialism and development. Grounded in the temporality of its method, ethnography cannot fail to do justice to both the continuities and discontinuities of post-independence experience and to trace how different life is for people variously positioned in society. In this respect, post-colonial literature and critical theory are ambiguous partners to ethnography. Even though they share its interests and ethical vision, they tend to highlight post-coloniality among different contexts and to sideline its schismic character within a single context.

A synergy of idealist and materialist aspects of language that respects the integration of "the multifunctional nature of the linguistic sign" (Irvine 1989, 249) allows us to see students at school engage with religious training at the same time as they plan their professional future, shape their cultural identity, and debate their political views. It is through this more comprehensive approach to language learning that I demonstrate just how multifaceted subjectivity actually is. During leisure-time activities and through virtual sociality, Moroccan youth both experience and creatively move away from the contours of the knowledge economy and its linguistic tensions. Their online writing techniques allow them romantic intimacy through a linguistic code over which they have substantial control. When they engage both online and offline in romantic activities and flirting—both of which are class- and gendered-specific practices—young people use Morocco's several languages in novel combinations in writing and oral communication. However, I do not claim that such practices do away with social hierarchy and that such practices are always undercut by gender. What is noteworthy about this realm of creativity is that it lays bare the school's porousness by demonstrating that school languages can and do flourish in other spaces that define competence and fluency differently.

The uncertainty of students such as Lahiane, educators such as Inspector Zirari, and parents such as Hanane's mother about the mission and effectiveness of public schools suggests that no official mechanism can predict with accuracy the outcome of learning and paths to social mobility. Those who are engaged in public schooling are acutely aware of the discrepancies between the structure and functioning of the school system and its underlying premises. However, their awareness, I emphatically claim, does not allow us to view the institution as deceitful and coercive.

Nor do the linguistically plural and socially divisive Moroccan public schools, as well as the means to circumvent them, point to a stable system that shapes dispositions in a durable manner. These phenomena, by no means unique to Morocco, invite us to revisit centralized theories of education (Bourdieu and Passeron 1990; Althusser 1993). Alarming student dropout rates, large numbers of unemployed graduates, and widespread cynicism about public schools seem to go against social science expectations that the public school constitutes a mechanism for social stratification. On the contrary, the modern Moroccan school becomes a space for the disruption of this stratification. By disruption I do not imply that the Moroccan school ceases to stratify altogether or that it inadvertently becomes the site for liberation in Freirean terms (1986). Rather, I propose that this process is less regulated, less hegemonic, and therefore less predictable than prevailing educational theory would have us assume.

An understanding of all schooling as a rite of passage into citizenship or adulthood is equally tenuous because school participants seriously doubt the legitimacy of this rite and of its orchestrator, the state. Further, reintegration into society is simply not a reality for many school graduates. Hence, although research on schooling has underscored the instrumental role of the public school in consolidating nationalist, capitalist, or other political agendas, here participants in the school strongly question both Arabization and the state that legitimized it. This realization should unsettle understandings of culture as normative and of individual development as coercion into collectivities (Miller 2010). Indeed, the crisis surrounding the ideology and policy of educational Arabization appears to be less the result of its ineffectiveness in producing an emerging labor force or a unified national public and more as the outcome of a multi-referential and open-ended experience of learning that enables students to respond to the state's objectives regarding their own socialization.

IN CRISIS

Since my first visit to Morocco in 2005, I have sought information, built relationships across generations, and navigated educational landscapes amidst an all-pervasive rhetoric of schools in crisis. According to this rhetoric, the inefficiencies of public schooling already had and, chances were, would have even greater effects on the ways Moroccan students viewed themselves, their prospects, and their state. The subsequent Arab Uprisings, which brought to the fore the predicament of unemployed graduates and demanded that educational reform become a strategic component of political transition, reified this rhetoric in even more urgent tones. Moved by the agreement around this pedagogical impasse and the palpable anxiety it caused in the students, their teachers, and their families I knew, it took me a while to critically unpack the concept of "crisis," shift it out of the classroom, and bring it into dialogue with educational experiences outside the region. What made this change of perspective possible was the recognition that the most helpful way to see the school is not as an instrument or mirror of the state, but rather as one of its key empirical spaces. In other words, the school becomes the object of observation of another object of study, the state, which exists most distinctly in the ideological realm (Abrams 1988; Trouillot 2001). The school roots the state, itself an effect of power that eludes yet shapes the interaction of governance and society. In this vein, school and state emerge as mutually constituent phenomena of lived modernity, albeit with the former being more empirically perceptible than the latter.

The modernist paradigm around education attributes to secular, mass-based, formal schooling qualities that appear transhistorical and universal. We should remember, however, that such an arena and its mission were a historical product of Enlightenment modernity wrought by the demands of the nation-state. From the Enlightenment until roughly the decolonization wave after the Second World War, national educational systems responded to a political desire for the existence of a unified, centralized state. This state defended its existence and shape through the strategic dissemination of narratives of coherence, equality, and relative homogeneity. Concomitantly, the ostensive self-sustained unit of the state would cultivate and maintain these features through specific modes of protectionism around spending and regulations. The global dissemination of capitalism, which accelerated after the Cold War and the third wave of democratization, necessitated some modification to this synergy for the purposes of facilitating transnational exchange—fiscal, legal, migratory, and cultural.

Often this modification prescribed the relative retreat of the state from its regulatory role and, as a result, from its status as the central address of citizenship. Educational privatization and the intensive commodification of knowledge and skill do point to a reconfiguration of the state's role, but we would be wrong to consider them state-undoing gestures dictated by the external logic of globalization. For one, the term "globalization" obfuscates the specific histories and politics that continue to operate under its auspices. Hence what often poses as external to state frameworks is in reality deeply implicated in encounters between specific countries. Moreover, the idea of globalization as the downfall of the nation-state presumes that the state is a locatable object of deliberation and action. Yet if we tried to pin down the Moroccan state, despite its personification in the figure of the monarch and the royalist circle, we would find ourselves foraging through multiple entities, attitudes, and interactions that make up the state at any specific time. In fact, formal schooling both anchors and veils this elusive, contradictory, and rapidly evolving state that nonetheless exercises a substantial amount of power on the lives of students and citizens.

As this book's stories taking place within the classroom, schoolyard, and living room will reveal, the post-independence Moroccan state has straddled a delicate balance between being a monarchical, theocratic regime and a restructured and rationalized bureaucracy. Not only have schools needed to contain and combine these two visions but also these visions developed during the period in which neoliberalism was thriving in accordance with global objectives around decentralized governance and market democracy. In some ways, the state's evolution has always been out of sync with that of the global market. Language policy responded to these complicated conglomerations of authority and legitimacy inconsistently, at times ameliorating and at others exacerbating tensions around resources, culture, and social configurations.

There is value in refusing to see the Moroccan case as an exception to this more global transformation of the state by looking beyond the shaky category of the "developing" state. As cultural studies, critical pedagogy, and educational research have suggested, public schooling in the global north has neither ensured social mobility nor alleviated cultural and gender disparities (Willis 1977; Giroux 2006). In fact, since the 1980s formal reports on failing public schools in the United States, Canada, and the United Kingdom have exploited feelings of anxiety to cultivate a general willingness to reform public education along neoliberal lines (Mitchell 2003). As mentioned earlier, these neoliberal policies commodify the individual and his or her skills, including language, accent, and communication tone, with unprecedented systematicity. Thus the national and international rhetoric of crisis in Morocco is not just the description of a tenuously decolonized and only partly democratized North Africa but is also the instrument of coercion to a new global logic of social transformation. The issue is that, as the public school falters, the virtual and disjointed nature of the state enters lived experience more forcefully, penetrating people's lives through surveillance, and the neoliberal conception of the skilled self gains strength. Could that be the greatest impetus for seeing in the abandoned school one of the strongest signs of a broad historical change in experiencing collective life and power?

FIELDWORK, LIFE, AND DREAMS IN NEOLIBERAL TIMES

I visited Morocco regularly from 2005 to 2011, spending eighteen months between 2007 and 2009 in and around urban public high schools located in the center-western industrial zone of Morocco. The school experiences featured in this book draw on extended observations inside two high schools, one in the Rabat-Salé-Zaïr-Zemmour region and another in the region of Gharb-Chrarda-Béni Hssen. Both schools, for which I use pseudonyms as I do for their participants, are in medium-sized cities with populations ranging from 250,000–400,000 and have had long exposure to French administrative and educational influence. These towns are economically mixed—containing both noticeable affluence and expansive shantytowns—and are culturally diverse, in part due to ongoing migration from rural areas. The high schools enrolled students of urban, lower, to lower-middle class backgrounds, most of whom had access to twelve years of public education regardless of their gender. My observations in these schools gave me insight into gender hierarchies and urban-rural disparities that affect student life elsewhere in the country, including the predominantly berberophone regions and the considerably less francophone area in northern Morocco.

As a foreign researcher who wished to examine classroom life in the public school, my trajectory of access was not always smooth. Yet it was precisely the challenges I faced that gave me insight into the semiotic complexity of language and the importance of thinking about the cultural and economic dimensions of learning in tandem. My first contacts were with higher levels of the educational hierarchy, with inspectors of education and then teachers, who in turn introduced me to their high schools. I attended numerous teacher assemblies and visited twenty high schools where I observed instruction in most courses and met, however briefly, with a large number of students. At first, I spent most of my time with teachers during class and during breaks in the staff lounge. I had the opportunity to observe how educators engaged with the complexities of the system, most often with perseverance and ingenuity, though sometimes with pessimism and disengagement. It soon became clear to me, however, that my entering and exiting the classroom with a teacher or an inspector did little to establish more consistent contact with students. Through the intervention of an inspector who supported my project, I got permission to become involved with a senior-year class and to engage in intense participant-observation that required my daily presence inside the school. After six months, I moved to another region and a second high school. During this period when I had intense contact with classroom life, I attended courses from the two academic tracks, sciences and humanities, each day—observing approximately 300 hours of instruction. In addition to observing them in class, I stayed with students throughout the entire school day, from morning to early evening, following them from class to class and joining them during breaks. Whereas I arranged semi-structured interviews with school administrators, ministry executives, school inspectors, and some teachers, I engaged with students in a less structured way. I had multiple discussions with them in class, during breaks and free periods, and on their way to and from school.

I recall feeling tremendous relief when I first got access to students without the mediation of a teacher or inspector. However, at that point, the formerly collegial attitude of some teachers turned into suspicion and ambivalence. Some expressed their distrust in teasing ("Still here? Not tired of us yet?"), in inquisitiveness about my field notes, and once in a kindly worded request to leave the classroom. At the time I was startled and even hurt by these incidents. I later came to appreciate how closely intertwined these reactions of teachers were with the vulnerable state of public schools, aspects of which only became apparent to me once I got closer to student life. In a climate of rampant disappointment with public education, my triangulation between administrators, teachers, and students opened up aspects of the public school that had not been visible before: extensive teacher absenteeism, widespread student cheating, and various practices of educational circumvention including types of privatization, nepotism, and bribery. These dynamics are by no means peripheral to the phenomena in question and have deeply shaped my interpretation of ideological interpellation and sociocultural reproduction inside the public school.

The warm reception of the inquisitive high school students I met compensated for the misgivings of some of the teachers. Students appeared very positive about the fact that a researcher sat among them and were hardly unsettled by my incessant note taking and questioning. They did, perhaps inadvertently greatly influence the way I juggled the multiple sides of my own identity. As a young female PhD student at the time—the age difference between the senior-year students and me was roughly eight years—who looked Moroccan though was not, I appeared to many as the embodiment of their elder sister or older friend. I was the object of curiosity and admiration because I came from Greece, a country made familiar by their philosophy and history textbooks, and had traveled and lived in the United Kingdom and the United States, dream destinations they pined to visit. However, in addition to aspiring to my privileged experiences for my age, students also understood me to be in a state of "waithood" (Jeffrey 2010): I was educated but unemployed and unmarried, much like their elder siblings and themselves. Although at the time I consciously handled my guilt around my access to opportunities in the global landscape, it took me years to understand that the affinity I felt to these students originated in part from my shared frustrated dreams of social mobility, considering my educational efforts. Over the years, I have realized that my investment in chronicling their skepticism and critiques sprang from my own anxieties about economic insecurity, an uncertain social position, and increasingly limited political agency in the neoliberal configuration of political institutions both in my home country, Greece, and my current host country, the United Kingdom.

A combination of these feelings, plus my continuous presence at the back row, created an unforeseen degree of comfort between the students and me. This sense of comfort made spending time with students at their homes, watching and commenting on TV shows, or chatting with them online a natural continuation of our exchanges at school. These informal encounters revealed the way educational dilemmas intersected other spaces and practices, such as fighting with parents over the choice of academic disciplines, preparing for exams, and flirting offline and online. During the first year of my fieldwork, I had the incredible good fortune to stay with the Tazi family that had five children in public education, from middle school to university. Members of the family, whose living room scene I described earlier, debated with me the theoretical hypotheses of my project and the parameters of my methodology. They also gave me the opportunity to observe the emotional dimensions of academic uncertainty and economic insecurity for Moroccan youth and their families. When not studying for school, the Tazi children acquired new skills while surfing the internet, patterned their style on Moroccan and other figures they saw on TV, and dreamed of romance and marriage. It was they who invited me to consider formal linguistic barriers as permeable and to see that a plethora of spaces and practices escape the binds of grammar, dictionaries, teacher admonishments, national exams, and job interviews. These activities, along with a set of interpretive tools that highlighted contingency and contradiction, framed my conversation around language ideology, subjectivity, and learning.

Attending to the ways high school students experienced learning in relation to their professional visions, their cultural identity, and their political engagements required further contextualization provided by an analysis of curricula for secondary education and of government documentation issued by the Ministry of Education. Historical research on educational policies under the Protectorate and an analysis of post-independence debates in the press on language and professionalization corroborated the continuities I unearthed between colonial hierarchies and the linguistic and disciplinary layout of the modern school.

Although I read educational curricula in *fuṣḥā*, I spoke with students and teachers exclusively in *dārija* and French. Here, ethnographic practice mirrored the wider complexities of multilingualism in Morocco: despite the fact that Arabization imposed instruction in *fuṣḥā*, the register used in informal everyday talk, as well as in classroom conversations, was *dārija*. French words were part of *dārija* vocabulary, and French was the first foreign language of state education, as well as the language of instruction for certain scientific and technological courses. Among young students, French featured strongly in online communication and flirting practices. The irony of my formulating the arguments of this book in English was never lost on me, especially because this language was not my first language, either. Throughout my fieldwork and the process of writing this book, I have been deeply enmeshed in the unequal academic and professional landscapes that make anglophonie a hegemonic scholarly register and mode of access to academic and professional opportunity. Constant reflection on these, albeit partial, affinities with the school participants who generously offered me their time and insights has continued to renew and strengthen my sense of academic purpose over the years.

BOOK OVERVIEW

In Part I, I examine the material (Chapter 2) and symbolic (Chapter 3) ramifications of Arabization inside the public school and illustrate how neoliberal rhetoric and policy rework older linguistic and cultural hierarchies into "valuable knowledge." The scientific high school track exemplifies this shift because it is associated with the prestigious skills of technological aptitude, problem solving, and logical reasoning, abilities that are contingent on speaking French. Language hierarchy informs not only the academic and career choices of students but also their ideas around creativity and innovation. While students, their teachers, and textbook authors display their awareness of the politics of language policy and try to evade its material and symbolic trappings, they also end up producing equally knotty language ideologies such as the myth of unified Arab knowledge or of the extra-linguistic nature of science.

In Part II, I relate the socioeconomic set-up of the Arabized school to the state's moral (Chapter 4) and political (Chapter 5) visions. In addition to being a vehicle for national scientific and technological advancement, the post-independence school constituted a foundational element in the religious legitimacy of a state headed by a monarch claiming prophetic lineage. Yet a language ideology that promotes the inflexibility of Arabic due to its intrinsic sacredness has proven to be highly problematic for the current job market. Humanities students, more closely tied to Arabic in professional terms, suffer more from this discrepancy between language and economics. Moreover, the hegemony of this Arabo-Muslim national narrative and its association with despotic systems of governance have been strongly challenged by Morocco's ethnolinguistic "minority," the Berbers. Public education is central to Berber advocacy for cultural pluralism, which activists consider coterminous with genuine democratization. Students voice critiques over both aspects of the Arabized school: some endorse religious figures who contest the state's appropriation of religion, whereas others support the agenda of Berber linguistic and cultural advocacy.

Part III traces the social and cultural experience of Arabization outside the school. During leisure-time activities (Chapter 6), students negotiate and temporarily outwit institutional tensions through their use of French for romance and flirting and through their innovative creation of multilingual online codes. In the concluding chapter (Chapter 7), I delve into the relationship between classroom experience and political unrest before and during the Arab Uprisings (2011–2012). Drawing on the visible disengagement of high school students from public education, I suggest that we need to seriously reconsider the function and meaning of the school in the neoliberal era.

This book contributes to our knowledge of contemporary North Africa and the Middle East in two ways. First it reframes older debates on the language situation in colonial and post-colonial Maghrib. Through a focus on language ideology and policy, it explains how language contributes to the streamlining of school knowledge to align with new workplace values by sidelining earlier ideologies of language repertoires in favor of their contemporary commodification. Second, by demonstrating how young Moroccans take learning and the circulation of knowledge into their own hands, the book depicts the school as both an embattled and outdated public space. This depiction harkens back to development discourse and theories of education that assume mass public education to be the driving motor of the future. The book complicates this assumption by showing that the demise of the Moroccan school has been caused by more than colonial, nationalist, and international development or market initiatives. It is, in fact, the harbinger of a broader historical shift that invites robust intellectual imagination to envisage otherwise the educational future of the next generation of young Moroccans and youth across the globe more generally.

PART I

2

---❦---

Study Antigone *to Become a Scientist!*

Le choix d'une filière d'études ne relève en rien du hasard
(The choice of an academic discipline has nothing to do with chance)

    —Pierre Vermeren, *École, elite, pouvoir au Maroc et en Tunisie au 20ème siècle*

In September 2007 Zineb was a fifteen-year-old public school student who had graduated *al-iʿdādī* or *collège* (middle school) and was about to enter *al-thānawī* or *lycée* (high school). Invited to her home for early evening tea, I sat in on a conversation she had with her parents and four siblings about the academic discipline she would choose for the next three years. The first year of high school comprises *al-jidhʿ al-mushtarak* or *le tronc commun* (the common core), and the second and third years the *maslak al-bakālūryā* or *le cycle baccalauréat* (the Baccalaureate cycle). The second year culminates in a regional exam and the third year in a national examination, called *al-imtiḥān al-jihawī* or *examen régional* and *al-imtiḥān al-waṭanī* or *examen national*, respectively. These two exam grades, along with those earned on *al-murāqaba al-mustamira* or *le contrôle continu* (mid-terms) for the duration of the Baccalaureate cycle, contribute to the final average score that determines access to higher education.[1] That final average is the Baccalaureate score, which goes by the abbreviation le Bac. The structural and terminological affinity between the Moroccan and the French educational systems is hard to miss. The affinity was especially conspicuous in the urban schools in which I conducted fieldwork; there, school participants used Arabic and French interchangeably to refer to school levels, evaluation tools, academic disciplines, and examinations.

Relishing the shades of dusk flooding their colorful tiled living room and savoring freshly made [dar.] *rghaif* (sing. *rghifa*, flat pastry) covered in honey, I listened in silence to what started as a cheerful speculation about Zineb's professional future, but ended in an animated disagreement over her imminent educational choice. Zineb wanted to join the scientific high school track and had earned respectable grades in science courses with an average of 14 out of 20. This average theoretically qualified her for one of the branches of this track, perhaps *al-ʿUlūm al-tajrībiyya or Sciences expéri-mentales* (Experimental Sciences), which would allow her to pursue a university degree in one of her two preferences, chemistry or pharmacy (see Figure 2. 1).[2] Yet despite her good grades in scientific subjects, Zineb was worried that the school committee, which assigned students to tracks, would reject her choice of the scientific track:

> ZINEB: My grade in French is very low, I'm just not good in it, she said, forcing a nervous giggle.
>
> Her mother, Hind, visibly irritated by this self-defeating statement, retorted.
>
> HIND: This is nonsense, open a [French] book and read it!
>
> ZINEB: I don't know the basics in French; I read the lines but I don't get it.
>
> Her father, Ahmed, reprimanded her and the rest of his children.
>
> AHMED: You should speak more French outside of class for practice! Why don't you ever use French among yourselves or with your friends?
>
> Zineb intercepted, trying to mitigate her parents' irritation.
>
> ZINEB: French is not that important, is it?
>
> HIND [noticeably angry]: You are so misled! Try out a *concours* (entry exam) for any of the scientific faculties at university or for any job for that matter. They will reject you the moment you open your mouth to speak in French!

I felt sorry for Zineb being put on the spot, and the conversation left me very perplexed. How could the study of French literary texts such as Jean Anouilh's *Antigone* (c. 1946)—along with other classics such as Honoré de Balzac's *Père Goriot* (1835) and Voltaire's *Candide* (1759) in the Bac curriculum be considered a predictor of Zineb's academic and professional success in the scientific track and a factor in entry into it?

Zineb's quandary unveils a central though officially masked element of the theoretically Arabized public school: the school assigns students to tracks based on their French language skills, not their grades in the track subject area. This practice promotes the Sciences and French over the Humanities and Arabic in line with the broader socioeconomic hierarchy that links individual advancement and collective progress to technological and scientific savvy. The conflation of progress with science is by no means unique to the Moroccan educational system. What is remarkable here, as well as ironic, is that achieving technological savvy depends on mastering the French language, which belies the stated goals of educational Arabization as anti-colonial policy. School participants use the metaphor *ascenseur à deux vitesses* (two-speed elevator) (Zejly and Achehbar 2014) to describe this linguistic bifurcation of the system, which essentially pushes some francophone Moroccan students faster and further up the socioeconomic ladder. This metaphor is too dichotomous to account for the multiplicity and complexity of educational experience on the ground, but its binary character is itself instructive of how people experience these academic disparities.

Drawing on Zineb's efforts to navigate the system, this chapter maps out the structural organization of secondary public education. It pays particular attention to the tools that ensure the masking of this linguistic bifurcation within the system. Zineb's experience, which exemplifies the predicament of many students I met, exposes the key role of the French language in determining entry into the scientific track in Moroccan public high schools and the symbolic value placed on this track and its graduates within Moroccan society. The persistent promotion of francophone science refracts contemporary tensions around the continuity of colonial visions of social reproduction in national educational planning. It also indicates the recasting of French and science as the most valuable skills for neoliberal labor. Not only do the educational objectives of neoliberal agendas on a global scale exacerbate the devaluation of Arabic inside the Arabized public school but they also reformulate the function and type of French-language skills that the current market requires. Most significantly, these objectives, which appear as inexorable responses to the needs of the market, allocate the risk and the responsibility of integration and mobility onto individual students and their families rather than onto the state. Hind's and Ahmed's admonishment of their children's lack of initiative in cultivating French-language skills outside of class suggests their awareness of this risk.

Because this continuous promotion of francophone science remains under the surface of pedagogical planning, and because the neoliberal recasting of French makes the link between these skills and work opportunities more questionable, school participants struggle with uncertainty. They express this uncertainty in generational and class terms, which reflect their efforts as lower-middle and middle class Moroccans to readjust the aspirations they had placed on public education. The strategies of students, parents, and teachers to circumvent the structural inequalities of the public school system through cheating, parallel lessons, and bribes reveal both their obligatory complicity in this shift of responsibility and their contempt for government recommendations regarding the official rules of meritocratic promotion. In light of the uncertainty that saturates the educational landscape and the obvious circumvention of the public school, the conventional understanding of the role of the school as a mechanism for social reproduction becomes insufficient. Doubt and difficult compromises probe the perceived boundaries of institutional logic and emerge as forms of a critique of sociocultural hierarchies and the political economy of contemporary Morocco. They also point to the current difficulties of legibility wrought by the workings of state power (Mitchell 1991; Comaroff and Comaroff 2000).

The fissures in the official curriculum, the ambiguous concept of "skill" (Urcuioli 2008), the reconfiguration of education as commodity (Lukose 2009), and the negotiation of generational shifts and class boundaries help us understand a non-elite experience of citizenship. This experience demonstrates that the relationship between the public school and the state is neither new nor the direct product of the world-making currents of development or globalization. Rather, it constitutes the current form of a long encounter that is specific both to the modern history of Morocco and its position in the French imperial project, and to the currents of global market integration. In sum, the unequal articulations of progress that hinge on the primacy of science and French demonstrate the continuity between colonialism and its aftermath and become the scaffold on which economic liberalization promotes its desires.

THE SYSTEM AND ITS MASKS

Zineb's and her siblings' schooling took place during the last twenty years of educational and social Arabization. As members of a lower-middle class family, they all attended arabophone public schools and communicated with their friends and family in *dārija* (Moroccan Arabic). Satellite networks such as ARAB SAT and NILE SAT brought them into intimate contact with the more or less standardized media Arabic and with the spoken registers of Egypt, the Levant, and the Gulf. Both parents came from a rural area and moved to the city as adults in pursuit of professional opportunity and a better standard of living. Ahmed, a low-ranking civil servant in governmental service, was the only breadwinner of a family of seven. His wife Hind had graduated high school, got married soon afterward, and was now a housewife.

As mentioned, all the children in Zineb's family attended public school, except for preschool for which there was no state provision. Zineb's three elder siblings attended the neighborhood *msid* (mosque school), but as the family's finances improved over the years, Zineb and her little sister went to an affordable private *crèche* (nursery) near their home. Because the state does not regulate preschools, nursery teachers use Moroccan Arabic and French with their pupils. The family rented a light-filled apartment on the first floor of a three-story building in a central though unassuming neighborhood of their city. I lived nearby and found the neighborhood pleasant and comfortable, but the children of the family called it *sha'bī* (popular, working class) and distinguished it from middle class neighborhoods, which they called *classe* (classy, bourgeois), and the unapproachable *quartiers des villas* (affluent neighborhoods) or *quartiers des richards* (ultra-rich neighborhoods); these names indicated the demarcation of urban space in class terms. I first met Zineb through her eldest sister Houda, who was my age, when I was on a short summer visit to Morocco. When I later settled in their city, I occasionally volunteered to help Zineb with her French homework. Though I did not expect it, this tutoring gave me a good deal of insight into the undeclared linguistic hierarchies of the public school system.

Every public high school has an Orientation Committee that organizes the student transition from *collège* to *lycée* and determines students' allocation into tracks and branches. Although students can declare their preferred track on a form that their parents have to sign, ultimately it is the Orientation Committee that makes a decision based on each student's grades. Zineb was cognizant of the fact that even though the majority of students choose the scientific orientation, the committee prefers to push students with the lowest averages into the humanities track (see Figure 2.1).[3] Her parents fervently rejected the humanities option because they feared that a high school diploma in humanities and a university degree in Arab Literature or Religious Studies would condemn Zineb to unemployment. Their concern was understandable given that the dominant language in most of the public sector and across the private sector is French. Even the Training Institute for Teachers, which traditionally offered spaces to teachers of Arabic, had temporarily closed its doors to exclusively arabophone graduates.

Within the scientific track, students with mid-level averages (10–12 out of 20) can join the economic and technical branches, whereas those with the highest averages have access to the science branches. This institutional privileging of the sciences is not unique to Morocco or the Middle East. What is vexing here is that entrance into the scientific track hinges on mastery of a foreign colonial language despite a fifty-year-old language policy explicitly opposing this language. School principals, who lead Orientation Committees, are candid about the impact of the French-language grade as the guarantor of a student's ability to manage the scientific track. In the words of one principal,

> In general, all good students will choose and will be accepted into the scientific track based on their score in the core courses. However, the Committee pays great attention to the French grade since science courses contain many French terms and therefore it is crucial for students to be competent in this language. Science students do not have any other option but study in French at university. The economic branch and the technical orientation also heavily depend on French because is it their main language of instruction.

As the principal disclosed, the economics and technical branches of study are entirely francophone. In the other scientific branches, students study science in Arabic but have to switch to francophone instruction at the university level.[4] This abrupt transition into francophone higher education

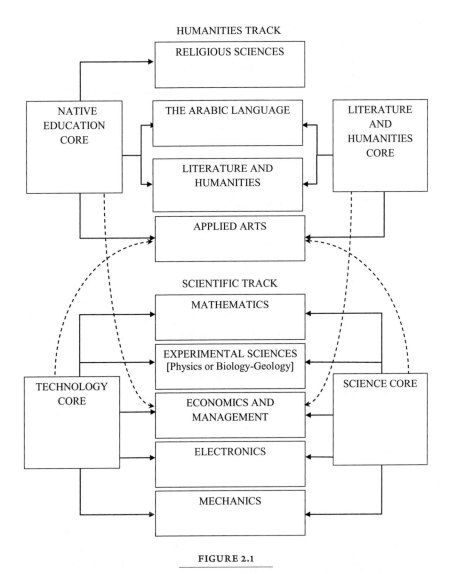

HUMANITIES TRACK

RELIGIOUS SCIENCES

NATIVE EDUCATION CORE

THE ARABIC LANGUAGE

LITERATURE AND HUMANITIES CORE

LITERATURE AND HUMANITIES

APPLIED ARTS

SCIENTIFIC TRACK

MATHEMATICS

EXPERIMENTAL SCIENCES
[Physics or Biology-Geology]

TECHNOLOGY CORE

ECONOMICS AND MANAGEMENT

SCIENCE CORE

ELECTRONICS

MECHANICS

FIGURE 2.1

Diagram of disciplinary orientations in the secondary level and possible
transitions from the common core (one year) to the Baccalaureate cycle
(two years). From *Mudhakira raqm 43, Wizārat al-tarbiya al-waṭaniyya
wa-l-takwīn al-mihnī, 2006/2007* (Memo 43, Ministry of National
Education and Professional Training).

triggers rampant failure and high dropout rates among science students at university. This high rate of failure is hardly astonishing if we consider that public school students study French as a foreign language for only three to four hours per week and that for the majority of these students French is not a language of daily communication. The demands of French-language competency at university are so great that during the three years of higher education students in many departments take compulsory remedial classes in French. Thus the teaching of scientific subjects in Arabic throughout high school is problematic in practical terms and also misleading to students because it conceals the role of French in scientific disciplines in higher education.

The structure of higher education underscores the circuitous promotion of francophonie through science. In the tiered higher education system, the most prestigious institutions are not universities but the *écoles professionelles* (professional schools), such as the *École Normale d'Administration,* the *École Mohammedia des Ingénieurs,* and the *École Polytechnique.* A student can only gain entry into these institutions by earning an excellent score in the scientific high school track. There are two pathways to access. Students who possess a Baccalaureate diploma have to either complete a scientific degree at university first or must score high on a *concours* (entry exam) for the *classes préparatoires aux grandes écoles* (preparatory classes for professional schools, CPGE). After two years in these preparatory classes, students can apply to one of the Moroccan professional schools, which have institutional ties with their French counterparts, or apply directly to the French professional schools. Only the top students in the most competitive *Sciences Mathématiques* (Mathematics) and *Sciences Physiques* (Physics) branches of the scientific track dare apply for the *classes préparatoires.* Tellingly, these classes are available only in few highly regarded urban schools such as Moulay Youssef in Rabat, Mohammed V in Casablanca, and Moulay Idriss of Fes. Students exert tremendous intellectual effort and pay a hefty tuition to gain entry to those classes in hopes of ensuring their academic and professional success. As is apparent by their name and institutional ties, these prestigious educational spaces conduct instruction solely in French (see Figure 2. 2).

The wider structural bifurcation that privileges francophonie and scientific training is supported by less visible pedagogical tools for the evalu-

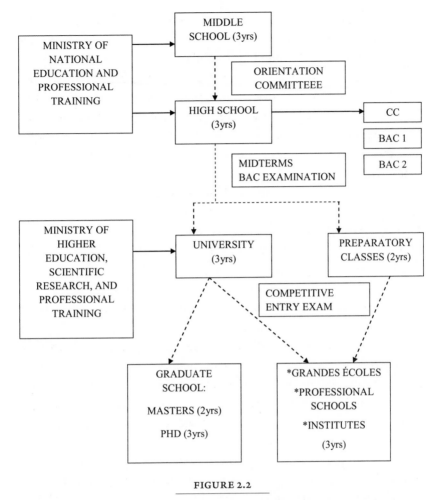

FIGURE 2.2

Diagram of the organization of secondary and higher education in Morocco. Please note that the map is simplified. For more detailed and up-to-date information, consult the Ministry of National Education at http://www.men.gov .ma and the Ministry of Higher Education at http://www.enssup.gov.ma

ation of student performance within high school. A look at a final examination report for the scientific track indicates why the *coefficient* (course weighting) is at the center of student concerns. Each semester and Baccalaureate exam grade is weighted by a multiplier ranging from 1 to 7 according to the importance of the course.[5] During the academic year 2007–2008, the weighting for French in the Experimental Sciences branch was 4. Its value was high both with respect to the core courses of Geology and Biology (7), Mathematics (7), and Physics and Chemistry (5) and in comparison with the non-core courses of English (2), Arabic (2), Philosophy (2), and Islamic Education (2). Even though the specific value of a course may fluctuate from one academic year to the next, the relative ranking suggested by the weighting remains stable. For instance, for the academic year 2006–2007, the weighting for French was 6, whereas the one for Arabic was 2 (see Figure 2.3). Course weightings not only assign significance to each course but also determine the number of hours in which it is taught and even whether it is taught. Notably, during the senior year the school administration may reduce the number of hours of lower ranked courses and give additional hours for the core courses or remove the former courses from the weekly schedule altogether.

Hence the weight given to the French course lies at the center of this macro-systemic incongruity regarding the power of the French language in the Arabized public school. In this context, assigning this weight appears to be a political choice disguised as a neutral pedagogical tool that could and does orient important socioeconomic decisions. Structurally, it is an a priori assignment of importance to the French language in the Arabized curriculum just before it becomes the language of instruction in higher education. The course weighting also functions as a filter that helps select students for promotion only after they adapt to a French-language curriculum. It is not always clear to what extent a student is aware of the power of the weightings because they fluctuate from one year to the next. In fact even teachers are often in doubt as to the current course weighting of their course. The fluctuation of course weightings and the largely unacknowledged linguistic priorities they carve out contribute to student uncertainty about how they fare within the system. What is certain is that the course weighting is inextricably linked to social selection, but only for a particular group of students whose ambition for upward mobility is dependent on public schooling, in which they study French as a foreign language for three to four hours per week. It certainly does not affect students from upper social strata who have already made this linguistic choice at a very young age, attending French and increasingly English-speaking private schools and speaking French at home.

Royaume du Maroc
Ministère de l'Education Nationale, de
l'Enseignement Supérieur, de la Formation des
Cadres et de la Recherche Scientifique
Département de l'Education Nationale

14/07/2007

A.R.E.F : **RABAT-SALE-ZEMMOUR-ZAIR**

**RELEVE DES NOTES DU BACCALAUREAT
(CANDIDATS LIBRES)**
Session de   Juillet   2007

Nom et Prénom :   Code Candidat : **27566225**

Série : **SCIENCES EXPERIMENTALES**

Né le : **26-11-87**   A : **RABAT**

MATIERE	Note/20	CF	Note*CF
LANGUE ARABE	10.00	2	20.00
INSTRUCTION ISLAMIQUE	15.50	2	31.00
HIST.-GEO. ET INSTRUCT.CIVIQUE	19.00	2	38.00
LANGUE FRANCAISE	08.00	6	48.00
TRADUCTION	14.00	2	28.00
MATHEMATIQUES	10.00	7	70.00
SCIENCES PHYSIQUES	08.00	7	56.00
SCIENCES NATURELLES	10.00	7	70.00
PHILOSOPHIE	10.00	2	20.00
2EME LANGUE ETRANGERE	17.50	2	35.00
LE FAIT LOCAL	12.50	**	02.50
EDUCATION PHYSIQUE	09.00	1	09.00
TOTAL		40	427.50
MOYENNE			10.69

DECISION DU JURY

ADMIS(E) AVEC MENTION **PASSABLE**

Chef de la division des
affaires pédagogiques

AREF
Rabat Salé
Zemmour Zaer

FIGURE 2.3

School report of a scientific track student, Experimental Sciences class,
for 2006. The report shows the allocation of course weightings.

The timing of when school participants realize the influence of French
in academic promotion is crucial for the management of this systemic
incongruity. For Zineb and other students in her position, the concealment of this linguistic contradiction only becomes obvious late into their
school life, at the moment they have to choose their high school orientation. Her family did not have prior experience of this quandary because
her elder siblings had pursued vocational training, and her younger sister,
Mouna, was still in middle school. Her parents belonged to the generation
that preceded the full implementation of educational Arabization, which

meant that they had studied subjects in French, except for Arabic Literature, Religion, and History-Geography. As a result, they spoke French
better than their children, a fluency they had acquired inside the
classroom—and not through personal initiative, which is the path they
proposed to their own children. Assuming responsibility for language
competence given these gaps in language training, Zineb's family struggled to manage a systemic contradiction alone.

As expected, this devolution of educational risk onto the student and
family, which is attuned to the neoliberal rhetoric of self-management and
entrepreneurship, leads to stress, frustration, and, quite often, a personalized
sense of academic failure. By June 2009, Zineb had managed to enter the
Experimental Sciences branch and was about to sit for the end-of-junior-
year examination. I visited the family for Friday couscous three days before the exam. As soon as I entered, I found Zineb in a state of panic so I
offered to help her before lunch with some last-minute revision of French.
Once she sat down with her notes, the extent to which she was struggling
to prepare for the exam became strikingly apparent. The demands of the
exam were indeed great: students had to be familiar with the terminology
of literary stylistic elements such as *parallélisme, antithèse, métaphore, al-*
légorie, oxymore, and *métonymie* (parallelism, antithesis, metaphor, allegory, oxymoron, and metonymy) and apply them to an analysis of a text
as demanding as Anouilh's *Antigone.* From what Zineb had grasped in
class about the story of *Antigone,* she could tell that the text centered on
the heroine's agonizing decision whether to follow the law set by her uncle
or to honor the memory of her slain brother. Beyond this basic summary,
however, she could not understand the text. Her brother Younes, who had
passed the national examination after two failed attempts, tried to help
her by downloading online translations of the play into Arabic. He urged
Zineb to smuggle these translations into the examination room. To comfort her, he disclosed that he had also cheated in French for his Bac exam
by producing miniaturized photocopies of other people's essays and carry-
ing them in the pockets of his military-style trousers. Zineb seemed completely lost. I strongly encouraged her to read the text again, but she insisted
it was beyond her: [dar.]*"Ash ngulek ukhtī, maʿndish maʿ a l-fransiyya!"*
(What can I tell you sister? I'm not good in French!).[6]

IN CLASS

Inside classrooms and in homes I encountered many situations similar to Zineb's self-avowed weakness in French and her parents' anxiety over her academic future. Conversations centered mostly on the operational use of French for academic and professional promotion: passing an entry exam, succeeding in a job interview, managing in the workplace. Interestingly, acquiring these language skills did not hinge on the knowledge of French culture, history, or civilization. Rather, these skills emerged as the transparent and malleable communicative tools for use by a chemist, a doctor, or an engineer or, at worst, a low-level employee in the call center of Orange Telecom, a tourist resort, or a local factory owned by a French pharmaceutical company such as Sanofi-Avenis.[7] Yet the curriculum for the French course during the Baccalaureate cycle unsettles this surface of newness and of harmonization with emerging economic realities. It bears witness to earlier ideas and earlier functions of French in Morocco, rendering the continuities and discontinuities of the colonial project in the neoliberal present uncomfortably visible.

One of the schools where I spent considerable time was located five minutes away from a cluster of [dar.] *brārek* (slums) that housed approximately eleven thousand people. High schools in this neighborhood differed greatly in appearance. Older ones boasted Andalusian buildings dating back to the French Protectorate, whereas newer ones were more basic square blocks of concrete. Some offered respectable facilities; others had non-functioning restrooms and rundown classrooms furnished with broken chairs and written-on desks. One of the newer schools, the Ibn Battuta high school, was tucked into a side street. Newly built, clean, and featuring a vast schoolyard, it was definitely not among the worst I had seen. Its only drawback on that freezing February afternoon was the absence of central heating that forced students and teacher to keep their coats on in the classrooms. I sat on a desk covered with multilingual football slogans: F.A.R, FAR 4 Ever, TIFOSI, ULTRAS.[8] Students had sparsely decorated some walls with photos clipped from a tourist magazine: the beach of Agadir, the square of Jemaa al-Fna in Marrakesh, and the sand dunes of Merzouga.

Mrs. Elgasmi devoted a double class session to a Moroccan franco-phone novel by Ahmed Sefriouri titled *La boîte à merveilles* (The Won-derbox) (1954). The novel narrates retrospectively the early childhood and schooling of a Fassi boy at the onset of French colonialism. The in-structional objective was the analysis of the *axes de lecture* (main themes) of the novel and the definition of self-fiction and autobiography. The teacher's analytical focus was on Sefriouri's francophonie, specifically on this question: "how to be oneself in the language of another." At first the lesson format appeared sterile to me—an uninterrupted lec-ture from a teacher who allowed little input from the students. I gradu-ally realized, however, that the students were not able to engage in a conversation about the novel and, in fact, could not even transcribe the teacher's comments. As a result, she wrote everything she said on the blackboard. In her effort to encourage her otherwise tongue-tied class to speak the language, Mrs. Elgasmi launched into a series of questions in French:

> MRS. ELGASMI: What is the function of autobiography?
> There was no reply.
>
> MRS. ELGASMI: It starts with a t . . .
> After a long silence, a student ventured a guess.
>
> STUDENT: A testimony?
>
> MRS. ELGASMI: Yes! It is a testimony of Moroccan society at the time.
>   Anything you would like to add?
> Faced with another prolonged silence, the teacher spoke to them in an im-
>   ploring tone.
>
> MRS. ELGASMI: Make an effort so that we get out of this impasse!
> Still getting no answer, she insisted.
>
> MRS. ELGASMI: Do you have anything to say at all?
>
> ANOTHER STUDENT: No Madame.
>
> MRS. ELGASMI: I was sure of it [murmured in evident disappointment].

During break, she rushed me out of the classroom and confided the fol-lowing to me:

> The curriculum is just a *vitrine* (showcase); the students cannot reconcile with this level of French. These ones are scientific track students, so they

are the best at school. As for the literary ones, they are hopeless. With the latter, *on pédale dans la semoule* (we try to fight quicksand). You see, we teach *à deux vitesses* (in two speeds).

Seizing the opportunity, I asked her whether the scientific students were equally good in both languages, Arabic and French. She replied that these students were more motivated to learn French than Arabic because French was their passport to the *Écoles*: "We don't hide it from them: the key to success is Math and French."

The expression *à deux vitesses* (in two speeds) points to bifurcation and hierarchy on many levels. On one level, it alludes to the inability of high school students to catch up with the French linguistic demands of the Arabized educational system. It also references the varying opportunities available to the "slower" arabophone humanities track caught in quicksand versus those in the "faster" francophone scientific track.

The teaching of Sefriouri's francophone novel illustrates, on the micro level, Zineb's dilemma with regard to reading *Antigone* and ensuring a good grade in French and, on the macro-systemic level, the historical ironies that undercut the contemporary nationalized educational system. Nearly sixty years after independence from the French Protectorate and the implementation of Arabization policies, these students are almost as dependent on the French language as their colonized counterparts. Despite this dependency, these students have markedly inferior skills than the flawlessly bilingual Sefriouri who wrote the novel they studied; as we saw, in a class where there was a ban on speaking Arabic, students either spoke little or were voiceless. Furthermore, Mrs. Elgasmi's assertion regarding the key to educational advancement qualified French as the passport to success in the scientific domain. However, this domain demotes French literature to anachronistic and even superfluous knowledge, given that what these scientific track students urgently need is mastery of francophone scientific terminology. Paradoxically, the curriculum itself and the unanswered questions raised in class about identity and testimony peel the language away from its current position within the neoliberal logic of speaking French and make visible its long-term embroilment in Moroccan society. Hence this multilayered and disjointed French lesson displays the historical bases on which linguistic resources may now be associated with a cycle of novel meanings.

In positioning language mastery as the outcome of power relations within society, scholars of language and communication resist an understanding of linguistic competence in the universal practical sense as a language spoken by its users. Instead, they envision communication as a far more intricate activity than the outcome of rational motivations internal to individual speakers (Bourdieu 1991; Hymes 1996). Their insights resonate strongly with research in post-colonial settings such as Morocco on the capacity of students to handle bilingual education. In many such settings, post-colonial pedagogical bilingualism has been more competitive than complementary, more suffered than mastered; in fact, it remains the primary cause for school failure among students of modest backgrounds who find it a stumbling block to learning. For Moroccan students, researchers have characterized this official bilingualism as "savage," meaning not only rough and incomplete in terms of imparting skills but also cruel in terms of the student experience (Moatassime 1992, 82). Using this evolutionary term to contest bilingualism's naturalness and to emphasize its political nature instead, Ahmed Moatassime connects it to the larger context of under-development, claiming that the inability of a post-colonial society like Morocco to grow is due to linguistic discrepancies that hinder the academic performance of Moroccan youth.[9] What happens in schools refracts the broader manifestations of bilingualism in contemporary Moroccan society: "Bilingualism does not invoke an image of two gladiators advancing upon each other armed with nets and tridents; rather, it suggests that one of the two combatants is already sprawled in the dust awaiting the fatal blow" (Kilito 2001, 108). Moving this bifurcation from the colonial period into the post-colonial delineation of social stratification, Pierre Vermeren calls Arabization "the instrument of a true social apartheid" (2002, 429).

The historical experience of colonial bilingualism remains relevant to the neoliberal governance and rhetoric around mass public education. Neoliberal imaginaries have recast workers' employment value as dependent on the soft skills of communication, leadership, and innovative thinking, characterizing those abilities as "aspects of personhood and modes of sociality" (Urcuioli 2008, 211). Language skills are central to this pairing of school knowledge with new workplace abilities, a pairing that shelves the ideological backdrop of language repertoires in favor of their use as neutral commodities. As the earlier classroom scene demonstrates, the apparent neutrality and novelty of these skills deserve some probing. In fact, the figure of the francophone science student that Mrs. Elgasmi sees as the pinnacle of school success has featured prominently in Protectorate schooling, nationalist campaigning for independence, and the broader processes of nation-building and economic development. Situating this figure at the center of the political entanglement between Morocco and France during and after the Protectorate allows us to detect the specific interlacing of colonial dynamics, nationalist agendas, and neoliberal paradigms. This interlacing makes neoliberalism appear not as a deviation, but actually as the latest push in the long *durée* of imperial modernism.

THE LEGENDARY *INGÉNIEUR* BETWEEN PAST AND PRESENT

The francophone science student, destined to become an *ingénieur* (that is, a graduate of a prestigious and specialized professional school), is the product of the agendas of demarcation, stratification, and orientation of the Moroccan schooled population since the time of the French Protectorate. Schooling under the Protectorate was not important in terms of the numbers educated because "only a tiny percentage of the Moroccan population bore the brunt of the French educational and cultural effort," but it acquired symbolic prestige through its formation of a native colonial elite—this situation was equally true of Algeria and Tunisia (Waterbury 1970, 82–84).[10] The landscape of colonial schooling was fragmented. For one, strategies that originated in the metropolis changed by the time they made it to the colonies because of the divergent convictions of the principal administrative officers, the Resident Generals (chief administrators), and the French settlers in Morocco. In addition to these unanticipated alterations, these strategies themselves embodied fragmentation. Both the French and Spanish Protectorates created multiple systems of education for what they considered to be different local realities: Arab and Berber, urban and rural, elite and non-elite (Zouggari 2006; Hoffman 2008b).[11]

This multiplicity was instrumental to the two Protectorates' policies of intense surveillance. Therefore, from the beginning of the twentieth century there were several clearly demarcated educational systems set up to maintain, or produce, social hierarchy. The maintenance of social hierarchy connected with the goal of the French colonial campaign in Morocco to use "association" rather than "assimilation" as an organizing frame for relations between the colonists and the native peoples. This meant that the Muslim population would remain separate from the French settlers, but would nevertheless approach them in mindset and objectives.[12] Tellingly, Maréchal Lyautey, the Resident General of France in Morocco from 1912–1925 and a veteran of the Indochina and Madagascar campaigns, appeared very keen to assure the existing elites that he would not disrupt traditional hierarchies (Hoisington 1995).

In line with these objectives, the Protectorate competed with, though did not eradicate, traditional education—which began at the *msid* (mosque school), continued through the *madrasa* (religious school), and culminated at prestigious religious universities such as the Qaraouine of Fes or the Youssoufia of Marrakech—by molding a triangular system of education: Franco-European, Franco-Muslim, and Franco-Berber. Franco-European schools were elite institutions under the control of the central administration that educated, almost exclusively, the offspring of French expatriates. The Franco-Muslim schools provided separate educational options to two native groups: one recruited from the rural population and the other from the privileged urban Moroccan strata. For the former, General Lyautey envisaged vocational and agricultural training and thus oriented the curricula away from humanities and scientific subjects. Schools for the Moroccan elite consisted of primary education establishments, *les écoles des fils de notables* (schools for the sons of notables), and secondary education establishments, the *collèges musulmans* (Muslim colleges). Both enrolled students from urban families involved in commerce. These *collèges*, such as Moulay Idriss in Fes, Moulay Youssef in Rabat, and Sidi Mohammed in Marrakech, were fee paying and screening for entry was vigorous. Following the principles of association, their intent was to cultivate bilingual and bicultural dispositions by teaching Arabic and the Moroccan culture in Arabic and "modern" and "secular" subjects such as science and math in French. In this context, bilingualism did not provide the opportunity to compete with the dominant colonial culture, but rather created candidates for low- and mid-level administrative positions (Kinsey 1971).[13] The acquisition of French-language skills thus led neither to unlimited social mobility nor to full immersion in French civilization. The intentions of the Parisian government and French settlers notwithstanding, students and parents pursued socioeconomic advancement through the means available to them and showed great interest in francophone schooling and new subjects, among them the sciences.

Based on its own ethno-racial classification of the schooling population, the Protectorate administration founded special *franco-berbères* (Franco-Berber) schools. These schools, such as the *Collège Berbère d'Azrou*, would hypothetically produce a powerful Berber constituency kept away from the dangers of nationalist propaganda. To ensure such distance, the colonial administration banished Arabic and the teaching of the Qur'an from the curriculum (Benhlal 2005). Reformist ulama and proto-nationalist groups reacted to the general orientation and unequal foundations and resources of protectorate schooling and decided to set up a type of renovated *msid* called *madrasa ḥurra* (free school) during the 1920s and 1930s. Few in number, the free schools offered an arabophone alternative to French-administered schooling while dividing the students into pedagogical levels and introducing modern disciplines (Damis 1970; 1974).[14] In addition, the *Alliance Universelle Israelite* founded its first school in Tetouan in 1872. *Alliance* schools, which gradually spread across the country, enrolled a mixed population of Moroccan Jewish and Muslim students and used French as the language of instruction (Laskier 1994). Thus, the divergence between planning and policy within the Protectorate administration, the widespread fragmentation of schooled populations, and native attempts to counter the effects of colonial schooling suggest that the colonial educational landscape was considerably messier than the orderly modernist colonial enterprise depicted in other scholarly works about this region (Mitchell 1988).

For the purposes of this discussion, the *collèges musulmans* are especially interesting because they attracted the sons of the urban elite (the institutional equivalent in Tunisia was the *Collège Sadiki*). Using their school ties and their alumni organizations, graduates of these institutions formed the proto-nationalist groups that would eventually lead the struggle for emancipation. Unlike graduates of the Franco-Berber schools and the free schools, *collège musulman* graduates had access to the French *lycées* inside Morocco and, eventually, to universities in France.

Administrative and military independence from the Protectorate did not spell the end of the pedagogical involvement of France in North Africa (Vermeren 2002). On the contrary, in the domain of education, what occurred after independence amplified and intensified earlier tensions between traditionally educated elites and the emerging French-educated ones. The latter, most of whom initially chose to enter the medical and legal professions, antagonized the religious elites of the Qaraouine and the Youssoufiyya and undermined the prestige of these institutions (Eickelman 1978). They shaped the new indigenous elite that defined itself through the modern educational path and professionalization in accordance with new norms of expertise.

Despite their internal competition, the two elite groups came together to fashion the nationalist discourse. Their joint anti-colonial campaign, with the support of the *salafi* (religious reformist) movement, was the precursor to the policies of Moroccan Arabization that vindicated the Arabo-Muslim character of the country.[15] Post-independence Arabization was led by the nationalist party *al-Istiqlāl* (The Independence), and particularly by Mohammed al-Fassi in his capacity as the first Minister of Education and Allal al-Fassi, one of the leading figures in the nationalist struggle and leader of the party from 1959. The party's agenda displayed a conservatism that echoed the French Protectorate's ideals of non-assimilation and support of traditional hierarchies in Morocco. However, despite its search for authenticity, the nationalist ruling group did not adopt a singular cultural vocabulary. In fact, it combined political Arabism with an appreciation, sometimes more and sometimes less explicit, of French intellectual production and technological advancement. Indicatively, Mohammed al-Fassi was educated both at the Qaraouine and the Sorbonne and wrote in both French and Arabic. Yet the personality that school participants referred to as the personification of this double-ness was the iconic leader of Istiqlāl, Allal al-Fassi himself. In his long political career from 1959 to 1974, Allal al-Fassi displayed the most ardent support of the Arabic language and the Islamic religion. Still, he educated his children at entirely francophone secular mission schools. In fact, his first-born son became a cardiologist—that is, a francophone scientist. However reductive, this popular skepticism of Allal al-Fassi's commitments reveals a bifurcation of the ideal of Arabization since its inception. King Hassan II, heir to Mohammed V, was even less inclined than the nationalists themselves to associate Arabization with a suppression of French.[16]

Therefore, the post-independence state, created by a number of actors and institutions that as we saw translated their tensions and internal ambivalence into pedagogical policies, founded a public educational system that was both the structural heir of the French school and the symbol of *salafi* (religious reformist) nationalist ideology. The conversion of curricula into Arabic reflected this dual character. In 1957, in the aftermath of independence, Minister of Foreign Affairs Ahmed Belafrej signed cultural conventions with France that guaranteed the dissemination of the French language in Morocco. Hence at the same time as the Ministry of Education recruited teachers from Egypt, Iraq, and Lebanon for help with Arabization, French teachers, called *"coopérants,"* either remained or moved to Morocco to support francophone teaching in all levels of education (Vermeren 2002, 289–292; Segalla 2009, 252). What is key to Zineb's dilemma discussed earlier is that the scientific subjects remained francophone long after the Arabization of the humanities. The Arabization of the sciences for the secondary level was not put in place until 1983.

The complete Arabization of the public school's curriculum and cultural direction would theoretically lead to incremental access to social and material opportunities. Yet the delays in translation from French to Arabic, the division of subjects according to language, and the value attributed to scientific tracks maintained the Protectorate's deep-seated elitism despite official statements to the contrary. For a long time, these scientific tracks, which were francophone, carried a double potential for individual success inside the public education system and for the development of the nation. In 1966, Minister of Education Benhima made this clear when he declared, *"Le pays se construit et attend ses élites"* (The country is being constructed and awaits its elites) (Vermeren 2002, 281). The elites Benhima was addressing would theoretically emerge from the highest performing students of the public school system. The metaphor of construction underlines the fact that the promotion of scientific disciplines inside schools

tied in with the national imperatives of infrastructure, technological up-
grade, and economic diversification. Despite the Arabization of the sciences on the secondary level in 1983, the French language remained the
language of instruction in higher education.[17] Moreover, under the spon-
sorship of the French professional schools, the Ministry of Education
restructured the scientific high school track in a way that allowed students
to bypass the standard educational path by taking preparatory classes.
This way, as we saw, students in the most esteemed branch of the track,
Sciences Mathématiques, could study science in French, skip the public
university, and enroll in the entirely francophone écoles professionelles and
grandes écoles (professional schools) in Morocco and Europe.

Given the high bar to entry into the Sciences Mathématiques branch and
the official narrative about the need for scientists to build the nation, the
scientific professions steadily acquired material potential and undisputed
prestige. This prestige contrasted with the devaluation of the overloaded
Arabized humanities that admitted the majority of public school students.
In the 1980s, when the civil service, the main recruiter of arabophone
graduates, reached the capacity of employees that it could absorb, the already difficult-to-enter scientific track became the sole opportunity for
upward mobility in the public and the private domains. This phenomenon
has perpetuated, until this day, widespread admiration of the figure of the
ingénieur. The ambiguous meaning of the term in Moroccan society clearly
reveals the politics of science promotion: it refers not only to a member of
the engineering profession but also to any applied scientist graduating
from the elite professional schools. It is interesting that some of these
professional schools, such as the Haute École d'Administration, do not
teach scientific subjects at all, but respond to the globalized economy by
cultivating communication, team, and leadership skills (Urcuioli 2008,
212). Yet, although the Moroccan economy in the first two decades after
independence was able to absorb some scientists, it did not develop in
ways required to incorporate a large, highly skilled workforce. Some en-
gineers and architects were hired for infrastructure and real estate projects, but industrial development outside the phosphate industry was not
impressive, and neither were the country's advances in scientific, medical,
or pharmaceutical research. After the liberalization of the market in the
1980s, the demand for non-elite labor in outsourced companies and the

expansion of the service sector required employees with skills that were neither scientific nor technical. Language competence in French was and continues to be a key skill for this latter type of labor.

The historical trajectory of the academic and professional status of the *ingénieur* reveals that what may at first glance appear to be the manifestation of the global market and the types of knowledge that underpin it—that is, foreign languages and science—are collusions that date back to earlier configurations of the Moroccan educated person. What is novel in the current push for scientific skills is their increasing disjuncture with the expertise or competence that new workplaces in Morocco require. In fact, the only skill that remains relevant is French fluency in a type of communication that does not necessarily correlate with knowledge of French literature, history, or culture. This overview of twentieth-century educational planning attests to the fact that the public school has thwarted the mobility of worthy arabophone students. Despite these barriers, school participants have always pursued their own strategies to achieve integration and mobility. These strategies, which I call "strategies of circumvention," align with the government's endorsement of the self-pursuit of mobility and financial security, but do not accept the rhetoric of meritocracy inside educational institutions. These complex and sometimes problematic strategies also derail the public school from achieving state objectives regarding social reproduction.

CIRCUMVENTING COLONIAL AND NATIONALIST SPECTERS

At the end of a full school day, Mrs. Elgasmi offered to give me a lift to the bus station. She lived in a neighborhood that, in her own words, was "less populated" and "calmer"—proxy words for describing a more affluent suburb than the poorer area of the Ibn Battuta high school. During the ride, Mrs. Elgasmi divulged that she believed Arabization made the public school "not the place to send your child." In fact, she had enrolled her youngest daughter in a private pre-school for which she had to pay fees equivalent to the monthly salary of a junior civil servant (1300MAD, 136 USD).[18] Her child's private school did not break mid-day for lunch or have Friday afternoons off in accordance with the Friday *khuṭba* (sermon), as do public schools. This *horaire continu* (continuous school day) imitated the rhythm of private enterprises in Morocco and more and more of chain supermarkets and commercial centers in the affluent parts of the city. To ensure her daughter's fluency in French, Mrs. Elgasmi and her husband spoke to her predominantly in French: "I love Arabic," she confessed with some grief, "but I pretend to my child that I always speak French." She assured me that most parents, even those who do not earn a lot, do their best to enroll their children in a private institution. Her own family was following this practice. One of her sisters sent her children to an even more prestigious Moroccan private school for 1500MAD per month. Her brother-in-law, a taxi driver, worked day and night to afford tuition for his child in a medium-quality private school with a monthly fee of 500MAD. Many lower and lower-middle class parents agree with Mrs. Elgasmi's evaluation of the implementation of educational Arabization and engage in similar strategies of circumvention of the public school.

In addition to being involved with the private school as a parent, Mrs. Elgasmi openly admitted that she taught part-time in a private school as well: "The private is a different world, this is where I actually enjoy my work. The students are good in all subjects and especially in French since the school is a continuation of their home." I gradually came to learn that many public school teachers also teach in privately owned institutions or in parallel tutoring centers for Bac students referred to as *murājaʿa* (revision), corresponding to remedial classes. The Regional Academy tolerates this parallel engagement so long as it does not exceed eight hours per week, in addition to the required minimum commitment of twenty hours per week in the public school. In reality, however, many teachers dedicate more than eight hours weekly to private school teaching at the expense of their public school duties. I heard stories, and subsequently witnessed, cases of teachers who rarely show up for class at the public school because they are teaching private school students (see Sobhy 2012 for a very similar description of Egyptian schooling). According to some indignant parents, teachers routinely bribe school principals to ensure that they overlook their absences.

The primary justification for involvement in the private school is material need.[19] The average salary for a high school teacher with a few years of service is respectable, but given the rising cost of life in the urban centers and their desire as parents to educate their children in private schools, teachers consider it a necessity to engage with private schools. Yet, as Mrs. Elgasmi intimated, the prospect of material gain is not their only motivation. The few times I followed teachers of the public school to their private school classrooms, their pleasure in teaching there was unmistakable and their attitude toward their students was noticeably different. Inside private school classrooms, the same teachers were more dynamic, more attentive to student needs, and more punctual. Certainly, the patron-client dynamic with its mechanism of direct compensation was one cause for this shift. However, teachers seemed to genuinely enjoy interacting with a more linguistically confident student body that benefited from using French at home and displayed a general confidence born from their social position and communicative success within Moroccan society. Although this educational dynamic holds for many countries, Moroccan private schools are remarkable for their distinct linguistic organization. Unlike foreign or mission schools, Moroccan private schools are officially under the control of the Ministry of Education and are officially bound by the national curriculum. Yet, despite this regulation, a considerable number of private high schools only offer the scientific option and often train students using scientific textbooks published in France, Belgium, and Canada. This effectively means that private schools do not use French as the main language of instruction, but as a foreign language.[20] By virtue of teaching in French, private schools become more effective in pushing students through the Baccalaureate exam and therefore become more attractive to parents anxious for the academic promotion of their children.

After watching a TV documentary on a local private high school with the family of Samir, a high school student, I realized that the experiential distance between public and private school student life is greater than I had imagined. Three things surprised Samir and his siblings the most: the cost of books, that the students of the private school spoke French with the reporter, and that the cafeteria food cost about 40MAD per meal. The children of the family laughed heartily at the lunch prices, which they found utterly exorbitant—they returned home for lunch each day because they could not afford to buy lunch. They did look impressed by the school cafeteria, where students had a choice of fast food such as chicken nuggets and French fries. But it was hard for them to believe that the school in question was less than a fifteen-minute car ride from their house because everything seemed to them to be so exotic. Their mother, Asma, who was watching the documentary with us, expressed her disdain for private education. She claimed that the private school mapped onto familiar patterns of clientelism within Moroccan society because parents put pressure on headmasters and teachers to inflate semester grades. She reassured her children that public school students are in reality better students "since their teachers do not do them any favors and do not sell semester grades." On the contrary, private school students were [dar.] "*walu*" (zero, worthless), except for the fact that they spoke really good French and English. Her observations were valid, but the irony was that by virtue of mastering foreign languages alone, many private school students manage to prosper in their chosen academic and professional fields.

Despite accusing the private school of clientelism, however, Asma also engaged with private incentives that overcame the inconsistencies of the public system. Her son, Samir, like most high school students I knew, spent most of his evenings and weekends in remedial classes for his core courses. More often than not, these classes took place in centers run by the same teachers who taught these students in public school. Language centers equally overflowed with students who wanted to improve their French and English skills for the final Bac examination. At the time of my fieldwork, the price of remedial classes ranged considerably according to the location and quality of the center. In one neighborhood, these centers charged about 150MAD per course per month, which was unattainable for the students who lived in the slums but manageable for middle-income parents. In other neighborhoods, the course cost could reach 800MAD. Tuition for private tutoring provided at home for the most affluent students ranged between 150MAD to 200MAD per hour, with the higher cost applying if the instructor was a senior professor or an inspector. Parallel tutoring seems like a tactical choice for parents and students who have lost faith in the public system with its overcrowded classrooms and frequently absent teachers. It is also motivated by their fear that high school teachers are more likely to award a good semester grade to students who attend their own evening remedial classes. In a grading system where the semester grade counts toward the overall diploma average, investing in your child's teacher's revision center seems like the most sensible choice.

In my experience, families used additional strategies to help their children succeed in the absence of true meritocracy: explicit forms of bribery were commonplace in all higher education institutions that require special entrance exams. Like Zineb's brother, many students cheated any way they could, including at the national Bac examination: some brought written essays inside the examination room, and others used their cell phones to send and receive messages from friends or parents. Cheating extended well beyond the school walls, however. During my June 2006 visit, a national scandal erupted when Bac exam topics were leaked on the internet on the eve of the examination. Rumors of such incidents have since accompanied these high-stake examinations year after year.

Although it dates back to the Protectorate (the *écoles des fils de notables* and the *collèges musulmans* imposed fees), privatization in its many facets has become so prevalent, especially in the urban centers, that it constitutes a key site for the negotiation of linguistic and social hierarchies. This negotiation provides new combinations of social promotion through low-cost private schools or remedial classes to those whom the public school system has left most vulnerable.[21] Far from being exclusive to the educational experience, privatization underpins a broader neoliberal approach to managing citizens, whom it construes as led by the desire to optimize their choices, efficiency, and competitiveness (Ong 2006, 6). Indeed, privatization has been simultaneously a policy of the Ministry of Education and the recommendation of Morocco's international donors such as the United Nations Development Program and the World Bank. The rush to privatize education is so strong that administrative staff and educational personnel openly discuss private bids for the purchase of some public schools in their area. On one occasion, I saw an inspector-coordinator of education in one region mediating between private offers and the Regional Academy to take over one of the local public schools and make it private.

Yet, however directly they respond to this official drive for educational reform, strategies of circumvention do not readily map onto official visions of ambitious and entrepreneurial citizens who accept the structural hierarchy and operate within it. These practices in fact confront the structural hierarchy through both a negotiation of the hypocritical tools of meritocracy—such as assessment methods and entry exams—and through their visible distancing from the space of the Arabized public school as the guarantor of social mobility. Not all circumvention involved cheating and bribery. The inspector of French, Mr. Zirari, told me about an association he had launched with the aim of assisting high school students of the slums by offering remedial classes in French. The association also created and maintained modest libraries from which students could borrow French books. "By helping them in French," he told me, "I am trying to help them get over a whole inferiority complex and break down the wall between them and life here in Morocco. It is not about professional success, it is about survival." One day Mr. Zirai took me to a school where his association runs these remedial classes and showed me the room reserved for such activities. The association had modestly equipped the room with a limited number of books. Nour, one of the volunteer teachers in the association, guided me through it with pride, opening drawers and lockers and showing me the audiovisual and art materials for the use of the students. Mr. Zirari then explained that the association is funded by "private benefactors whose doors [he] had to knock," as well as by Moroccan publishing houses and bookshops in Rabat and Casablanca, with which he had struck advantageous deals.

After this visit, we drove around the area, inviting Nour to accompany us. The inspector guided us through the slums, pointing out the crowded living conditions, the unpaved roads, and the unhygienic neighborhoods without sewage, electricity, or running water, all while describing in detail the lifestyle of the youth and their families. Although he did not explicitly share his reasons for giving me this tour, I sensed that Mr. Zirari wanted me to see the slum as a symbol of official abandonment against which I could interpret his charitable work. It occurred to me, though I did not ask him, that his view of the slum reflected his take on the public school as an equally forsaken space. As we drove through the slums and came across students on their way back from school, he pensively launched into a monologue:

> These are the children we are addressing through our association. You see, the more the social status is high, the more multilingualism is rich and

code switching from Arabic to French is easy. A language has no value in itself. It is all about the opportunities it offers, its prestige and its connection to people's aspirations. It is a means of social promotion, finding a place and getting integrated. Arabic does not participate in this fulfillment. Arabization has not succeeded because reality is much stronger.

Nour took over:

> For the rich, the ideas are clear: one should not waste time with Arabic, identity comes afterwards. They are the ones who write texts defending Arabization. There is also the mass: these people still preserve the imagination of the 50s, they think that school still means a work and life guarantee and they follow it blindly. For them, the state has to offer everything. But now there is privatization, it will come quickly and we will pass from one extreme to the other.

Both of these scathing commentaries illuminate how class and generation are the axes on which depend the awareness of inequality and the possibilities for responding to the system. Class and generation are therefore central considerations within the general drive for circumvention. However, the fact that these strategies end up fitting well with the government's push for self-reliance—as a replacement for welfare provision—is not the outcome of an agreement between citizens and state nor even among people who occupy similar socioeconomic positions. That is because, as Nour claimed, some of these strategies operate on outdated information about the role of the state in educational provision. Furthermore, whatever socioeconomic divisions looked like "in the 50s," they are much changed in the present moment, not least due to the topsy-turvy quality of privatization. The individualization of strategies of circumvention reflects and affects people's sense of social hierarchy even if it does not alleviate their respective marginalization. In short, the very idea of the consumption of pedagogical privilege reorganizes principles of value and identity both in individual and collective terms (Comaroff and Comaroff 2000; Peterson 2011). Yet the relationship between this reorganization and the vocabulary of class and generation is still unclear to school participants. Their uncertainty over how to take advantage of educational and socioeconomic transformations overrides visions of consensus that both the public school and theories of schooling have long posited as key to the work of sociocultural reproduction.

IN TWO SPEEDS [À DEUX VITESSES]:
IRONY, MULTIPLICITY, AND VOLATILITY

The uncertainty that Zineb, her parents, Mrs. Elgasmi, and Inspector Zirari express in this chapter and the numerous strategies of circumvention used to respond to this anxiety expose the historical substratum of the notions of "mastery" and "competence" and the experience of such notions inside the school. In a school system that has partially absolved French of its colonial past and has recast the language as a valuable skill for a neoliberal job market, French and science continue to provide the most appropriate combination for productive labor in Morocco and abroad. As students live through the school's linguistic inconsistencies it becomes clear to them that the logic of the institution is fraught with internal contradictions concerning the role of skills, academic success, and the school in general. Circumvention through engaging in private education and corruption not only becomes complicit in neoliberal agendas but also complicates the assumptions of automatism and linearity that are usually attached to formal schooling. The ingenuity, tensions, and ironies that undergird circumvention offer a good opportunity to see how school participants rework their perceptions of the state and of themselves as citizens.

Starting from the insight that the definition of language mastery is the product of political negotiation, it is clear that Moroccan education achieves what Pierre Bourdieu aptly describes as a "certain kind of objectification in which formally defined credentials or qualifications become a mechanism for creating or sustaining inequalities in such a way that the recourse to overt force is unnecessary" (1991, 24). Yet, although Bourdieu's analysis of the school's mechanisms for social selection is perceptive, we should not accept his take on the effectiveness of those mechanisms. This assumption of effectiveness may have evolved out of conditions and settings that do not reflect a wide spectrum of educational experience. It certainly does not adequately explain the experience of the ideologically ambiguous and socially divisive Arabized school.[22] For example, Zineb may accept the institution's demands, but she is not convinced by its logic, especially as she progressively endures the intricacies of discipline orientation and processes of academic promotion. She may partially comply with the institution out of necessity and to facilitate her success, but she also circumvents the institution through parallel schooling. Her brother circumvented it through cheating.

Certainly, by understanding the context in which Arabic is incapacitated and not investing in the language for its future development, Zineb and her family have maintained some of the unequal features of the institution. Her awareness and her maneuvering does not actually mean that she rationalizes this accommodation at all times. In the complex experience that is education, a student may internalize some of the tensions of the institution as personal inadequacy and thereby suffer from them. Thus instead of saying, "As a native speaker of Arabic educated in the Arabic language, I am not supposed to be able to translate all my knowledge into French, yet I am forced to do so," Zineb says, "I am not good in French." Timing is crucial in understanding this tension. As public school students reach the final levels of high school and the intricacies of higher education and the job market become more apparent to them, their lack of mastery of French turns into a personal problem they have to handle. Until then, the importance of French is more concealed, especially if we consider the fluctuation of course weightings from one year to the next. Evaluation tools such as the course weighting are noteworthy because they point to the moment the state summons the student to compensate for its hierarchical language politics. Hence the different timings of educational experience encourage diverse engagements with the logic of the system.

After her painful initiation into the politicized linguistic and scientific training, Zineb demonstrates a deep understanding that the way things are deviates greatly from the official discourse of the Arabized school that promises to make Arabic a language of equal socioeconomic opportunity. When she studies Anouilh's *Antigone* as a scientific track student, she strips the text of its intellectual weight within French literary tradition and turns it into a dictionary for the mastery of science and technology. This way, she maintains the instrumentalization of French encouraged by the school but in a way that furthers her own aims. In Mrs. Elgasmi's classroom near the slums, the irony, one would say even farce, of learning French to become a scientist by reading a Moroccan francophone novel becomes all the more poignant. However, school participants reappropriate a number of ironic and farcical conditions for a chance at social promotion, for the dream of immigration, or out of the desire of academic excellence for its own sake. The contemporary pedagogical experience of the majority of public high school students seems so divisive and so unfair to school participants that the objectives of the neoliberal market of skills become an object of debate and contestation. Given the obvious educational fragmentation since the colonial era, it is fair to assume that Moroccan students from the Protectorate onward have been observing and comparing their experiences with each other—thereby unsettling the rhetoric of sociocultural homogeneity promoted by Arabization and exposing several hidden agendas of educational policy.

Theorists who have exaggerated the success of ideological interpellation inside the school consider teachers to be exemplary mediators of pedagogical dogma: "The majority do not even begin to suspect the 'work' that the system (which is bigger than they are and crushes them) forces them to do, or worse, put all their heart and ingenuity into performing it with the most advanced awareness" (Althusser 1993, 31).[23] In sharp contrast, Mrs. Elgasmi and Inspector Zirari seem to be acute evaluators of the system. Their deep recognition of generational shifts informs their assessment of the transformation of French from a colonial imposition to a neoliberal soft skill and reveals the incompleteness of Arabization as a decolonizing project. Yet, certainly, one does not need to be duped by the dominant discourse to become complicit in perpetuating the inequalities of the system. Material and social anxiety plays a key role in how teachers operate. First, by accepting that it is through the French language that the current generation will acquire mobility, many teachers do little to promote Arabic at school. Second, in their role as parents and professionals, they orient themselves toward private education, a practice that perpetuates the valorization of French. In this light, even Inspector Zirari's charitable work has equivocal meaning: although it displays an appreciation of the linguistic conundrums of public schooling, it perpetuates the language hierarchies of this schooling by providing remedial classes in French. Third, in their acceptance of this double juxtaposition of French and *fuṣḥā* (Classical Arabic), teachers disregard the potential of *dārija* (Moroccan Arabic) and Berber within the educational institution, thereby maintaining the linguistic erasures of the nationalist ideology.

I was by no means immune to this complex ideological interpellation. At the same time as my ethnographic research looked to disentangle the ways colonialism and neoliberalism colluded in the demotion of Arabic, I continually advised Zineb and many other students to work harder in their French courses and systematically assisted them with their homework. I convinced myself that it was possible and even necessary to give up the long-term expectation of Arabic promotion for the short-term privileges of French: the price to pay for making the opposite choice was too high. Hence resolving the cultural incongruities of the Arabized school may present school participants with another set of dilemmas. These difficult compromises show that analytical accounts of the workings of ideology in people's lives need to leave considerably more space for ambivalence, doubt, and the ability to maneuver.

The unanimity around the necessity of French-language skills should not disguise the very tenuous process of social reproduction inside public schooling. The volatile nature of this process appears more forcefully at the juncture of generational and class tension. There, social groups such as lower-middle or middle class parents and public school teachers realize that they are unable to pass their status onto their own children and students, respectively. In the Moroccan public school, the explicitness of social hierarchy neither brings about nor reaffirms a triangular—upper, middle, working-class—consciousness. Instead, what emerges is the inability of school participants to define the limits and methods of class formation. Having been educated in the public schools, the parents and teachers here were able to achieve a degree of social integration and even mobility by earning a stable income and some social status. Nevertheless, they find themselves losing their status because of the rising costs of urban living and are doubtful that they can pass it onto their children and students through the same educational system. For example, Mrs. Elgasmi, a graduate of the public school system in the 1980s, has chosen to educate her own children not in the schools near the slum where she teaches, but in private institutions.

The negotiation of generational differences in relation to opportunities for mobility becomes the impetus for this book's reconsideration of the salience of social class as a point of consensus and continuity. Influential educational theories have been based on a triangulated model of class structure even when theorists acknowledge that this class configuration does not exactly map onto real life manifestations of class consciousness and class action (Bourdieu 1991).[24] Both theory and public policy in Morocco have often projected onto the middle class the hope of achieving social consensus through mediation between the elites and the agricultural labor force or the precarious urban strata (Bouderbala 2006). What happens, however, when people struggling with the consequences of socioeconomic inequality find it hard to demarcate class limits, let alone position themselves in any one group?

Research examining the post-independence trajectory of class formation in Morocco has argued that market liberalization in the era of global market integration has the power to engender new social groups. Because the experience of these groups unfolds against the horizon of the global—even when they remain in the periphery of global activity—these groups constitute a highly heterogeneous "global middle class." The two commonalities among its members are their lack of identification with national politics and their feelings of "ambiguity, loss of principle and purpose" (Cohen 2004, 138). Still, this conglomeration of feelings does not bring about any consciousness of group belonging or identity among its members. Reflecting on the earlier vignette of public school students watching a TV documentary about their private school counterparts, I see that what separates young educated Moroccans, namely language capacity and professional potential, is more powerful than what brings them together. My critique of the analytical potential of a triangular class model points to the numerous and profound divisions that make the idea of class consensus extremely vulnerable, and today's fragmentation—exemplified by the newly urbanized inhabitants of the slums and the crowds of unemployed or underemployed educated youth—only makes this identification more tenuous. These two groups are even less likely to reproduce the conditions of their own formation. The events of the Arab Uprisings have shown that, despite the temporary uniting of different segments of society brought about by collective grievances with the state, socioeconomic fragmentation remains a real obstacle to achieving a lasting consensus over the economy or a political system that can make economic progress possible.

The multiple agendas, volatility, and ironies of the educational landscape have important ramifications for the fashioning of the student body as a local and global labor force. We should note that the same dynamics complicate the role of the state in relation to these students. Because the state in the singular is often too amorphous a construct to tackle, we can break it down into mechanisms of state power such as the *Makhzan* (the Palace), governmental institutions such as the parliament and ministries, regional administrative instruments like the Regional Academies of education, and transnational capital flows and the political pressures they impose. Arabization, a post-independence project positioned betwixt and between the above mechanisms, has been only partially implemented, making inconsistent the status of languages through which generations of young Moroccans would integrate into society. That this inconsistency continues indicates that the contemporary experience of learning is not the result of external neoliberal forces writ large. Rather, it is the consequence of a virtually uninterrupted, though considerably transformed, mode of social engineering from the Protectorate onward. Although critics of neoliberalism acknowledge these continuities, they attribute them less importance than they actually deserve.

The neoliberal state does not retreat from this picture. Something more complex is at play. The increasing privatization of schooling distances school participants from the state's nationalist message of Arabization while reinforcing aspects of state elitism present since independence. Yet it is unclear to what extent this elitism profits the state, given that global competition has opened the national market in ways that the state cannot entirely control. More seriously for the state, the education delivered by private schools through these schools' language choices and curricula breaks with the historical and symbolic role of the state as the sole educator. But the thing about neoliberal states is that they are never just neoliberal. They carry forth, even in spectral shape, a legacy of their modernist nationalist formation. Hence the Moroccan state does not only exist as an apparatus for facilitating the unfettered market. It is also invested in projects of ideological interpellation that require a degree of centralization. A feature of the current situation is that the lines of action and reaction for both state and citizens appear blurry. As they move between public education and their various involvements with privatization, school participants do not pit the state against the market so that the former represents the public domain and the latter the private—after all, the state monitors private schools as well as public schools (Lukose 2005). Rather, through its symbolic importance to the state and its pragmatic enmeshment in privatization, schooling partakes in a sociocultural turmoil replete with unintended consequences.

The experience of high school students, parents, and teachers with the system exposes the material meaning and impact of a linguistic strain underlying the foundation of public education. This strain, despite its masking by technical and structural elements of the system, suggests that colonial schemata of hierarchy and the language ideologies that they promoted are still operating inside the contemporary school. The preservation and recasting of the French language inside the public school, the tenuous role of the public school as the space of individual investment, and the questioning of the educational authority of the state give us important clues about people's consciousness of change. Consciousness of change is a vital element in studies of change that we often speculate on rather than record. Moroccan schooling provides a strong concretization of this consciousness in everyday life despite or perhaps precisely through the ambient uncertainty around the rules of the game regarding learning. Consciousness of change lets us appreciate how Moroccans assess the passing of time, for which the image of Morocco as an elevator *à deux vitesses* (in two speeds) is a good though agonizing trope. This metaphor, at once temporal and technical, indexes the local face of processes that are often too hastily described as development and globalization.

3

Paradox and Passion in the Tower of Babel

All cognitive experience and its classification is conveyable in any existing language. Whenever there is deficiency, terminology may be qualified and amplified by loan words or loan translations, neologisms or semantic shifts and, finally, by circumlocutions . . . . Languages differ essentially in what they *must* convey and not in what they *may* convey. [emphasis in original]

—Roman Jakobson, *On Linguistic Aspects of Translation*

Please welcome the fifty-first student of your class!" exclaimed the [dar.] *mudīr* (school principal) of the Ibn Battuta high school as he introduced me to the SVT senior-year class. The SVT class belongs to the Experimental Sciences track and takes its name from the abbreviation of its key subjects, Biology and Geology: *Sciences de la Vie et de la Terre* or *ʿUlūm al-Ḥayāt wa-l-Arḍ*. His announcement, followed by a wink he cast in my direction, alluded both to the fact that the class would have to endure me for a few months and that it already had fifty registered students. This large class size is common for urban public schools, but is certainly not ideal for a senior-year class. His encouragement to students and teachers to see me as a student sought to make my presence as unobtrusive as possible. This aspiration remained entirely unfulfilled. Even after teachers overcame their initial reservations, I regularly became the addressee of their commentaries around topics as varied as Greek philosophy, mathematics, French literature, and English-language lessons. Students matched

71

their teachers' curiosity. My varying desk mates in the back row questioned me constantly about my work and life in Morocco and elsewhere, often while class was in session. After sharing a desk, spending time together during break, or taking the same bus home, I came to know some of these students very well.

It was late January, and because the national Baccalaureate exam was only six months away, the SVT students were focusing almost exclusively on their core subjects: SVT plus Mathematics, Physics, and Chemistry. Students were attending Philosophy and English classes more sporadically, and the lowest weighted subjects such as Arabic Literature, Islamic Education, and Physical Education rarely, if at all. There were two noticeable exceptions to this subject hierarchy. Two courses that were not part of the final year examination had a high and steady attendance rate: *Français* (French) and the Translation Course for Scientific Terms, commonly known as *Tarjama*.[1] The Translation course entered the curriculum after the Arabization of the scientific track in 1989. It was intended to assist students of science and technology as they made the transition from an Arabized curriculum to university instruction in French. *Tarjama*, even though it was not part of the final exam, had a high course weighting of 4 so students felt compelled to attend it consistently. What drew my attention to this subject was that its translation vector was enigmatic, given the policy of Arabization: instead of translating arabophone scientific texts into French, the course focused on the translation of francophone scientific passages into Arabic. This privileging of French scientific terminology in an arabophone curriculum is a critical paradox that frames a set of reversals of Arabization as a process of the decolonization of knowledge. These reversals speak to dilemmas around symbolic emancipation that reflect the material implications of language hierarchy.

Science sits at the center of the symbolic competition over knowledge in post-colonial societies. Along the path from colonialism to nation-building in Morocco and elsewhere (Anderson and Pols 2012), science has emerged as the means of symbolic emancipation and the metric for a broader understanding of individual and collective creativity. However, emancipation through scientific creativity—namely, the possibility of taking part in knowledge production—is by no means a simple process. Arabophone science in Morocco has materialized through a vigorous translation effort from French into Arabic that was contingent on linguistic transformation. Because many translators of science in Morocco also work as authors of textbooks used in public schools and as educators in the public educational system, the Translation course does not simply reflect this transformation but also is one of its principal instruments. As this chapter shows, the Translation course, which posits French as the original scientific language, clearly constitutes a pedagogical corrective of Arabization and confirms the renewed promotion of the French language in the academic and professional domains. Yet, when probed further, the course reflects a chronologically longer trajectory of Arabic translation as the mediator of momentous political claims—of which the French Protectorate was one instance and Morocco only one of its settings. Awareness of such chronological depth is important for understanding translation as always tied to larger political processes. Hence the Translation course becomes a conceptual site for an exploration of the history of the Arabic language in motion and in interaction. This should not detract from the discomfort students experience today in learning science in two unequally positioned languages or from the passionate dedication of translator-educators to invert this power balance. The students' and teachers' respective understandings of the language of science are not identical, but these ideological nuances are what make scientific translation such an ethnographically captivating and analytically potent topic.

The act of translation exposes the "mythologization" of French and Arabic; that is, the privileging and naturalizing of specific narratives around them. I borrow this concept from Roland Barthes (1993) to analyze the process by which scientific terms become potent messages of intellectual and political authority inside classrooms. The students' awareness of the political nature of knowledge production and the translators' deeply affective stance toward this process reveal the stakes involved in challenging some myths, often by promoting or producing others. Interestingly, such affective responses expose qualities of scientific translation that both linguists and sociolinguists have so far neglected. Scientific translation has as much to say about the multilayered nature of translation as does literary translation. In fact, in the current Moroccan landscape, scientific translation emerges as the central practice in managing both decolonizing and globalizing aspirations.

Jacques Derrida has asked the provocative question, "To whom is the translator indebted?" which resonates strongly within debates on translation inside the Moroccan school. The title of Derrida's essay *"Des tours de Babel"* (Towers of Babel) (2007) spells out this work's cogent connection to these debates. In the parable of the Tower of Babel from Genesis 11:1–9, God punishes an ambitious monolingual Semitic community for attempting to build a tower to reach the heavens. God imposes multilingualism as a way to thwart their efforts to communicate and cooperate effectively. In this light, the Tower of Babel, which is the illustration on the cover of the textbook used in the Translation course and the archetypal frame for translation theory, stands for the public school. Like the Tower, the public school is both destabilized by contention and instilled with ambition to achieve a restored understanding. The metaphor is as compelling as it is risky, because one of the major hurdles to tackling the translation of science into Arabic as a national emergency is precisely its immersion in the mythologies of arabophone and francophone knowledge production, both of which circulate zealously in and out of class.

ARISTOTLE'S FEET AND HEAD

In the first Translation class I attended, I sat next to Mehdi, a tall and intentionally scruffy-looking student in shredded jeans and tousled hair. The session started with the teacher, Mrs. Khouaja, dictating the following passage:

> *Relation entre alleles*
> *Si le phénotype d'un hétérozygote ne rend compte que de la présence d'un seul allèle, cet allèle est dit dominant. L'allèle dont on n'observe pas l'expression au niveau du phénotype est dit récessif. Il peut arriver qu'un hétérozygote présente un phénotype intermédiaire entre ceux des deux allèles, on parle alors de codominance.*

> (Relationship between alleles
> If the phenotype of a heterozygous pair only reveals the presence of a single allele, this allele is considered dominant. The allele whose expression in terms of phenotype we do not observe is considered recessive. It is

possible that a heterozygous pair presents an intermediate phenotype between the two alleles, in which case we speak of co-dominance.)[2]

After the oral dictation of the passage, the rather stern-looking Mrs. Khouaja read out the following instructions in French: "Define the genre, the discipline, and the type of text. Give the two general ideas of the text. Give the equivalent ideas in Arabic. Translate the text into Arabic." As students jotted down the passage and instructions, the teacher went around the room to check their notebooks. Finding them full of grammatical and syntactical errors, she asked Soufia, a high-performing student, to stand up and write the text on the blackboard.

My desk mate Mehdi looked bored, practically on the verge of sleep, and astounded by my diligent note taking for a course that he found, as he said, "completely dull." Mehdi had not come to the Translation class during the first semester, but was obliged to attend in the second half of the year so that he could boost his semester average. His dream was to study architecture, for which he needed a Bac score of 15 out of 20. So far, the dream seemed unattainable because his average was close to 10. Mehdi was also doubtful he could ever pass the *concours* (entry exam) for the *École Nationale d'Architecture*, which required high grades in both Science and French. Like many young men his age, Mehdi exuded an adolescent malaise evident in his disdain for classroom instruction, homework, and any other disciplinary aspect of the school. He often skipped class, and whenever he was present he would either doze off or flirt with the girls in his class. Yet on that day he seemed uneasy. As he looked left and right at his fellow students who were hard at work translating the French passage, Mehdi looked uncomfortable. He eventually fixed his eyes on his notebook and attempted a translation. Twenty minutes later, he had not written a single phrase. Sensing his embarrassment, I averted my gaze.

The teacher finally started the correction process. She specified that the genre of the passage was "scientific" and that the discipline of the passage was "biology." Before moving on, Mrs. Khouaja provided the translation of scientific terminology from French into Arabic:

Allèle:alīl (allele)
Phénotype:maẓhar khārijī (phenotype)

Hétérozygote:mukhtalif al-iqtirān (heterozygous)
Homozygote: mutashābih al-iqtirān (homozygous)
Dominant:sāʾid (dominant)
Récessif:mutanaḥī (recessive)
Intermédiaire: wasīṭ (intermediate)
Codominance: tasāwī al-siyāda (co-dominance)

She then asked students to read out their Arabic version of the passage. She spoke to them exclusively in French, a linguistic choice that was unique to the French and the Translation courses: instruction in other science courses was in a mixed *fuṣḥā* (Classical Arabic), *dārija* (Moroccan Arabic), and French register. Several students tried their versions out loud, their body language and hesitation signaling that they found the process grueling. In the middle of the correction process, the bell rang, much to their relief.

I found the Translation course puzzling both because of its demanding requirements and its designation of the French passage as the original text. Were SVT students, who had previously studied science in Arabic, capable of engaging with French scientific texts of that level? Attendance at subsequent sessions of Translation made clear the answer to my question. When Mrs. Khouaja scheduled a quiz, she let me sit in despite her reservations that I would find it very boring. Quite on the contrary, observing this quiz was highly instructive because it confirmed the gap between curriculum expectations and the students' language skills. As in the lesson format, the students were given a French passage the length of a paragraph and asked to answer questions on it, analyze aspects of the passage such as *figures de style* (figures of speech), and translate the text into Arabic. The assigned topic discussed neuropathy:

> *Les signes avant-coureurs de la neuropathie liée à une intolérance au glucose sont essentiellement des troubles sensitifs. . . . Contrairement à ce que l'on pensait, l'atteinte nerveuse n'est pas irréversible à condition d'intervenir précocement . . .*
>
> (The harbingers of a neuropathic condition linked to glucose-intolerance are essentially sensory disorders . . . . Contrary to what we used to think, brain injury is not irreversible provided that intervention is timely . . .)
> (*Parcours de traduction*, 75)

Having studied French for more than a decade, I was astonished at how linguistically demanding the passage was. Yet to my dismay students looked thankful and reassured when they saw it on the quiz. As it turned out, the teacher had taken the passage straight out of their textbook and had made sure that the class had worked on it before. Given their familiarity with the text, students relied on their memorization of the Arabic translation, rather than their capacity to translate. Even more, as the best performing students who completed the translation left the classroom, they handed their notes to those who had not already memorized the passage, all of this under the nose of the teacher who may have pretended not to notice.

During the break, everyone rushed toward Soufia, the diligent student whom Mrs. Khouaja had invited up to the blackboard. They asked her to corroborate their translation of this or that term. Soufia answered everyone's questions courteously, but could not help boasting a bit about her determination to study thoroughly for this course. "Why is it so important?" I asked her. She replied,

> It's crucial! While technology is produced in America, it comes to us through France. They [America and France] make, we imitate and they advance while we stay still. It's a pity because there was a time when the Arabs were the greatest civilization in the world; now we have stagnated.

Another classmate, Mohammed, interrupted with a witty comment: "French goes on the bicycle; Arabic follows on foot!" Both Soufia and Mohammed linked creativity to technological advancement, which in Morocco is mediated through another country and another language with an inevitable delay. We should not understate the global hierarchies in knowledge production and dissemination, so evident in Soufia's comment, that imbue the dichotomy between Arabic and French with irony; after all, the scientific lingua franca is English, and the United States ranks higher than France in scientific and technical expertise. That Soufia does not even mention English in her comment implies that, although English is steadily gaining ground in the Moroccan marketplace and public life, French remains the dominant institutional language in science education and practice.

This portrayal of scientific and technological knowledge extends well beyond the casual comments made by high school students. French sociolinguist Lelubre calls the characterization of arabophone science as delayed a *"banalité"* (platitude): "The question is raised specifically in the case of translation into Arabic from French and English texts of scientific and technical nature, where one aims at diffusion of knowledge and techniques that are developed in occidental countries and then come to the Arabic world, which finds itself in the position of receptor" (2004, 46). This convergence of opinion around the role of the Arabic world in advancing science clarifies the positioning of the French text in the Translation course as the de facto original and of the Arabic as its de facto translation.[3] This positioning demonstrates the ideological weight of studying science at school and perceptions about the possibility of Moroccan and even, as Soufia suggests, Arab creativity.

Given the Arabization of the scientific curriculum—itself a translation of the Protectorate francophone curriculum—the course of Translation tries to compensate for the delay in the transformation of Arabic into a language that can accommodate contemporary technological innovation. In this sense, the Translation course is not simply one more course in a scientific curriculum, but rather is a "course symbol" of the incompleteness of an independent Moroccan modernity. The course marks a double deferral: of the terrain that Arabic has not yet conquered (modern science in Morocco) and of a language that Moroccan students have not yet mastered (French). The existence of the course may create the false assumption that students happily navigate the scientific landscape in both languages. As Mehdi's case shows, however, although students should theoretically use the course to enhance their bilingualism, in reality they understand very little French and memorize entire passages in order to pass exams. University entry exams and oral interviews raise the stakes by requiring an adequate knowledge of French, and the need for good French-language skills continues throughout higher education.

Consequently, the Translation course is the arena not only for a class struggle for economic opportunity and social integration but also for an ideational battle over which language can mediate an agenda of Moroccan modernization. Noticeably, by discussing a delay in the transformation of Arabic rather than its inherent incapacity, speakers posit the Arabic language as a malleable and changing entity as much as French or English, emphasizing its evolving relationship to global scientific and technological knowledge production. This characterization is worth scrutinizing because the specific features of language and science it appropriates enter a dialectic that often passes unnoticed by researchers and practitioners of translation. An analysis of the textbooks used for the course yields insights into these "modes of objectification, the potential for reflexivity they capacitate, and the specific character of their respective vulnerabilities to contingency" (Keane 2003, 423).

The Translation course, which spans the last two years of high school, makes use of two textbooks: the *Manuel de traduction* (Translation Manual) in the junior year and the *Parcours de traduction* (Course of Translation) in the senior year. Examining these bilingual textbooks, with titles and prefaces only in French, alongside the other arabophone scientific textbooks of the junior- and senior-year levels, is very instructive.[4] The preface to *Parcours* states the main objective of the book: "to help respond to student needs of bilingual training and communication, both written and oral" (*Parcours*, 3). Yet even at first glance the quantitative presence of the two languages throughout the textbooks shows a bias toward French. Most units start with French scientific passages that serve as the basic text through which students learn to make grammatical, syntactical, and terminological points of comparison. The first few units of the junior-year textbook offer a general French lexicon—*table des matières* (table of contents), *index* (index), and *sommaire* (summary)—and focus on how to use an online dictionary and a specialized encyclopedia. The units conclude with observations on the differences between literal versus interpretive translation and advice on how to summarize passages. Yet, in their great concern for factors that complicate or inhibit translation between the two languages, the textbook authors choose to single out only elements of the Arabic language that resist scientific translation: for instance, in a unit dedicated to acronyms, such as SIDA (AIDS), the authors remark that the morphology of the Arabic language does not allow for the formation of acronyms (*Manuel*, 29).

What is curious given the scientific focus of the textbooks is that they do not limit themselves to scientific terminology of scientific texts. Instead they address general phraseology and metaphors or idiomatic expressions. For example, a homework exercise asks students to find the translation for "*le talon d'Achille*" (someone's vulnerability or weakness), "*donner sa langue au chat*" (the cat ate my tongue), and other idiomatic expressions of the French cultural repertoire (*Manuel*, 31). Hence the textbooks for scientific translation function as general manuals of translation from French into Arabic. Instructions on translation technique set up a relationship between the two languages as systems theoretically devoid of hierarchy. However, because the original texts and terms are the French ones, the Arabic language appears mainly through its ability or inability to communicate similar notions in effective ways. In this light, the resistance of the language to acronyms appears as a translation difficulty loaded with meaning. The textbooks subtly validate Soufia's and Mohammed's interpretation of a declining Arabic civilization. In turn, this narrative of decline corroborates the current dependence of arabophone knowledge on foreign models for imitation instead of harvesting Arabic's own creative potential.

Thus, although they explicitly envision bilingual competence in the domains of science and technology, the textbooks enfold layers of hierarchy between the two languages. They designate hierarchy via a linear timeline according to which francophone terminology precedes Arabic terms. This hierarchy does not remain unchallenged; at certain points, the same textbooks offer an alternative timeline. This alternative chronology reinstates arabophone science as the generator of scientific concepts and, thus, as a consequential contributor to global scientific production. One example of this is the exploration of the Arabic origin of several French scientific terms:

> Arabic constitutes one of the principal loan languages of the French language. In fact, more than 300 French words are borrowed from Arabic (some of which were borrowed by Arabic from other languages, such as Persian), among which:
>
>> *Alchimie* comes from *al-kīmyā᾽* (chemistry)
>> *Alcool* comes from *al-kuḥūl* (alcohol)
>> *Algèbre* comes from *al-jabr* (algebra)
>> *Algorithme* comes from *al-khawārizmiyya* (algorithm)
>> (*Manuel de traduction*, 27)

This reversal of chronology corresponds to textbook sections that narrate the biographies of arabophone translators and producers of science from the distant past.[5] These biographies, which are tellingly written in Arabic, are not part of the testable component of each unit and thus constitute optional reading. Still, they saturate each unit with an awareness of a golden age of Arabo-Islamic knowledge production (*Manuel*, 29). This golden age narrative refers to the Umayyad (661–750 AC) and Abbasid periods (750–1285 AC), during which arabophone Muslim scholars synthesized, expanded, and diffused philosophical, mathematical, astronomical, and medical notions through translations of Greek and Persian sources.[6] *Parcours* introduces some of these translators—Ibn Qura (died 900), Ibn Batriq (died 800), and al-Kindi (801–867)—as scientists and polymaths who exemplified the superiority of the scientific and philosophical production of the classical Islamic era: "Muslim scholars were the first ones to study Greek philosophy and science and to transmit them into the Arabic language; for this, they were called philosophers. They worked on the transformation of science, its analysis, and on the corrections of its mistakes" (*Parcours*, 100).

These views are neither unusual nor particular to the textbooks. In fact, they seem to have been widespread even among French colonial educators in Morocco. In the Protectorate's main educational publication, "*Le Bulletin de l'enseignement public au Maroc*," one contributor characterized earlier intellectual encounters between France and what he called the "Muslim world" in the following terms: "The intellectual centers of Europe and especially the French ones find themselves in the first half of the 13th century literally invaded by Muslim thought" (Théry 1941, 307). The use of the term *envahir* (invade) is provocative, especially given the time period it refers to, because it implies that Arabic intellectual dominance was a type of military victory over Europe. The same contributing author establishes the circular path of Greco-Latin intellectual production that arabophone scholars preserved and updated during the rather stagnant European Middle Ages: "Aristotle entered the occidental world—and by this I specifically mean the French world—with Latin feet and a head covered by a fez" (Théry 1941, 308).[7] Hence the historical vignettes in Arabic, as they intermingle with French texts on environmental issues, the structure of the human cells, or the ethical problems of cloning, feature as balancing acts. These acts renegotiate a dominant, though far from hegemonic, modernist and imperial narrative of French superiority. In her work on Tamil language nationalism, Ramaswamy discusses this type of move as "compensatory classicism" (1997, 39), which contributes to an oppositional discourse to the colonial linguistic promotion of Sanskrit. In this light, the presentation of information on the classical Arabo-Islamic scientific production as the perpetuator and innovator of world knowledge is a *coup de force* to the French narrative of civilizational superiority.

Nonetheless, both arabophone translation and Arab intellectual achievements appear to belong resolutely to the past: the contemporary contribution of Arab scientists and translators is conspicuous by its absence. By contrast, the textbooks feature twentieth-century French translators such as Émile Benveniste (1902–1976) and Danica Seleskovitch (1921–2001) As do their textbooks, Mehdi, Soufia, and Mohammed wrestle with the idea of French supremacy in scientific production because it competes with the history of an Arab golden age. As Soufia indicates, this negotiation between France and the Arab world is crucial to Morocco's position within a global network of knowledge production: "they produce, we imitate." Given the openly competitive rhetoric and structure of global market integration, it would seem that this negotiation should feature centrally and urgently in nationwide debates and policy making around education. Paradoxically, this negotiation takes place in the unmarked Translation course under the guise of bilingual competence in science. This choice is not inconsequential and deserves a closer look.

LAYERS OF MYTH

The Translation course, which Mehdi considered dull while Soufia and Mohammed treated as indicative of the Arab position in global knowledge production, illustrates how larger political tensions fashion prevailing ideas about the Arabic language. Historical and sociolinguistic analyses and observations of everyday language practice have strongly argued that power relations at once contextualize and are constituted by language use (Bauman and Briggs 2000). Colonial and post-colonial encounters are particularly privileged sites for exploring the interaction between language and ideology because of the obvious collusion of "representations of linguistic structure and colonial interests" (Errington 2001, 20).[8] Along these lines, the Translation course and its textbooks can be taken as "myths," by which I mean linguistic items that simultaneously constitute ideological messages. These messages may promote values that actually undermine the explicit purpose of a course in translation; that is, achieving bilingualism in science.

Inspired by the broader undertaking of semiotics (the study of signs and symbols), Barthes has analyzed myth as the manipulation of history through form.[9] The concept of myth helps us see clearly that the materiality of language such as its transcription and syntax is vulnerable to a number of appropriations that create motivated systems of communication. For instance, any scientific term in Arabic that appears in the Translation textbooks, such as *"mazhar khārijī"* (phenotype), is not simply a "sign"; that is, the associative total of a concept and an image. By placing it next to the French terminology as its translation, the textbook momentarily empties the Arabic term of its "first-order meaning," "phenotype," and imbues it with a supplemental "second-order meaning": namely, the Arabic word becomes the "more or less successful rendering of the French original word." This "second-order meaning" does not make the "first-order meaning" disappear altogether, but pushes it aside so that *mazhar khārijī* is both phenotype and the translation of the French original term. In this sense, Soufia's phrase "they make, we imitate" echoes the entire Translation course that mythologizes French as a value that establishes French as the original scientific language.[10] Barthes describes myth as a "motivated" form that attempts to distort its historical and political origin by giving it the aura of nature: "We reach here the very principle of myth: it transforms history into nature" (1993, 116). Likewise, the Translation course does not exactly erase, but does depoliticize France's continuous presence in Morocco as a colonial power and development partner, by purifying and reshaping French as the language of science. The organization of academic disciplines and pathways supports this symbolic purification and reshaping for the benefit of a neoliberal job market and the emergence of a labor force aligned with that market.[11]

The Translation textbooks present one more mythologizing maneuver that is especially tantalizing. As already mentioned, on the cover of one of the textbooks is the famous painting "The Tower of Babel" by Pieter Brueghel (1563). The painting is inspired by the Old Testament parable that portrays multilingualism as divine punishment for and as a brake on human ambition (see Figure 3.1). The use of this Judeo-Christian parable

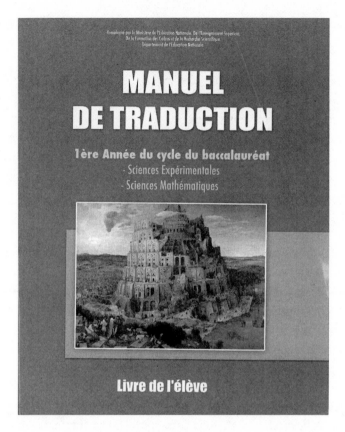

FIGURE 3.1

Cover of student textbook *Manuel de traduction,*
1ère année du cycle du baccalauréat, Sciences Expérimentales
et Sciences Mathématiques, 2006.
(Translation Manual, First Year of the Baccalaureate Cycle, Experimental
Sciences and Mathematics). Courtesy of *Dar nachr al-maarifa,* Rabat.

uncouples linguistic friction not just from colonialism but also from the
entire realm of world politics because it relocates this communicative
rupture from between people to between God and humans.[12] The choice
of the cover illustration is both fascinating and utterly puzzling. Could
this be the ironic choice par excellence on the part of the textbook authors,
who thereby critique the presence of this textbook in the curriculum? Or
is it the exact opposite, a gesture of extreme mythologizing that distances

school participants even further from the historical moment when multi-lingualism in Morocco became a necessity? I found Brueghel's painting on the textbook cover enigmatic and provocative, but the students I spoke to were neither familiar with nor intrigued by the Genesis story. To them, the cover was a picture of a half-torn tower—an impression that constituted one more inadvertent act of translation.

Its insights notwithstanding, Barthes's approach needs further quali-fication in a context where there is no single gesture of ideological domina-tion, but rather a fierce competition among many such gestures. Processes of linguistic ideologization, though more visible during colonial situa-tions, affect the entire experience of language. Hence a second type of myth inside the textbooks used in the Translation course is the direct opposite of the colonial myth: the textbooks put forward an image of continuity between classical Arabo-Islamic civilization and the Arabized Moroccan school. They establish this continuity through their coverage of the Umayyad and Abbasid periods during which arabophone scholars expanded and disseminated mathematical, astronomical, and philosophi-cal knowledge through their translations and commentaries.[13] In her com-ment "there was a time when the Arabs were the greatest civilization in the world," Soufia alluded to this historical period. As expected, however, the counter-myth about knowledge production in Arabic has its own his-torical and political depth, which the textbooks tweak. Although this counter-myth acts as a gesture of rebellion inside the course and its text-books, it also performs its own distortions by "reconstitut[ing] a chain of causes and effects, motives and intentions" (Barthes 1993, 104).

Hence regardless of its role as a balancing act and voice of revolt, this counter-myth is a myth itself. In other words, whereas the Arabo-Islamic contribution to scientific knowledge is undeniable, the direct connection the textbook draws between the caliphate of Baghdad and the Moroccan classroom constitutes a new intention that structures the past. Notably, the trope of the classical Arabo-Islamic civilization as the shared basis of all modern Arabs undergirds the nationalist ideology of Pan-Arabism and its manifestation in nation-building throughout the region. What this counter-myth silences is diversity, antagonism, and disagreement among Arab states in processes of nation-building and engagements with mod-ernization. These processes overlap with translation practice because they are contingent on the standardization and modernization of the Arabic language during the nineteenth and twentieth centuries. Significantly, they highlight the fundamental role of metaphor in the service of linguistic modernization.

CONQUEST, LANGUAGE, AND THE FRENCH BICYCLE

The story of scientific translation in contemporary Morocco reflects the protracted and deeply politicized role of translation in the history of the Arabic language. Debates on translation have been robust ever since the early Islamic period and have related to a variety of visions of Arabization that were not all aligned with the prerogatives of twentieth-century nationalism (Stetkevytch 2006, 57). An interest in language expansion and standardization intensified with the Arab conquests that culminated during the Ummayad and Abbasid caliphates. At that point, the divergence between the Bedouin language—according to some, the purest form of Arabic—and the varieties spoken in the newly acquired regions became a potential impediment to the administration of the empire. After the central administration settled in Baghdad, it took up the project of language standardization and the expansion of the lexicon, both processes deemed necessary for the effective administration of the empire's lands. Standardization involved fixing the orthography, classifying the vocabulary, and developing a stylistic standard (Versteegh 1997, 53). At the same time, the Arabic lexicon was in perpetual contact with other languages, in particular, Persian, Greek, and Sanskrit (Hodgson 1974; Lapidus 1988). Many foreign words entered the Arabic lexicon with slight modifications in phonology and morphology based on what later became the central principle for linguistic development: *al-qiyās* (analogy).[14] The Basra grammarians adopted the principle of analogy and the method of *ishtiqāq* (derivation from a three-letter verbal root) to create scientific terminology for Arabic.

Debates over methods of translation through analogy—such as *ishtiqāq, taʿrīb* (assimilation of foreign words), and *naḥt* (the formation of compound words)—intensified during the nineteenth century due to the experience of Western imperialism. This historical juncture, what we call the *nahḍa* (renaissance) of Arab cultural production, brought about a systematic conversation around Arabic's capacity to communicate the experience of contemporary life. This conversation took place in the institutional framework of the Arab language academies. As early as 1892, Muhammad Tawfiq al-Bakri, an al-Azhar scholar and engaged intellectual, hosted a language salon in his home in Cairo that gave birth to an academy in that city dedicated to the study and transformation of the Arabic language. Language academies then opened in Damascus, Baghdad, Rabat, Tunis, and Algiers. These institutions, explicitly modeled on the *Académie Française*, took on the task of producing contemporary scientific and technological vocabulary in Arabic. It is important to note that one of the main methods they used was *al-waḍʿ bi-l-majāz* (figurative semantic derivation), which entailed shifting the meaning of a word through metaphor. For instance, *maṭār*, which formerly meant "the place which or to which a bird flies," also became the term for "airport."[15] This linguistic operation inside the academies competed with the efforts of other language professionals such as poets, translators, editors, and journalists who were coining neologisms around the same time. Because this activity was fragmented, many of the words produced within the academies and by other professionals did not gain literary or scientific acceptance. For instance, one member of the Damascene academy, ʿIzz al-Din al-Tanukhi, wrote an essay on the topic *"Tashrīḥ al-darāja"* (Anatomy of the Bicycle; 1935) in which he translated the parts of the bicycle from French into Arabic. For the word "front wheel, he drew on the French term *"la roue directrice"* (directing wheel) to create the Arabic term *"al-dūlāb al-muwājih,"* its literal translation. Yet his terminological suggestion did not override other translations of the French term such as *"al-dūlāb al-amāmī"* (front wheel), which became more widespread (Sawaie 2006). Tanukhi's case indicates why the assortment of Arabic translations and their relationship of dependence on the French term have led many students, among whom Mohammed, to think that "French goes on the bike, Arabic goes on foot." Regardless of such complexities, the language academies came together in the period of decolonization—the 1950s and 1960s—to promote Pan-Arab nationalism through language transformation and standardization.

In colonial-era Morocco, a discussion of arabophone science was not really on the table, even though archival material testifies to the difficulties

students had with scientific subjects. In 1939, in his report on the teaching
of mathematics inside Moroccan schools, primary school teacher Mr.
Debraye deplores the fact that his students faced the double challenge of
learning "an entire foreign living language" at the same time as they
learned scientific concepts (1939, 251). In post-independent Morocco, the
Maʿhad al-Dirāsāt wa-l-Abḥāth li-l-Taʿrīb (Institute for Studies and Research on Arabization) opened in 1961. Its proclaimed mission, according
to its first director, Ahmed Lakhdar-Ghazal, was to "re-establish the Arabic language everywhere where the French language was used" (1976, 9).
He understood Arabization to be "in its origins, an engaged notion connected to the colonial presence. In the aftermath of independence, Arabization meant re-conquering the terrain heretofore occupied by the foreign
language and culture" (1976, 9). Because the Institute's goal was to replace
the French language with Arabic, its modernization of Arabic hinged
primarily on a vigorous work of translation (1976, 9). The immediate concern that arose was that of equivalence: "Can the Arabic language today,
as it appears in usage, express the reality of the contemporary world at the
same level of efficacy and precision of the foreign language?" (1976, 9). The
pursuit of equivalence entailed that the foreign language would serve as
model and support to Arabic's "opening to the world of progress" (1976,
64). Hence from the very beginning translators found themselves in the
tenuous position of using French as a model to empower Arabic so that
the latter would eventually displace the former language. Many similar
efforts have taken place around the world; for example, in Tanzania, English remains until today the language of higher education in anticipation
of Swahili attaining "its full language-ness" (Blommaert 2005, 399).

Lakhdar-Ghazal devotes his essay explaining the Institute's mission,
"*Méthodologie générale de l'arabisation de niveau*" (General Methodology
for Arabization of a High Standard) to elaborating on the technical impediments that delayed or inhibited the work of Arabization. He argues
that the first hurdle was the large number of terminological lacunae in the
domains of science and technology. These lacunae persisted inside French-
to-Arabic and English-to-Arabic dictionaries because they tended to
provide one-way translations of foreign terms into Arabic. The language
academies reproduced these translations in their scientific and technical
lists and dictionaries, even though doing so made the Arabic term, which

was usually a new coinage, appear isolated and less authoritative than its foreign, already standard counterpart (see Liu 1995 for an investigation of a similar phenomenon in twentieth-century China). What exacerbated this incongruence was that the activity of translation took place not at a time when scientific progress was stagnant but instead in a era of global acceleration in the scientific and technological domains: "In the modern world," writes Lakhdar-Ghazal, "a few million new terms are being coined every year in the different branches of science and technology, while only a few hundred appear in the Arab world to catch up with a terminological delay" (1976, 63). New coinage emerged in a rapid and anarchic way because there was no formal authority and publication in Arabic dedicated to explaining the origin, etymology, references, or the context of usage for neologisms. In the absence of such a platform, it was hard to compare, evaluate, and settle on new coinages (Stetkevych 2006). Consequently the work of standardization of scientific terms did not advance at the envisaged pace despite the establishment of institutions in Morocco and Algeria specifically for that purpose.[16]

IMPASSIONED DISCUSSIONS ON FORM:
TRANSLATORS AT WORK

The Translation course and the larger historical context of scientific translation attest that the form of the Arabic language has been a terrain on which is waged a threefold struggle for emancipation, modernization, and creativity. The symbol of science has woven together these three goals, making them appear interdependent. Given that the translation activity has taken place across arabophone contexts, those Moroccans who took responsibility for producing translations of scientific terminology shaped and led this struggle at a national level. As it turned out, I did not need to look far from the classroom to meet these translators; many were or still are educators in high schools or universities. These translators have engaged with the topic of arabophone science in different historical moments and approached the issue of arabophone science from diverse angles, yet share a passionate attitude toward the practice of translation. Their perspective both contextualizes and accentuates Mehdi's, Soufia's, and Mohammed's denunciation of Moroccan imitation of French and American technological advancements. It also elucidates the high stakes vested in scientific translation for the symbolic decolonization of knowledge at school and in the country.

Mr. Bentaleb was the regional coordinator for the course of Translation in the area I worked and a contributing author to the textbooks. An elegant suited man in his mid-forties, Mr. Bentaleb shook my hand firmly and swiftly turned on his laptop and plugged in a foldable Arabic keyboard. While he was starting up a PowerPoint presentation that clarified the rationale for the curriculum design for the course, Mr. Bentaleb began to narrate his own professional trajectory. "I became a translator overnight!" he exclaimed. In 1989, when the Arabization of scientific subjects was completed, Mr. Bentaleb was a teacher of mathematics. Like all other teachers, he had to immediately switch his language of instruction from French to Arabic. To prepare him to make that switch, he attended several *journées d'études* (workshops). He then pursued a two-year training program for teachers of translation. Acceptance into that program required a background in mathematics, physics, chemistry, or the natural sciences. Mr. Bentaleb fit the candidate profile and became one of the first teachers to complete formal training in scientific translation in 1991. As he explained, the most obvious problem for the Ministry of Education at the time was how to help students handle the abrupt transition from an Arabized high school to a French-speaking university. The Translation course was designed to help students cope with the transition, though the Ministry did not immediately produce a curriculum for it. Initially, translation classes ran as sessions in textual analysis in French using texts that teachers chose on an individual basis. In 2001, the Ministry of Education created positions for inspectors for the course and Mr. Bentaleb got a promotion. The new inspectors were given the task to oversee the creation of a curriculum. At that point, Mr. Bentaleb saw the need and opportunity to write a textbook. Evidently, not only had former science teachers turned into teachers of translation but also some became textbook authors with the authority to disseminate their own terminological choices for scientific terms. To elaborate further on these inspectors' approach to scientific translation, Mr. Bentaleb described his PowerPoint slides:

> For the translation textbooks, we [the authors] use notions that already
> exist in Morocco even if we personally don't agree with them. Whenever
> we have to translate a word anew, we research the historical range of the
> Arabic language, even ancient versions, to find a word that can approxi-
> mately evoke the same core meaning. An example for this would be the
> translation of *"atome"* into *"dharra"* (atom). The word *dharra* is old and
> it previously signified "a tiny particle." If the above method fails, we can
> always use the foreign word and transcribe it phonetically into Arabic.
> An example would be the word *"electron,"* which we use as is.

In this description of the translation process, Mr. Bentaleb raised two
translation challenges. The first one is how to translate acronyms such as
SIDA (AIDS) because Arabic does not use acronyms; they therefore
require another type of representation. The second challenge is how to
translate scientific phrases, such as *"limite de résolution microscopique"*
(microscopic resolution limit).

Diverging from the discussion of translation techniques, I asked
Mr. Bentaleb to evaluate the capacity of high school students to respond
to the bilingual requirements of his translation course: "Of course they
are capable," he answered, but with some defensiveness, and in the same
breath he added,

> Students have to be able to communicate in the two languages. They have
> to become truly bilingual. This course was a rescue-course at first, but now
> it is moving beyond the initial idea of accessing higher education. With
> this course, we can also tell the Other that we exist. If we don't engage
> with science, we'll always need the Other and we will never be free.

The moment he finished uttering this phrase, Mr. Bentaleb cleared his
throat and fidgeted slightly in his seat, looking as if he had surprised himself with such overt declaration of his investment in translation as a post-
colonial balancing act. He swiftly changed the subject back to curriculum
design.

If science is emblematic of contemporary attempts at knowledge emancipation, then the perseverance of French as the original scientific terminology suggests an ideological defeat. A series of discussions with a senior
inspector of French-language instruction probed this defeat by unpacking
the political reluctance around the Arabization of science and the impact
of this reluctance on students. Mr. Lamrini was one of the inspectors who

took me under their wings. His years of experience inside the public schools—he was approaching retirement—made him especially outspoken, and he often launched into lengthy explanations of less known aspects of educational policy. Mr. Lamrini had started his career as a teacher of French, but ended up working on the Translation course for more than a decade as a teacher and then as an inspector. His narrative on the Translation course begins with this powerful statement: "We cannot speak of translation per se." The following is his account of the course:

> In 1983, the state decided that Arabization would extend to high-school education except for the fields of technology and economics that we still teach in French. This choice would facilitate the relationship between the Palace and the parties of *Istiqlāl* and *Itiḥād Ishtirāqī li-l-Quwāt al-Shaʿbiyya* (*Union Socialiste des Forces Populaires*, USFP), both of which considered *fuṣḥā* integral to Moroccan identity. The Palace responded positively, but France was also implicated in this conversation. Mittérand and then Chirac kept reaching all sorts of agreements of co-operation with Morocco, and the country remained open to them. In 1989, when we translated the sciences for the *lycée* level, what used to be the Pedagogical Activities course turned into the Translation course. At once, we became ad-hoc translators of science and realized that we had to train teachers of translation. We recruited them from the scientific disciplines and the Faculty of French literature.

Mr. Lamrini recalled that the Translation course caused considerable friction between science teachers and French teachers around their respective ability to teach the Translation course:

> At first, there were disputes between teachers trained in translation and science teachers who worked with their own terminology. Then, there were tensions between teachers of French and science teachers. The latter argued that teachers of French without a scientific background did not have the necessary competence to translate. It was chaos!

Mr. Lamrini had not made up his mind, he said, about which academic background suited the task of translation better, but he did firmly believe that the majority of students did not benefit from the Translation course: "There are some bilingual students, but the question is, are they an exception? Can the system shape true bilinguals?" He said that he would gladly opt for an overtly bilingual system in which students studied all scientific subjects in French and the humanities in Arabic. But because the current system was unable to shape a bilingual cohort of students, Mr. Lamrini was against scientific Arabization. He emphatically distinguished between an ideal Arabization and what happened in Morocco, characterizing the latter as "a mere translation." I was curious to know what he meant by the phrase "a mere translation." He responded that the Arabization of sciences was a "mechanical translation of French terms and not a creation of a coherent whole." He referred to the fact that mathematical writing in Morocco was not in tune with other arabophone countries where both questions and formulas are written in the direction of the Arabic script, from right to left. Instead, in Morocco, students transcribe formulas from left to right.

Mr. Lamrini's historicization and politicization of the practice of translation at school were explicit throughout our conversations. On one occasion, however, he went in a different direction, establishing a direct link between translation challenges and linguistic form. "Either way," he said, "within a pedagogical and logical frame, French is Cartesian; it's a cause-and-effect language. Arabic is a juxtaposition." He justified this distinction by discussing the history of Arabic expression and its propensity for formulaic and ornate language. I found this double take on language form bewildering: Mr. Lamrini acknowledged the foundational role of political decision making in the work of scientific translation at the same time as he deplored the inherent inability of Arabic to communicate about science.

The most ardent opponent of this assessment of Arabic linguistic form was a prominent retired professor of statistics who had been engaging with the process of Arabization for the past forty years. Originally from Fes, Professor Merzouki attended school during the Protectorate when most subjects were taught in French except for Arabic literature, which was taught in Arabic for three hours per week. He pursued his undergraduate degree in Paris and then moved to California to complete a doctorate degree in statistics. Compelled by what he called his "nationalist duty," Prof. Merzouki decided to return to Morocco after earning his doctorate. In 1972, while a university professor in Rabat, Prof. Merzouki was asked to translate a university entry exam from French into Arabic. The venture excited him greatly: "I had to use an old language for an advanced scientific purpose!" The research he undertook to accomplish this translation made him consider translating other "wonderful advancements" of modern statistics from English into Arabic while bypassing French altogether: "Why do this favor to the French and fill in the gaps in their literature?" This led him to his writing a manual of mathematics. Prof. Merzouki recalled that writing the manual had been challenging both in terms of the translation itself and in figuring out layout and printing: "This book had to include Latin, Greek and Arabic characters on the same page, arranging mathematical formulas from left to right and descriptions from right to left." The professor made daily trips to a printing press in Casablanca to supervise the printing process: "Employees at the press looked like jewelers, taking one letter at a time and sticking it carefully onto the page." He published this book in Arabic first and then translated it into French. Poignantly, the book's recognition came via its French translation because parents and teachers considered francophone science books more prestigious than arabophone ones.

Throughout my fieldwork, Prof. Merzouki and I enthusiastically delved into the topic of science translation during our many meetings that took place in his professional translation office at the center of town. To the question of how he approached translation as process, he responded,

> It was through mathematics! Math gives you the power of abstraction and absorption of new systems through which you are able to comprehend everything. And let's not forget that the best researcher in translation and especially in the idea of automatic translation, which artificial intelligence will eventually bring to completion, was Noam Chomsky. Did you know that Chomsky was trained as a mathematician?[17] Linguistics is all about abstraction of language as system and the game of symbols, and Arabic is the perfect example of a mathematical language.

Contrary to what Mr. Lamrini claimed, Prof. Merzouki thought Arabic to be especially fertile for new scientific coinage because of its inherent generative potential emanating from the radical three-letter root:

> We begin with 26 letters in the alphabet, which can be combined in any three ways, so already we have the options: 26 x 25 x 24. Then you can add combinations with the *shadda* (symbol for letter doubling), or you can combine the three-root system with *alif* and so on. On top of this,

consider the addition of long vowels. The number of new words you can create is vast! We should also bear in mind that the regularity of the Arabic language is remarkable. You can teach a computer to conjugate in Arabic more quickly than in French or English since the latter are ridden with irregularity.

Evidently, Prof. Merzouki views language from the perspective of its formal units (letters, verbal roots) and appreciates what he deems to be the inherent regularity of both classical and modern Arabic. As we saw earlier, achieving this regularity was an explicit goal during the classical Islamic period and remained a core technique in language modernization in the early and mid-twentieth century. His take on the capacity of the three-letter root unswervingly refutes the evaluation of Lakhdar-Ghazal, director of the Institute of Arabization quoted earlier. According to Lakhdar-Ghazal, the three-letter root is "economical and efficient" but resistant to lexicography and neologism: "Our language resists borrowing for semantic reasons. . . . The three letter root, the most frequent, is the semantic matrix from which we can derive a lexical terrain. . . . The introduction of foreign terms may disturb this communicability in many ways" (1976, 38–40). In our discussion, Prof. Merzouki dismissed Lakhdar-Ghazal's assessment as "the propaganda of a non-patriot" who hid his ideological views in a technical review of translation practice. In contradistinction to this review, the logic underlying Prof. Merzouki's translation activity was that translation had to be based on the mathematical concept: "Once the student understands the universal language of mathematical symbols, translation is easy and successful." Here, the universal deep structure of mathematical science thus trumped the diversity of world languages.

Inspired by his own achievements in translation, Prof. Merzouki founded an entirely arabophone post-graduate program in statistics in a public School for Advanced Studies and invited professors to join him in teaching in it. Some of these professors went on to occupy key positions in the government, including the Ministry of Education. Prof. Merzouki described the program as a success in terms of ensuring job opportunities for its graduates, who later found work in prestigious government agencies. This success, he claimed, "destroyed the French thesis that science could not be taught in Arabic." For that reason, according to Prof. Merzouki, the French Embassy, as well as the Ministry of Education, which in his view was under the control of the French Embassy, vigorously opposed his program. So much pressure was put on him to switch the language of instruction of the program from Arabic to French that he decided to temporarily leave the university and, later, the country as well. After his departure, the Ministry of Education converted the course back into French, which remains its language of instruction until today.

Equally frustrating were Prof. Merzouki's efforts as a member of ALE-SCO (Arab League Educational, Cultural, and Scientific Organization), an organization that promoted the use of Arabic scientific terminology in education throughout the arabophone world. Its mission was monumental, and according to Prof. Merzouki, disagreement about the translation of scientific terms was fierce. The delegations from other countries did not consider Morocco a worthy contributor to the modernization of Arabic because of their prevailing perception that *dārija* was further away from *fuṣḥā* than other dialects and hence had distorted Moroccan speakers' understanding of *fuṣḥā*. Prof. Merzouki recalled the debate:

> It was not evident to everyone that we should standardize only one term
> for each scientific notion. For Egyptians and Syrians, it was also hard to
> agree on terms suggested by Moroccans, Algerians, and Tunisians. They
> thought we're not very good in Arabic. The idea that the other Arabs have
> of Moroccans is that they are latecomers to Arabic since the Andalusian
> cultural production came much later than the Levantine and the Saudi
> one. But we know that the question of fluency is unrelated to this history.

Disdain of the Arabic dialects and the different colonial traditions that provided the original scientific texts (French and English) brought the process of standardization to a standstill.[18]

The views of the translators just discussed give historical depth and political insight to the complaints of Mehdi, Soufia, and Mohammed about uneven pace and uncertain status of scientific and technological production in the Arabic language. These translators' disagreements about the properties and capacities of the Arabic linguistic form do not detract from their consensus around identifying the practice of translation with the decolonization of knowledge. This identification sends an urgent message about the symbolic weight of language hierarchy: namely, student perceptions of their ability to participate as equals in the global production of knowledge informs their engagement with knowledge altogether.

SCIENTIFIC POSITIVISM AND AFFECT
IN THE TOWER OF BABEL

Student evaluations of science and technology in Morocco and the impassioned commentaries of the three translators depict scientific translation as a multifaceted encounter in space and time. In this encounter, speakers deconstruct some political and linguistic myths even as they simultaneously produce and consume others. Although I never saw members of these two groups—students and translators—discussing this issue with each other, I view them both as grappling with the dilemma of whether scientific translation should be considered the transportation of meaning or as the staging of an ideological confrontation. This dilemma maps onto a theoretical debate on the nature of language, a debate that gains significance beyond the halls of the academy because different language theories feed differently situated advocacy agendas for the right to creativity. Bringing the translators and some of the most prominent scholars of translation in direct dialogue makes possible the evaluation of theoretical formulations of language not in a theoretical void but instead in relation to everyday choices speakers make as they position themselves in society, and in knowledge production.

In addition to exposing the political intentions that informed the venture of colonial linguistics, linguistics scholars have also probed the metaphysics of colonialism. It was largely those same metaphysics that led to the development of structural linguistics during the twentieth century as best represented by Saussure (Culler 1986). Skepticism about the Western Protestant gap between ideas and matter instilled in the traditions of structuralism resulted in criticism of the Saussurian view of language and in the presentation of this view as one semiotic ideology among others. For example, Webb Keane resists Saussure's assertion that signification is essentially arbitrary and therefore radically open ended. He proposes instead that we should examine diverse ideas about the relationship between signs and the world along with their "representational economies"— the historical and social formations that underpin them (2003, 417). Yet, in our case, we cannot dismiss Saussurian linguistics as ethnocentric or historical on purely theoretical terms. Structural linguistics stages a claim to knowledge production in Morocco by constructing arguments about the primacy of form over meaning and about the transparency of scientific translation.

All three teacher-translators put to use aspects of structural linguistics to defend arabophone science. Their take on science as "the arrow of prog-ress" (Escobar et al. 1994, 212), reflecting a modernist narrative of human evolution, is useful to them because it provides them with a plan through which to recapture a sense of ownership and take part in global competi-tion. Mr. Bentaleb, author of the textbook, and Mr. Lamrini, the senior inspector of French, oscillate between assessing the political substratum of scientific translation into Arabic and treating translation as a linguistic operation along the axes of efficiency and conciseness as if these were definite features. Despite his awareness of the implications of science in neocolonial relationships—"we need to show the other that we exist"— Mr. Bentaleb chooses to invest in the elaboration of translation tech-niques. To establish a correspondence between the two languages, his textbook treats translation as the transference of meaning.

Mr. Lamrini's position is equally complex. On the one hand, Mr. Lam-rini refuses to distinguish between the linguistic operation of translation and the sociocultural context that places the two languages in contact. There is strong affinity between his views and George Steiner's qualifica-tion of types of translation. Arguing that the act of interpretation is inherent in translation (he used the Greek term *hermeneia* after Aristotle), Steiner contests the conventional distinctions among "literalism, para-phrase, and free imitation" in translation practice and recommends other descriptive terms such as "generosity," "aggression," and "morality" (1998, 319). A joint concern for Mr. Lamrini and Steiner is that "the hermeneutic act must compensate. If is to be authentic, it must mediate into exchange and restored parity" (Steiner 1998, 316). In the Moroccan case, however, the Arabization of science has so far undermined instead of compensating the very language it was meant to empower.

Notwithstanding his acknowledgment of the role of political decision making in the work of scientific translation, Mr. Lamrini comments on the inherent inability of Arabic to convey scientific terms and concepts: as quoted earlier, he says, "French is Cartesian; it's a cause-and-effect language. Arabic is a juxtaposition." This stance resonates with earlier portrayals of the "Arab soul" or the "Arab mentality." It carries the specters of the orientalist tradition in which oriental languages became proofs of cognitive and social primitiveness. This heritage anticipated and became a building block of colonial projects.[19] Jacques Berque, a prominent Arabist and colonial administrator in Morocco, has addressed the tensions of modernization in the Arab world in a way that echoes both the criticisms and the incongruities of Mr. Lamrini's position. Berque finds the stylistic virtuosity of Arabic expression burdensome. Language traits, such as the propensity for assonance and a bias toward rhetoric at the expense of precision, functioned for Berque as barriers to the language's straightforwardness (1978, 35). He advocates that Modern Arabic expression should endeavor to rid itself of ambiguity and strive for scientific amenability: "For it is through and in technology that the Arab world and the industrial West showed themselves most obviously out of phase" (1978, 36). Although he regrets the violence that modernizing the Arabic language might wield on arabophone culture, he does note the high stakes involved in this linguistic operation: "Restoring the creativity of Arabs in Arabic is the real problem and it arises in terms not of languages as 'vehicles' but of true intimacy with the world's motion" (1978, 56).

Restoring creativity to Moroccans is precisely the goal of Prof. Merzouki's translation activities. He challenges the widespread view of Arabic's relationship to modern science and technology through his conception of mathematical translation. Asserting that mathematical notions are a universal language, he disengages all types of science from its European cultural bounds. Free to describe the "world as it is," as the professor claims, Arabic should use its richness of vocabulary and flexible word structure to approach scientific notions more accurately than European languages. Having reinstated the structural potential of the language, the professor can demolish orientalist arguments and confront both colonial influences in educational planning and the fragmentation among Arab states. This is where Saussurian linguistics, which favors the exploration of language's deeper structures as units of arbitrary interconnections between sign and things, turns into a real asset for the professor. Prof. Merzouki uses Noam Chomsky's by now outmoded vision of automatic translation. This concept assumes that, on a deep level, languages belong to one coherent universal human language, the grammar of which can be scientifically retrieved (Chomsky 1971). Through its capacity for infinite rule-governed variations, this formal grammar escapes the dubious arenas of meaning and significance. According to this logic, automatic translation would theoretically erase all need for creativity by being essentially anti-creative, thanks to the direct correspondence between the linguistic categories of each language.

Prof. Merzouki is aware of critiques of Chomsky's linguistic theory and of the existence of multiple theories of translation, but he makes use of this particular model so that he can promote arabophone science on the world scene. He achieves this through the merging of mathematics, which he considers the epitome of logical thinking, with linguistic structures. The affinities he traces are reminiscent of structural linguistics that mapped formal linguistic categories, such as grammar, onto logical categories (Benveniste 1966). What the professor leaves out, however, is any interrogation of mathematical terms as dependent on meaning and interpretation because his narrative assumes that mathematics is a universal language free from the treacherous domain of world languages.[20] In a sense, Prof. Merzouki follows the Barthean suggestion for mythologizing: he positions both French and Arabic as second-order systems to the assumed universality of a first-order system (mathematics). This way the professor can combat the assumed superiority of the French language as the original communicator of science. Barthes has warned us, however, that even though mathematical signs are relatively resistant to myth, mathematical language as a whole can become victim to full mythical appropriation:

> When the meaning is too full for myth to be able to invade it, myth goes around it and carries it away bodily. This is what happens to mathematical language. In itself, it cannot be distorted, it has taken all possible precautions against interpretation: no parasitical signification can worm itself into it. And this is why, precisely, myth takes it away *en bloc*: it takes on certain mathematical formula ($E=mc^2$) and makes of this unalterable meaning the pure signifier of mathematicity. (Barthes 1993, 120)

This quote illuminates Prof. Merzouki's parallel act of myth production: he presents mathematical language as the epitome of all scientific activity and as the quintessential description of reality. Essentially, both Prof. Merzouki and Barthes advocate for the extra-linguistic quality of mathematical language and its relative imperviousness to ideological appropriation.

Their assessment is however mistaken. Since mathematical formulas have to be voiced in one language or another, mathematics is not inextricable from language and therefore remains equally vulnerable to the ideological working of metaphor.

By reinserting metaphor in scientific terminology, we can now see how the students' understandings of translation paradoxes and the teachers-translators' passion invite an examination of scientific translation that resembles literary translation. In both cases, it is clear that scientific terminology and mathematics do not escape metaphorical thinking: after all, in Mr. Bentaleb's example of translation of the atom, is not the meaning of *dharra* a semantic shift from "tiny particle" to "nuclear core"? This is the point where literary and scientific translations converge: both types of translation require an understanding of motivation and an appreciation of affect in the act of translating. Prof. Merzouki's dilemma reveals this convergence particularly well. He finds himself in the position of theoretically disengaging science from expressive language and yet personally resenting the fact that science in Morocco is expressed in French. His resentment is well founded because we cannot really reduce language, not even scientific language, to its formal categories.[21] Barthes argues that mythologists, who are in the business of undoing social myths, find it hard to connect with the community because they are condemned to operate in "the order of sarcasm" (1993, 146). On the contrary, Prof. Merzouki feels like the ultimate patriot, proving that mythologists can also be myth producers with the desire to reshape a community through other ideological agendas. In this light, Prof. Merzouki's insistence on the Arabic root system and its generative potential is the manifesto of the arabophone voice defending its roots.[22]

As it happens, the image of "root" is central to theories of translation that have posited a third shared term between the word and its translation, a third term that can be the universal human grammar or the messianic true language. In "After Babel: Aspects of Language and Translation," Steiner argues that Jewish intellectuals from Benjamin to Wittgenstein to Chomsky have embraced the "linguistic mystique" of the parable of the Tower of Babel, the second fall from heaven via the imposition of multilingualism (1998, 62). The parable became central to the imagination of utopia through the return to a shared root language that kabbalistic philosophy correlates with "a messianic moment of restored understanding" (1998, 61). Walter Benjamin's essay "The Task of the Translator" (1968), an exemplary work that explores that mystique, is based on the assumption that the two languages that enter into an act of translation are fragments of this pure third register. This register glimmers through the act of translation and will eventually bring the foreignness of all languages to an end.

Prof. Merzouki, who modifies this metaphysics to posit mathematics as his third register, agrees with the crux of Benjamin's argument: a good translation does not transmit information, but instead translates the communicability of a text (its *intentio*), a mode inherent in every original. It is this quality of the original, its communicability, that renders itself to survival and renewal through translation (Benjamin 1968, 72). In "Des tours de Babel," Jacques Derrida defines translation as enhancement, a way to make the original work live both "longer and better, beyond the means of the author" (2007, 179). Enhancement is a key term here because it resonates with student comments during the Translation class and the translators' narratives. Both groups posit a time in the Arabo-Islamic civilization when translation was much more than replication; in Soufia's words "once upon a time, the Arabs were the greatest civilization in the world." During the classical Islamic period, translation into Arabic took place within an atmosphere of civilizational confidence and hence became the foundation of intellectual elaboration and creativity (Hodgson 1974, 153–154). On the contrary, scientific translation in the present is merely sterile imitation and a form of indebtedness. The question Derrida asks, "To whom is the translator committed?" (2007, 207), is key. His response is that the translator commits neither to the author of the original text nor to a model that needs reproduction. The impetus of translation lies is the excess; that is, the desire to overcome the text and produce something better. Hence, to be creative is not to simply translate science but rather to anticipate producing new science in Arabic and disseminating it to the world. Commentaries about the scientific capacity of Arabic constitute a political critique against the stagnation of knowledge production that the ruling mechanisms of the country tolerate and perpetuate. These mechanisms resemble the God of Genesis who "at the same time imposes and forbids translation" (Derrida 2007, 170).

Students, who are critical of imitation in the domain of science, and translators, who dynamically reverse translation hierarchies, render the act of translation as much more than linguistic activity. Rather, translation becomes for them an arena for reclaiming creativity and redressing the inequity of both past experiences and their current immersion in global production. While discussing the acutely political and deeply affective nature of translation, school participants inadvertently draw attention to one type of objectification of Arabic: they treat Arabic as a flexible and malleable language in the hands of people. This epistemological stance, which carries an assumption about the relationship between language and the material world, and the representational economy that underpins it— scientific instruction and production in Morocco—is in stark contrast with other symbolic visions that underpin Arabic. The next chapter turns to these other visions.

PART II

4

Inheritance, Heritage, and the Disinherited: Sacred Arabic

What does it mean to modernize a sacred language? What do such processes look like? How do they intersect with political interests and official policies? And what is a modern language in the first place?

—Niloofar Haeri, *Sacred Language, Ordinary People: Dilemmas of Culture and Politics in Egypt*

On the bus ride home from school that we frequently took together, junior-year student Malika often initiated provocative discussions about piety, the moral problems that undercut Moroccan society, and the relationship between what she called the "Muslim World" and the "West." The child of two primary school teachers, Malika was articulate and authoritative beyond her years. From her flushed face and beaming smile, I could tell she took equal pleasure in quizzing me on other religions, mainly Christianity, Judaism, and Hinduism, and in instructing me on Islam. During one such ride, slightly dazed by the heat and the very crowded bus, we spoke about the various educational resources on Islam available to Muslims today. Malika insisted that she did not owe her knowledge of Islam exclusively to what she learned at school; she also learned about her religion from independent online study, exposure to radio and television experts, and her participation in regular discussions on moral issues in her neighborhood's charitable association called *Raḥma* (God's Mercy). Even though these sources of knowledge definitely did not all speak in one voice, she told me every single one had convinced her that "Islam was the most advanced and most perfect of all religions." When I asked her to explain further, Malika pointed to how congruent the religion was with both tradition and modernity, with the past and the present: "I appreciate how the Qur'an explained natural phenomena and scientific facts that societies discovered centuries later!" Because Malika was a humanities student and very committed in sharing her religious expertise, I asked her if she contemplated a degree in Islamic Studies at university. Her tone shifted from cheery to somber: "No way—where would I work? There are no jobs in this field! Then, I don't really want to study and teach in *fuṣḥā* (Classical Arabic), I know it's our official language and it's the language of our religion, but I find it old and heavy." Her reluctance to study and teach in *fuṣḥā* piqued my interest in the relationship between language and religion for high school students. A self-avowed pious young woman, Malika contrasted Islam as a religion that transcends time with Arabic as a language stuck in the past. Her view is all the more striking because it conflates the Arabic language of worship, Qur'anic Arabic, with the Arabic of public education. What was the context that framed such a view, and how did it inform the negotiation of Muslim identity at school?

Both in and out of class, students and staff conversed regularly about the parameters and meanings of "piety"—devotion to God and observance of religious principles—and of "morality," ideas of right and wrong and the adoption of virtuous attitudes. In their conversations, they related their religious identity, which they fashioned across multiple spaces and through many experiences, to the institutional intentions of school and state. In so doing, students and staff brought into sharp relief the double instantiation of the post-independence Moroccan state as both bureaucratic and theocratic: the bureaucratic state has given rise to new mechanisms of governance and modes of production, whereas the theocratic state has been instrumental to the ongoing legitimation of a religious-dynastic monarchy. However, at the intersection of these two faces of state power inheres profound ambivalence about the nature and role of Arabic in contemporary Morocco. This ambivalence in turn informs ongoing public contention over the shape and meaning of Moroccan modernity.

This contention separates the Moroccan experience from that of other states in the region. As is known, the nation-building campaigns of every arabophone state after formal independence from Western imperialism embraced *fuṣḥā* rather than the diverse vernaculars as the medium for unification and modernization (Caton 2006). Many such campaigns incorporated organized religion in some way or another into state governance. These similarities notwithstanding, the post-independence trajectory of these nation-states has not been uniform and, as a result, nor has their specific deployment of religion in agendas of sociocultural engineering. What is interesting about the Moroccan case is the way Arabic language has been used to promote a particular religious orthodoxy.[1] In this chapter, I locate the promotion of this orthodoxy within the Ministry of Education as it connects to the *Makhzan*, the Palace, or, more precisely, to the royalist circles that dominate state mechanisms and oversee state objectives. These royalist circles and the institution of the theocratic monarchy they sustain need to promote Arabic as a sacred language so as to strengthen the legitimacy of the monarchy's Islamic heritage.

Yet the promotion of Arabic as a sacred language presents the Arabized school with a difficult dilemma: on the one hand, the Arabization policy has been driven by the argument of the expansion of Arabic into the mutable spheres of society and economy, and on the other, the post-independence state has had a vested interest in the preservation of Arabic as a sacred language that would fortify the monarchy's Islamic heritage. As expected, this dilemma has affected the form, function, and meaning of Arabic. In short, would Arabic be a profane and neutral medium of communication, or would it continue to be part of a metaphysical bond that endowed it with sacredness and therefore assumed its own efficacy? Even though this puzzle has a strong impact on the way students flesh out their positions as Muslims as well as their roles in society and economy, it remains deeply vexed to this day—so vexed, in fact, that research postulating the ontological nature of Arabic as a question has been scarce.

The government-sanctioned course *Tarbiya Islāmiyya* (Islamic Education), the focus of this chapter, explores this unresolved question and its implications for the policy of Arabization. This course's structure and curriculum reflect the state's agenda to transmit religious knowledge to large sectors of the population. It also foregrounds a state formulation of Islamic tradition that guarantees the Alawite dynasty a paramount place in the Moroccan national imagination. The use of religion to strengthen political legitimacy did not originate in the modern Moroccan state, but the modern state strategically built on a prevalent understanding of Arabic as a language made metaphysical through the act of revelation. The linguistic choices of the course become a starting point for exploring the political interest in Arabic emerging through public school instruction as predominantly a sacred tongue. This sacralization both happens in parallel to and at the expense of the language's ongoing, multifaceted evolution in presumed to be secular domains of practice and experience. The promulgation of this sacralization at school and in the job market has strengthened the perception that Arabic is unsuitable for promoting technological advancement and Morocco's integration into the global market. As we saw previously, this impression seriously jeopardizes the recognition of public school graduates as potentially valuable members of the labor force.

Religion instruction in class regularly became part of conversations about morality, language, and the state held outside of class. These conversations suggested that other aspects of selfhood, such as gender and aspirations for professional and political empowerment, had a dialectic relationship to the students' religious identity. They also revealed the specific frustration of the humanities students, such as Malika, caused by the inconsistent articulation of Arabic at school versus in the wider Moroccan society. In contrast with the scientific track, these students do not have the opportunity to improve their French-language skills through the study of scientific subjects and are therefore structurally tied to the use of Arabic in higher education and in their efforts to join a profession. Because of their dependency on Arabic, humanities students were the most vocal members of the Bac cohort in calling the school and the state to account for the mismatch between the linguistic ideology of sacred Arabic and broader demands for socioeconomic integration. Some came to doubt state and school as the arbiters of piety and morality. They framed their dissent within the terms of the Arabo-Islamic tradition, therefore proving that the contour and context of this tradition are more pliable than what is conventionally assumed. The landscape that has emerged is one of constant redrawing of orthodox praxis and belief by students, staff, and other actors—such as international religious experts and national Islamic movements that contest the state's claim to moral authority. State fears of student dissent from its own moral injunctions, a dissent it condemns as "radical," are strong evidence of the unintended consequences the state faces from foregrounding Arabic literacy as essential to moral cultivation.

Hence language—learned, monitored, and discussed—plays a key role in the students' moral contestation of the Arabization policy, especially those who should theoretically be the policy's most direct products, the humanities students. The relationship between language and religion raises a unique set of questions about moral cultivation that have been largely overlooked by research on Muslim piety and subjectivation more generally. What are the linguistic challenges of becoming a pious Muslim? How do these challenges implicate one's moral agenda in broader questions of sociopolitical and economic order? In sum, how does language training reveal all learning to be an open-ended process that involves approximation, reflexivity, hesitation, and contingency?

INHERITANCE: MODERN ISLAM AND SACRED ARABIC

The structural organization of the Moroccan public school is based on the French Protectorate model, as manifest in the division and terminology of educational levels and discipline orientations, as well as in curricula and pedagogical methods. However, public schools are also replete with pre-colonial educational elements that have found their way, through nationalist appropriation, into the modern classroom. Religious education is one such key element. In the nineteenth century, religious education took place in various institutions ranging from the *msid* (mosque school) and the *madrasa* to Islamic universities.[2] During the colonial period (1912–1956), these religious institutions, especially Islamic universities, reformulated their curricula and methods so as to compete with the Protectorate's content and methods of instruction (Eickelman 1978, 2007). The *collèges musulmans* (Franco-Muslim schools), which were under the joint supervision of the French Residency and the Moroccan Sultan, were the first to introduce Muslim religious pedagogy into a French-modeled curriculum and timetable. The contemporary Islamic Education course is a postcolonial appropriation of the Franco-Muslim school curriculum. The modern bureaucratic Moroccan state reoriented this curriculum toward mass consumption for the entire schooled population. In addition to this course, there are other opportunities for religious training inside formal schooling. For one, students have the choice of an alternative path to the public school called al-taʿlīm al-aṣīl (native education). This path is also run by the Ministry of Education and focuses on religious subjects.[3] Additionally, the Ministry of Habous (Pious Endowments) and Islamic Affairs administers a fee-paying option called al- taʿalim al-ʿatīq (traditional education). Traditional education takes place in special Traditional Schools and Qurʾanic schools.[4]

The Islamic Education course is mandatory for all twelve years of formal schooling and for all discipline tracks: hence it constitutes the most prolonged and systematic religious training for young Moroccans who complete compulsory education. The centrality of the course for academic success does decrease during the high school Baccalaureate cycle, whose timetable and weightings favor the core courses of the humanities and scientific tracks.[5] However, and considering that Islamic Education is not a core course for either track, its content is part of the junior-year examination. Outside of the course, students and staff engage with religion in school on many occasions. Although the call to prayer from the nearest mosque does not interrupt lessons, that call reverberates through the open windows of the classroom, and on Fridays school is only a half-day so that students can attend the khuṭba (Friday sermon). Religious holidays such as ʿīd al-fiṭr, ʿīd al-aḍḥā, and al-mawlid punctuate the academic year, and Islamic calligraphy decorates classroom walls, teachers' lounges, and textbooks.[6] The school implements a code of gendered religious modesty through the tablier (mandatory knee-length white apron) worn by female students and teachers. In addition to these regulated practices, spontaneous discussions on Islam abound inside classes as diverse as English, biology, and physical education. In my experience, teachers and students initiated such discussions in equal measure. Thus, in light of the structural, visual, and lived syncretism of the school landscape, a clear distinction between secular and religious education seems inaccurate. Clearly, the Moroccan state school is both the structural product of the Protectorate and a key site for the reinforcement of an Arabo-Islamic morality conforming to the interests of the state.[7] The overall content and linguistic parameters of the Islamic Education course suggest that Malika's perception of religion and language—positing Islam as complementary with modernity but fixing

Arabic as sacred and therefore inflexible—is neither idiosyncratic nor accidental.

During one class session on the principles of the distribution of *al-irth* (inheritance) as laid out in the Qur'anic chapter *"surat al-nisā'"* (The Women), I sat next to Malika. She shared her textbook with me and offered clarifications on the material of what she called "that unit" (*Tarbiya Islāmiyya* Bac 1, 2010, 113–116). The format of the lesson was no less systematic than that of any other scientific or humanities course. Specifically, the unit on inheritance treated the topic mainly as a set of principles explicable through mathematical fractions. Because the first task of the class was to calculate rules governing the distribution of inheritances, the teacher, Mrs. Samira Said, started the session by writing down fractions on the blackboard:

> First case: If the deceased (man) was survived by two sons and a daughter, then the inheritance needs to be divided in five; each son gets two-fifths of the inheritance and the daughter gets one-fifth.
>
> Second case: If the deceased (man) had only one daughter, then she gets half of his inheritance.
>
> Third case: If the deceased (man) has two or more daughters, the inheritance is divided into three portions; the daughters share two-thirds of the inheritance.

Discussion of these calculations (already displayed in table form in the textbook) took up half of the hour-long class session. Malika startled me with her detailed knowledge of the inheritance rules. She explained that her father had passed away the year before, and therefore she had experienced firsthand those rules in practice. Her father had left a wife, a son, and two daughters. Malika pointed out to me which rule applied to her case. Knowing that some female students expressed displeasure over the inheritance rules, I asked her if she minded that she only got half of what her brother got. "No," she replied coolly [dar.] *"Ana bint"* (I'm a girl). Malika did not read the Qur'an daily before her father died, but since then she had taken on the habit of reciting an *āya* (verse) in his memory every night. He had been a pious man all his life, and to honor him, both his daughters donned the veil after his death.

Not everyone was as interested as Malika in the Islamic Education course. In fact, many students thought it a waste of time, particularly during their junior and senior years when they felt they needed to zoom in on their core subjects. Those who participated eagerly in the calculations of inheritance distribution, however, shared Malika's level of knowledge. Like Malika, they may have had personal experiences with inheritance issues or systematic contact with popular devotional literature, but they certainly benefited from twelve years of school training in the subject. As in other Muslim societies, religious education at school entailed a recurrent and systematic engagement with a specific set of scriptures and moral principles that gave students plenty of opportunity to build on and refine their knowledge. During our conversations, students claimed that they were interested in the course because of its relevance and compatibility with many facets of contemporary life. For instance, during the class session on inheritance, Narjiss, who was sitting at the desk in front of us, overheard us whispering and turned around to offer her view on Islamic Education: "It shows us that Islam is a religion of the past, the present, and the future." "Do you mean that inheritance rules ensure the continuity of conduct within the Islamic tradition?" I asked. "Not just that," she responded. "I'm talking about scientific facts or human rights principles that the Holy Qur'an was first to introduce and explain." This view was obviously meaningful to Narjiss, but it was also in tune with the state's formulation of Islamic tradition and Muslim practice.

The Baccalaureate curriculum for religious pedagogy was developed to reflect the prerogatives of the post-independence Moroccan state. This state took the responsibility for the interpretation of religious principles away from the ʿulamāʾ (religious scholars) and deployed school textbooks to standardize and disseminate its moral agenda to an expanding schooled population. Moroccan religious schoolbooks, much like the Egyptian ones, incorporated two operations that adjusted Islam to the needs of the modern nation-state: "objectification" and "functionalization" (Starrett 1998, 6). Objectification comprises the editorial processes that systematize religious knowledge to fit it into the structure of modernist formal schooling: this knowledge has been divided into units that are adapted to different age levels, and its pedagogical objectives have been made testable through standardized examinations. For example, the senior-year textbook begins with nine chapters on the origins of Islamic knowledge, followed by nine chapters on a theological exploration of the universe and its influence on the establishment of faith. The next thematic unit of nine chapters deals with rights, and the final unit of nine chapters is dedicated to social issues such as marriage, divorce, and the custody of children.[8] In addition to its programmatic division into units and chapters, the textbook achieves objectification through its summaries of the material in each chapter, inclusion of comprehension questions, and vocabulary clarifications. The reflexivity that these editorial processes encourage should not be taken as the inevitable product of modernization as if it were a universal teleological process: we can after all assume that all learning requires reflexivity (Mahmood 2005). Instead, objectification points to the link between different types of learning and the specific concerns that arise in certain historical moments. Its operation consolidates the connection between theological principles and the organization of piety for a literate audience.

This operation is inseparable from functionalization (Starrett 1998, 6), namely the harnessing of religious knowledge as politically and socially useful to the agendas of the Moroccan state. In the Islamic Education course, functionalization orients students to the compatibility of Islam with the modern Moroccan monarch as the negotiator between religious tradition and modernity. In the course's textbooks, this intention is realized both visually and thematically in prominent ways. The cover of the junior-year textbook features two juxtaposed images: the Hassan II Mosque in Casablanca and a group of surgeons in the operating room (*Tarbiya Islāmiyya* Bac 1, 2010). The grandeur and strategic location of this particular house of worship make the mosque representative of the merging of worship and political allegiance to the now-deceased King Hassan II. This visual symbolism extends to the photos of the current (Mohammed VI) and former (Hassan II) kings, showing them both dressed in robes that mark their descent from Prophet Mohammed (Waterbury 1970; Combs-Schilling 1989); these photos feature prominently in classrooms, teachers' lounges, and the offices of the school administration. Their ubiquitous presence in all schools intimates they are mandated parts of the school.

The cover of the senior-year textbook presents another meaningful collage: the solar system, snowy mountain peaks, the scale of justice, and an Islamic medieval astrolabe are grouped together with the slightly foregrounded open pages of the Qur'an. The cover reflects the contents of the textbook, in which Qur'anic verses help elucidate the intrinsic link between divine revelation and scientific ways of knowing the world—including the most recent geological and biological discoveries, progress in astronomy and physics, contemporary medical advances, and legal frameworks such as human rights. The textbook consistently cultivates the impression that the Qu'ran anticipated all these domains of knowledge and experience (*Tarbiya Islāmiyya* Bac 2, 2010, 23, 54, 56, 103). In sum, the religious curriculum puts forward two pedagogical objectives: the systematic elaboration of Islamic principles in harmony with a Moroccan dynastic heritage and the thesis that Islam features centrally in all facets of modern life. Many students are well versed in both objectives.

Yet it was the Arabic-language proficiency required by the course of Islamic Education that grabbed my attention. Mrs. Said gave me the impression she was very concerned to ensure that her students understood the vocabulary of inheritance principles. She first translated Qur'anic concepts into contemporary Arabic, taking her cue from the textbook's glossary of synonyms. She then guided the class through the commentary, comprehension questions, and written assignments on the topic. It was only after she had illustrated the inheritance principles on the board and clarified the vocabulary that the teacher read out loud the Qur'anic verse in Arabic to the class:

> Concerning your children, God commands you that a son should have the equivalent share of two daughters. If there are only daughters, two or more should share two-thirds of the inheritance, if one, she should have half. Parents inherit a sixth each if the deceased leaves children; if he leaves no children and his parents are his sole heirs, his mother has a third, unless he has brothers, in which case she has a sixth. (In all cases, the distribution comes) after payment of any bequests or debts. You cannot know which of your parents or your children is closer to you in benefit: this is law from God and He is all knowing, all wise. (Qur'an 4:11)

This part of the session approximated a method of Islamic Education that preceded the post-independence classroom and that focused on the correct recitation of the sacred text (Robinson 1993). Students took turns reading aloud the same passage. The teacher was strict in correcting the *ḥarakāt* (vocalization of the script) and *i'rāb* (case endings) and in admonishing students who read with a Moroccan accent. These points deserve elaboration. Vocalization and case endings are essential in clarifying syntax in the Arabic script and hence in fixing meaning. Their role is generally significant for readers of Arabic, but it is especially crucial for the study of religious texts because correct voweling leads to the accurate comprehension of the Qur'an. The same principle applies to the Hebrew script and the Hebrew scriptures (Olender 1992, 23). In fact, textbooks of Islamic Education use diacritical marks exclusively for Qur'anic passages, an exception to the vowel-less transcription of the rest of the Arabic text. Attention to vocalization has a long history and great significance in religious pedagogy in Muslim communities. In his work on the changing relationship between writing and authority in the history of Yemen, Brinkley Messick makes an important comment about the pedagogical value of recitation: "Preserved in its vowelled-consonant recitational form . . . a memorized text is one that has been embodied complete" (1993, 26). In this respect, having students read a text aloud allows the knowledgeable teacher to correct the student who may have introduced inadvertent errors into the text. Even in a classroom where students and teacher read without *tajwīd* (recitation), correct vocalization remains a focal pedagogical concern.

A further challenge for the Islamic Education teacher was to discourage a regional accent. Mrs. Said was very diligent in reminding students that they should not pronounce the fraction *al-thuluthu* as *al-tulutu* (one third), which they tended to do because *dārija* (Moroccan Arabic) does not distinguish between the consonants *ta* and *tha*. The students' use of *dārija* was frequent and largely unproblematic in all their classes, except when reading religious and classical literary texts. The correction of dialectal accents in Qur'anic recitation is common in religious training at schools across the region (Starrett 1998; Haeri 2003). As the session time ran out, the teacher gave her students a summary of the inheritance rules in *dārija*. Before she dismissed the class, she made sure that everyone was clear about the contents of the session, asking specific students whether they had understood: [dar.] *"Ash fhamti Layla ulā lā?* (Layla, did you understand or not)? Students did comply with the injunction to fully understand and properly recite the Qur'an in class, yet were conscious of the fact that some of their fellow Moroccans—often their own grandparents—fulfilled their religious obligations while being illiterate or only partially literate.

This raises the question: why does literacy in Qurʾanic Arabic remain important inside public schools?

After the class finished, Malika and I approached Mrs. Said. Malika wanted to ask more questions about the inheritance rules, and I wished to introduce myself. A soft-spoken middle-aged woman with a warm gaze, Mrs. Said invited us both for tea in the teachers' lounge. There I inquired about the relationship between linguistic mastery and moral cultivation in Islamic Education. She eagerly explained that both aspects were mutually enhancing: analysis and comprehension depend on linguistic mastery, while linguistic mastery for its own sake is inadequate without an appreciation of the applicability of religion in everyday life. Her role was demanding, she added, because the Qurʾanic text was complex and filled with words liable to misinterpretation. "Of course," she assured me, "this is already predicted in the text itself. The Qurʾan clarifies that only God has total understanding of its meaning." Nevertheless, she emphasized the need for students at school to be able to understand the text in order to "avoid misinterpretations and distortions of faith." Mrs. Said proceeded to delineate the cognitive relationship between meaning and form in the Qurʾan:

> The Bible was written by men and altered many times. On the contrary, the Qurʾan is the word of God; you can't change the word of God! This is why the teaching of *fuṣḥā* is so demanding for our students. Since its grammar and rules have developed from *al-ʿarabiyya al-qadīma* (old Arabic), we have to be extremely strict in how we use it. *For it is grave to make mistakes in Arabic, the language based on the word of God!* (emphasis added)

In her explanation, Mrs. Said states succinctly the semiotic view of Arabic endorsed by the school. On one level, she evokes a broader linguistic ideology that sees Arabic as the word of God.[9] This feature endows the Qurʾan with the quality of *iʿjāz* (inimitability), a quality that inhibits felicitous worship in another language, including the spoken Arabic registers. This quality not only ties revelation to language form in an organic manner but also has metaphysical ramifications for that form. On another level, Mrs. Said goes further by assigning the *fuṣḥā* taught at school the status of the "sacred heir" to Qurʾanic Arabic, making them equivalent. In our conversation, she underscored the centrality of this heritage by explaining that for many years public schools instructed Arabic grammar solely through Qur'anic verses "since its rules stem from the Qur'an." She expressed the conviction that using the Qur'an remains the best method for learning *fuṣḥā*. In fact, Qur'anic recitation has long served, and continues to do so, as children's introduction to literacy (Wagner 1993, 44–48).

Mrs Said's perspective echoes the systematic pedagogical support for the fluidity between older and newer registers of Arabic across the curriculum. In the textbooks for the Islamic Education course in every level, citations from the Qur'an and the hadith are interspersed with newer versions of Arabic. The course on Arabic Literature teaches texts from sources ranging from the pre-Islamic and the Classical Islamic (622–1258 AC) periods to the *nahḍa* (renaissance) in the nineteenth century. Students, teachers, and textbooks refer to all these registers without distinction as "*al-lugha al-ʿarabiyya*" (the Arabic language). It is worth highlighting that Mrs. Said's remarks on proper voweling and accent are a reminder to students that the embodiment of the sacred text demands their constant exertion to achieve this linguistic virtuosity. In brief, both literacy in Arabic and literacy in morality, which appear tightly connected at school, are aspirations fraught with difficulties and deferred goals.

During my discussion with Mr. Tawfiq, the inspector for Arabic in this high school, he offered a similar, though not identical, explanation of the metaphysics of Arabic form. In addition to his professional involvement with secondary education, Mr. Tawfiq conducted research on language training and had written a published essay on this topic. An ardent supporter of Arabization at school, Mr. Tawfiq was very disheartened by Moroccan students' level of *fuṣḥā*. Remarkably, after he attributed this low standard to a lack of funding for linguistic research and an insufficiently trained body of educators, Mr. Tawfiq advocated that the language's sacred inheritance was the most important limitation to its social evolution:

> Remember, there's a reason why the language has remained rigid in its rules and traditional. When it comes to Arabic, *religious identity is more important than education.* So even though languages develop along with the social, they are social animals, Arabic always needs to go back to the root, the Qur'an. This makes it a closed language that cannot develop very much. (emphasis added)

The fact that Mrs. Said's and Mr.Tawfiq's views only partially align reveals the school's ambivalence around *fuṣḥā*. For Mrs. Said, literacy in *fuṣḥā* serves to avoid misinterpretations of faith and therefore is instrumental to "proper" moral cultivation. Simultaneously, *fuṣḥā*, even outside religious practice, is replete with sacredness. It is this inherited quality that separates the language from the passing of time and from the social developments that affected other languages. This tautology between *fuṣḥā* and religion is a widespread view among many Moroccan speakers, yet it is not hegemonic. For some, the development of the Arabic language remains inextricable from Islam, yet for others the question of the metaphysics of the language gives way to a historical narrative of the relationship between language and religion.[10]

Mr. Tawfiq seems more prone to endorse the latter view. He agrees with Mrs. Said's linguistic ideology to a degree, but is critical of this ideology's effect on the project of Arabization. Although he points out the lack of logistical support for the instruction of *fuṣḥā* at school, he also indicates that this lack of support might be a result of ideology: "When it comes to Arabic, religious identity is more important than education." His somewhat cryptic comment implies a synergy between the dominant semiotic view around *fuṣḥā* and spheres of political decision-making. What have been the political uses of this synergy? The historical trajectory and ongoing motivations of the state's promotion of the sacred character of Arabic at school shed light on this question.

HERITAGE: ARABIZATION AND THE *MAKHZAN*

The designation of any language in the singular, even with the help of classificatory terms such as "classical" or "modern," complicates the sanctioning of certain versions of a language over others as well as the composite motivations that drive communication. *Fuṣḥā*, the Arabic promulgated by the Arabization policy, has served a multiplicity of purposes that cannot be subsumed into the singular English labels "Qurʾanic," "modern," or "standard." Beyond educational policy, the continuum between the Qurʾan, literary production, and everyday communication is impossible to miss.[11] Therefore it is by exploring the strategic way that Arabic has intersected state institutions that we can appreciate the state's formulation of religious orthodoxy. This formulation is closely related to the constitution of the Moroccan state and in particular to the features of its central institutions. These features are significant because they at times underpin and at other times undercut student efforts to vocalize the Qur'anic text, limit their regional accent, and negotiate a view of Arabic as sacred. At school, the shaping and experience of *fuṣḥā* have emerged as a means for national consolidation based on the religious authority of the monarchy. This pairing of nationalism and the monarchical religious heritage has defined a version of Moroccan modernity that draws heavily on the religious past, a past that is used to inform present and future deliberations on various domains of sociality and governance.

Significantly deviating from Benedict Anderson's (1983) narrative of European nationalism as enmeshed with the vernacularization of religion, colonized arabophone states imagined their sovereignty through the sustained dissemination and contemporary transformation of official written Arabic, *fuṣḥā*. This conception, however, has not coincided with a singular vision of the semiotic nature of the language—in broad strokes, as sacred versus profane. In the heated discussion over the foundations of nationalist movements throughout the region, the relative weight of religion in the constitution of Pan-Arabism has been the object of intense contention among historians (Khalidi 1991).[12] The secularizing experiences of Kemalist Turkey indeed influenced liberal constitutionalist groups such as *Lisān al-Maghrib* since 1907 and inspired nationalist figures such as al-Wazzani, al-Khattabi, and Ben Barka. Yet none of these groups or leaders was able to dictate nation-building agendas (al-Mansour 1994). Sultan Abdel Hafid, who abdicated his throne after signing the Treaty of Fez in 1912 that established the French Protectorate, aligned early on with *salafī* militants through a rhetoric that foregrounded Islam as a reaction to the Protectorate's ethnic, spatial, and judicial separatism.

The consensus among historians on Morocco continues to be that its victorious nationalist movement considered religion its anchor. Seeking to promote Islam as a unifying paradigm among Moroccans, early twentieth-century nationalists and subsequently the monarch in exile Mohammed V were outwardly hostile to the worship of the *murābiṭūn* (rural saints) and the practices of the *ṭuruq* (sing. *ṭarīqa*, sufi orders). The

newly formed Moroccan state of 1956 under the leadership of King Mohammed V and the nationalist *salafī*-inspired party *al-Istiqlāl* concretized
its unifying nationalist vision around an Arabo-Islamic identity (al-Fassi
1966). The leader of the *Istiqlāl* party Allal al Fassi strongly argued for a
sovereign and a unified judicial system based on the *mālikī* (one of four
schools of Sunnism) interpretation of Islamic law in terms that foregrounded the Arabic language: "We find ourselves faced with an internal
battlefield that denies us the right to speak our language or study it as well
as the right to get rid of a legislation imposed by the colonizer and substi-
tute it with Islamic law" (1977, 4).

Political leaders and the monarchy envisioned an expanded Arabic
literacy that would facilitate a return to an authentic Moroccan Muslim
identity and lessen the main cleavages of Moroccan society. The nationalist discourse, which bore the imprint of urban Islamic reformism, emphasized two principles: the importance of Arabic literacy and the conviction
that Islam had always anticipated modernity, including the chain of transformations based on scientific postulations (Geertz 1968).[13] The latter
conviction was as empowering as it was conservative—implying that the
mode of adaptation to contemporary life and power relations did not need
to change drastically from pre-colonial times. The Arabo-Muslim unity the
nationalists called for reflected only partially the linguistic and cultural
practices of the country, but their message drew on the shared religious
heritage of Arabic and the potent narrative of the classical Arabo-Islamic
civilization (Segalla 2009, 228). As evident both in Mrs. Said's concern
with the mastery of the Qur'anic text and the weight given to scientific
references in the Islamic Education textbook, both principles remain
important to state-controlled religious pedagogy at school.

Nationalist discourse sponsored the idea of heritage as the foundation
of modernity. This direction proved useful in legitimizing the hereditary
institutions of the Alawite dynasty (al-Mansour 1994, 58; Bourquia and
Gilson-Miller 1999).[14] In a sense, urban nationalism salvaged and revived
the monarchy and its symbols and ensured its continuity after independence (Aouchar 1990; Hammoudi 1997, 15). The modern evolution of the
Moroccan monarch with his double role as *Amīr al-mu'minīn* (Commander of the Faithful) through prophetic heredity and as popular ruler
through social contract—confirmed through the ritual of allegiance to

the new king called *bayʿa*—is a true political feat. The monarch owes his durability to his centuries-long designation as blood heir to the prophetic line and the continual performance of this affiliation through religious ritual and rhetoric, as well as his being a speaker of Arabic, "the Holy tongue of God" (Combs-Schilling 1989, 20). Therefore, the monarch's Arabo-Islamic roots, in which sacred Arabic plays a significant part, endow him with the exceptional moral character attributed to the Prophet himself and his descendants. At this juncture, the objectives of the course of Islamic Education at school and the formulation of monarchical legitimacy emerge in full congruence. Interestingly, the figure of the monarch embodies not only reformist Islam but also has also come to encompass the mystical element of intercession between God and people through the concept of *baraka* (divine blessing), formerly the preserve of saints and Sufi masters. The instrumentalization of this embodiment is obvious in the religious coating of state policies relating to the monarch. One such case was the solicitation of public donations for the construction of the Hassan II Mosque, the same mosque featured on the cover of the Islamic Education textbook, through the use of the repertoire of *ziyāra* that alludes to saintly compensation (Tozy 1999, 84).

The synergy between theocratic kingship and modern bureaucracy has produced an amalgam of governance that is both mystical and rational: "This way democracy has become mere *shūrā* (consultation), a delegate moved from a position of representation to that of appointment, he is at the service of his Majesty . . . and law is a *ẓahīr* (royal decree) imbued with the same infallibility than its source" (Tozy 1999, 85).[15] The use of the word *Makhzan* to refer to the monarchical institution to this day epitomizes the ability of the concept of heritage to endow contemporary instruments of government with historical legitimacy. The *Makhzan* was a pre-colonial mechanism of tax collection. During colonial times it alluded to the sultan's administration under the French Protectorate. Gradually, the term expanded to capture a conglomeration of elite actors, such as royal notables, top-ranking military officials, security personnel, and civil servants. Thanks to its political *savoir-faire* (know-how) (Hibou 2011, 5) dating back to the nineteenth century, the Alawite dynasty was able to present itself after independence as the encapsulation of religion, nation, and state.[16] The Moroccan national anthem, the central component of the morning assembly at public high schools, highlights this merging of religion, nation, and monarchy: "We Salute as Our Emblem, *Allah* (God), *al-waṭan* (homeland), and *al-malik* (the King)."[17] The intention to sustain the monarch's religious-dynastic legitimacy and extend it to confirm the state's moral superiority is embedded in the promotion of Arabic as a component of this sacred heritage. This heritage emphasizes moderation in matters of scriptural interpretation, which incidently helps placate a heretofore anxious Western discourse around the role of organized religion in the region.

Clearly, the policy of Arabization has always implied a degree of Islamization that would guarantee the validity of existing state institutions. While it captured the public's yearning for unity and stability at the time of decolonization, the policy began to cause widespread anxiety in the post-independence period. When Minister of Education Benhima responded to this anxiety by halting Arabization in 1966, Hassan II pursued Islamization instead by introducing prayer to public schools and by making the study of Islamic science and civilization mandatory for all levels of education. *Al-ʿAlam*, the newspaper of the *Istiqlāl* party, endorsed these measures as conducive to the wider diffusion of Arabic in all domains of life (Grandguillaume 1983, 88).

Even though Arabic and Islam have featured centrally in the moral self-presentation of the modern state, they have not taken part in the material processes of modernization. This tension between pushing forward the message of Arabization and the reality of institutionalized bilingualism, with its resources and prestige weighing in favor of French, has dictated the educational experience of post-independence generations. The extent to which the *Makhzan*-led state had planned this outcome is a matter of speculation, given the persistent involvement in the country's educational, professional, and development domains by France and other states. What is certain is that, although the actualities of finding a job and the mechanisms of achieving social distinction do not validate arabophone education or the moral principles exemplified in Islamic Education, the Ministry of Education continues to endorse this agenda. So long as French remains critical to educational promotion, the humanities track, which is more tied to arabophone education than other tracks, remains the default destination for all poorly performing students. It is common knowledge that its graduates constitute the largest section of unemployed youth in the country. Their deeply compromised position and their critique of their predicament illuminate both the anticipated consequences of the preservation of the metaphysics of Arabic and the unanticipated impact of this preservation on the moral legitimacy of the state.

THE DISINHERITED: THE "DEMORALIZED" HUMANITIES STUDENTS

The Islamic education course and its emphasis on language training illustrate how the theocratic face of the Moroccan state sustains itself at school. As expected, however, students and staff drew on this curriculum to deliberate unofficially on the meaning of morality in general and moral leadership in particular. This unofficial deliberation, which connects with other conversations within Moroccan society, exposed the inconsistency of state discourse around the role of *fuṣḥā* and unsettled the state's formulation of religious orthodoxy. A conflict between a teacher of philosophy, Mr. Guelmim, and a high school student, Badr, brought me closer to dissenting voices in the school that contest the official parameters of proper faith. The official tainting of these voices as "radical" proves that the policy of Arabization, which was meant to shore up state power, has turned into an instrument of a vigorous critique of the state. Yet accusations of radicalization and backwardness harm the humanities students not only because these accusations discredit student contestation, but also because they bolster public perceptions of the lower place of these students in modern Moroccan society. Their future being more tied to Arabic, humanities students have to endure the complications of the preservation of this language as sacred and old. In short, what the stories of humanities students make more visible is the fact that everyday life is in flagrant discord with the state's discourse of self-glorification through Islamic credentials under the banner of a sacred Arabic language.

Having started my sustained fieldwork inside the school in the scientific track, which both staff and students openly acknowledged to be "the better track," I was very eager to spend time with humanities students. The principal did not prevent me from doing so, but tried to discourage me from moving to humanities with the disclaimer that the [dar.] *adabiyyin* (humanities students) were "rowdy" and "academically mediocre." The scientific track students also tried to dissuade me, claiming that I would not find the *adabiyyin* interesting: "Their level is so low that not even their teachers show up for class." More confirmation of this assessment came from teachers in the teachers' lounge. Mr. Guelmim, who taught philosophy to senior-year students of both tracks, offered to introduce me to a humanities class, but was blunt about his personal antipathy toward these students: "They exasperate me," he said, lifting shoulders and arms in a gesture of resignation.

Despite this statement, Mr. Guelmim became my closest interlocutor among the teachers during my time with the humanities track. Although he often expressed his frustration with the track, he consistently showed up for class and made a serious effort to engage his students with the subject of philosophy. As it turned out, he was an exception: teacher absenteeism in the humanities track was considerably higher than in the scientific track, to the point that I ended up spending more time with students in empty classrooms or the schoolyard than in class. For example, after not having been to the school for three days, I asked one of the students, Sara, how the week had gone. She replied,

> On Thursday, we had a double period of French, Islamic Education, and Sport. We all showed up but none of the teachers came. On Friday, we had Sport and English but these teachers rarely come so I did not bother. On Saturday, we normally have four hours but only the Arabic teacher came.

Students were generally more punctual than their teachers, but sometimes responded to teacher indifference with matching disengagement. They recognized that teachers had no faith in them and referred to themselves as "*demoralizés*" (demoralized). This loaded French term points to defeated morale and the loss of hope about future prospects.

This demoralized attitude was shared by senior-year students in both tracks but was particularly acute among the *adabiyyin*. Because they were heading for the humanities or religious studies at university and did not possess marketable language skills, their professional prospects appeared bleak. The students in the *Adab* (literature) class I followed were generally older than other students (21–22 instead of the expected 17–18) because they had repeated several grades over the years. Close to half of the students did not aspire to continue their education after high school. Some girls were open about coming to school to "pass the time" and to avoid doing chores at home. A few boys disclosed that they came to "stay out of the street" and that the only thing they hoped for was some *furṣa* (opportunity) to get out of the country. Even though the devaluation of the humanities track goes beyond the Moroccan case and indicates a broader redefinition of knowledge in the discourse of neo-liberal utilitarianism, we need to examine how these global frames map onto engrained power relations that equate Arabic, and by extension the arabophone humanities, with conservatism and religiosity. It is precisely these features of Arabic—conservatism and religiosity—that seal the marginalization of the humanities.

An attitude of defeatism and educational discrimination led the humanities students I observed to distrust school and state and to express this distrust in socioeconomic and moral terms. A heated discussion during a Philosophy class convinced me that the state's moral authority was subject to serious contestation. The class session, titled *"al-dawla"* (The State), was structured as a lecture on the meaning of *"sulṭa"* (authority). Mr. Guelmim started with a presentation on Machiavelli and his ideas and then proceeded to summarize the thinking of Locke, Spinoza, Rousseau, and Ibn Khaldun. Students were usually bored during the Philosophy course, and Mr. Guelmim's class often resembled a café, with students coming in and out at will, chatting among themselves, and listening to music on their mobile phones. A pigeon nest just above the classroom door contributed to the general havoc as teacher and students regularly interrupted the lesson to kick out pigeons perched on the window ledges. On that day, however, the question, "What makes a good governor," stirred the class, and especially a group of boys, into a heated discussion. Instead of responding to the question philosophically, some of the students jumped right into a political argument:

> BADR: Teacher, whoever governs here in Morocco does not do so out of merit and *baraka* (divine blessing) but because he steals!
>
> MUSTAFA: The government is always far, teacher, the ministers who meet the demonstrators (unemployed graduates) outside the parliament stand there for a minute, shake a few hands, and then they leave.
>
> BADR: Once I happened to be passing by and a policeman came up to me and started beating me up! What could I do? I struck back!

MR. GUELMIM: What would you prefer? The state we have or the caliphate
envisaged by the Islamists? Their view is utopian! We want a state of civil
rights and of law.

MUSTAFA: We don't have law now, teacher . . .

BADR: The king does nothing, teacher. Where is the king?

ADNANE: [dar.]*Msha l-Amrīkā!* (He left for America)

The class burst into laughter at Adnane's joke, but Mr. Guelmim became
stern and thoughtful. This discussion explicitly implicated morality in the
domain of good government through the concept of *baraka*—*baraka* is a
particularly salient term because it alludes to both divine benediction and
to the blessing of abundance and economic prosperity (Eickelman 1976,
61). The discussion also linked morality to matters of social justice such
as the rule of law. Significantly, students did not spare the monarch from
criticism due to his sacred status, nor did they consider him a supreme
arbiter above the abuses of the government. By mentioning *baraka*, students implicitly challenged King Mohammed VI, a risky criticism given
that the public defamation of the monarch warrants arrest.

On another occasion, Badr deployed again the term *baraka* to persuade
his fellow classmates and me of his own worth as a potential political
leader. During break, I bumped into Badr while he was admonishing two
of his male classmates for smoking outside the school and for covering
school walls with graffiti. I considered Badr the male equivalent of Malika
because both were vocal on questions of right conduct, though Badr extended his criticisms to political matters. Badr referenced the sayings of
Prophet Mohammed to argue against the consumption of tobacco and
referred to *akhlāq* (morals) to criticize the destruction of public property.
Although he did not appear to convince the two smokers to stop their behavior, he impressed another of his classmates: "Wow, Badr, *tbarakllah 'līk*
(God bless you, well done), that was well said!" Badr replied humorously,
"I have *baraka* don't you think?" His classmate shook his hand in a half-
mocking, half-serious gesture of respect. Badr continued, "Only good
Muslims in power can show us how to be better people! Maybe I'll run for
office one day . . . if I graduate!" These explicit statements and many more
comments students made daily about the lack of virtue among the ruling
elites demonstrated that the state's effort to control the religious sym-

bolic realm was largely unsuccessful. These comments also revealed the conflation between king and government as the source of doubt and disappointment.

Badr's awareness of his lack of prospects as a humanities track student ("if I graduate!") is telling of the many ways in which humanities students face marginalization. The classroom scene just described uncovered yet another layer of exclusion. After this class discussion, Mr. Guelmim appeared unsettled by student opinions and singled out Badr as a student who displayed "signs of radicalization." Mr. Guelmim claimed that his students considered that "the rule of the *shari'a* (Islamic law)" would be a remedy to the inequalities undercutting Moroccan society. His in-class retort—"What would you prefer? The state we have or the caliphate envisaged by the Islamists?"—incited them to express such views openly. I gradually discovered that Mr. Guelmim thought of Badr as someone who constantly antagonized him from a perspective of piety that the particular teacher did not share. The fact that Badr was active in the youth wing of the moderate Islamic party *al-'Adāla wa-l Tanmiyya* (Party for Justice and Development, PJD), which was in opposition to the government at the time, added to Mr. Guelmim's concerns. As far as I could tell, Mr. Guelmim was not a supporter of the current government, but preferred the state's deployment of religion to alternative religious visions of governance. The principal's forewarning that this class was "rowdy" corroborated Mr. Guelmim's view of students like Badr as potentially threatening to the state's moral objectives. The fact that male students like Badr were the objects of suspicion more so than girls who espoused the same political views and religious ideas is indicative of the gendered reading of student religiosity by the modern state and society.

What proved to be a continuous clash between Mr. Guelmim and Badr during the Philosophy course indexes a broader competition between the state and other actors over the control of moral authority. In my conversations with the students in this class, I found that some, including Badr, strove to abide by a stricter code of ethical conduct than they thought state and social elites lived by, and they were open in their criticism of these elites for their immoral behavior, such as embezzlement, corruption, drinking, and sexual depravity. Such criticism had recourse to non-state voices that presented new avenues for moral guidance. Like Malika, some students expressed a moral sensibility mediated through the internet and televised religious sermons by prominent preachers such as Yusuf al-Qaradawi and Amr Khaled (for Egypt, see Hirschkind 2001a, 2006). However, students never adopted the deliberations of such figures wholesale: for instance, the female students I knew strongly disapproved of scholars who openly condoned polygamy.

Mr. Guelmim and other teachers who had similar concerns about Badr drew connections between his attitude and the Islamic opposition during Hassan II's infamous *al-sanawāt al-raṣāṣ* (Years of Lead; 1965–1993). This Islamic opposition, especially prominent in university student unions in Casablanca and Mohammedia, protested against the government's economic policies and its limitations imposed on political and civil rights.[18] The connection the teachers made was anachronistic but not irrelevant, because the PJD traced its origins to the oppositional youth movement *al-Shabība al-Islāmiya* (Muslim Youth) founded in 1970 by Abdelkrim Moti. Even though the PJD split from *al-Shabība al-Islāmiya*, providing a more moderate alternative, it has voiced popular frustration with state mechanisms in social policy, cultural planning, and economic opportunity. Even though the party's eventual ascent to power coincided with its alignment with *Makhzan* objectives, it has been undeniably popular among a sizable segment of the population, including high school and university students (Slyomovics 2005). Other students sympathized with the outlawed Islamic movement headed by Shaykh Abdelsalam Yassine, the *Jamaʿiyat al-ʿAdl wa- l-Iḥsān* (Association for Justice and Spirituality) that has openly challenged the status of the monarchy. In his long battle against the monarchy, Yassine contested the religious legitimacy of the theocratic state. Although they used different political strategies, the Association for Justice and Spirituality and the PJD agreed on the need for judicial reform, the coordinated Arabization of education and society, and the alleviation of vast socioeconomic divisions (Belbashir 2008).[19] It is hardly a coincidence that both movement leaders, Abdelkrim Moti and Shaykh Yassine, had worked as inspectors in the public education sector during the 1970s (Burgat 1995). Their appeal to social justice, a central element of their advocacy, was congruent with student desires for a more equitable society.

Badr's activism in and out of class illustrates how the public educational system has inadvertently created voices of opposition that perceive the *Makhzan*-led government as inadequately representative of the Arabo-Muslim character of the Moroccan society. The school's marking of these voices as "conservative" and "radical" contributes further to the marginalization of the humanities students and of arabophone graduates more generally. The irony is that the very ideology of *fuṣḥā* as sacred and old, which the state has promoted through education, has turned into a strategy for derailing these students from paths of modernity, moderation, and progress. Caught in the state's one-sided, uneven promotion of the Arabo-Muslim narrative, humanities students constitute a mirror that refracts the state's inconsistency. It is precisely because these students make this inconsistency most visible that they worry the state, a worry voiced by both Mr. Guelmim and the principal.

While walking to class one day, the history teacher expressed this inconsistency in the starkest terms:

> Arabization was a *jarīma* (crime)! Arabic is a language to pray with, but you cannot plan your future with it. If we cut off this connection with the outer world, we will not grow. This is the problem with radicalism! Monolingual arabophone youth are imprisoned in Arabic, which is always associated with the Qur'an; at the end of the [symbolic] spectrum, there is no difference between the two.

This conflation of Arabic, religion, and radicalism is more fascinating in what it omits than in what it incorporates. First, the attribution of stagnation to the language itself understates the fact that it was because French was upheld as the language with which "to plan a future" that Arabic had become, in the teacher's words a "prison." Second, the teacher posits radicalism as a stable, objective category. Yet what the teacher targets here as "radicalism" is neither stable nor objective, but, rather, a perspective that the divinely ordained state refuses to sanction.

When Arabization policies began to come to fruition, some scholars characterized contemporary *fuṣḥā* as a language without cultural references or community (Grandguillaume 1983, 25). However, it is obvious today that the expansion of school-based Arabic literacy in Morocco has created a new community of speakers that has entered the domain of public deliberation, leading to "an opening up of the political process and heightened competition for the mantles of political and religious authority" (Eickelman 2000, 130). Eickelman's correlation between literacy and public deliberation is certainly demonstrable in the Moroccan case, but it is only one side of the argument. The state's promotion of Arabic literacy has also assisted its agenda of legitimization through Arabo-Muslim unity. This agenda hinges on a view of *fuṣḥā* as timeless and relatively closed to today's world. Hearing humanities students describing themselves as demoralized, we cannot but recognize that the same literacy that has provided the means of religious deliberation has also deprived students in Arabized schools from domains of academic and professional engagement linked to the country's development. Hence, a generalized assessment of arabophone societies as literate ignores the contradictory meanings of Arabic literacy for different speakers.[20]

In this light, the Islamic Education course and the sacralization of Arabic signal the unanticipated consequences of the modern state's institutionalization of religious knowledge: on the one hand, the state's desire to direct religion through the development of widespread literacy laid the foundations for its uncontrollable dissemination. On the other hand, the same literacy has placed arabophone graduates, and especially humanities students, in precarious positions with regard to material opportunity and social mobility. This dynamic complicates a prevalent explanation of Muslim "fundamentalism" as the product of increased access to religious texts and of the technologies that allow these texts to circulate in unprecedented ways (Eickelman 2000, 643). In the Moroccan case, the attribution of "fundamentalism" solely to the opening up of the domain of deliberation through literacy runs the risk of reifying the inherent religiosity of Arabic and misconstruing the grievances of the students who are most affected by inconsistent state policies. The reification of sacred Arabic explains not only the devaluation of certain tracks within the school but also why Moroccan students turn away from the epitome of Arabo-Muslim symbolism—the king—and opt for other paths of moral guidance (see Figures 4.1 and 4.2). The students' experiences prompt a reconsideration of theories of learning as ideological inculcation: in light of the disappointment openly expressed by Malika, Badr, and others, what is the moral status of schooling?

FIGURE 4.1

Female students during break. Photograph by author.

ON MORAL CULTIVATION

When Malika extolled the relevance of Islam in contemporary life but deplored the inability of *fuṣḥā* to respond in a similar way, she conveyed a view that conforms to the state's promulgation of an Arabo-Islamic narrative inside the public school. This state narrative has been ambivalent about the meaning and function of *fuṣḥā* in Moroccan society. It has deployed Arabization as a legitimizing tool for Moroccan nationalism headed by the Alawite dynasty, which has in turn overshadowed a vision of Arabic as the medium of indigenous modernity in economic terms. The course of Islamic Education and the clarifications of Mrs. Said and Mr. Tawfiq laid bare the features of the official linguistic ideology of Arabic: the metaphysical link between Qur'anic Arabic and revelation and, by extension, the sacredness of all registers of Arabic jostle against the role of the language in other facets of life. This paradigm may be

FIGURE 4.2

Male students during break. Photograph by author.

meaningful to Muslims in Morocco and elsewhere, yet it has no doubt also been instrumental to the state's safeguarding of its religious credentials. The emphasis on the sacredness of Arabic in combination with the dominant role of French in the job market postulates *fuṣḥā* as a morally loaded but outdated language. Malika's claim of finding it "old and heavy" expresses this inconsistency most concisely.

Humanities students both experience this inconsistency and voice their disappointment more intensely with the school and the state than do than their scientific track peers. For some humanities students, the critique of the state's failed effort to fashion a consistent Arabo-Muslim agenda surfaces in their self-proclaimed demoralization. For others, this assessment is more explicit, and it manifests in their search for alternative moral leadership. This search has been central to the growth of the Islamic Revival, a broad movement since the 1970s that calls Muslims back to lives of piety by transforming themselves and the social landscape through social welfare, publishing endeavors, and informal educational activities (Mahmood 2001, 2005). The links between the Islamic Revival and institutional politics have been explicit in Morocco, as in Egypt, Tunisia, Jordan, and Turkey, even if some adherents of the movement did not intend their ethical edification to transform governance. For Badr, in contrast, this intention is clear. He both lectures his fellow students on matters of everyday religiosity and participates in the youth wing of a political party that trumpets faith and morality. Badr formulates his antagonism toward the king using the concept of *baraka*, which he understands as the essential characteristic of a moral leader. His critique is daring not only because it deconstructs the allusion of the *Makhzan's* separatedness from the mechanisms of state governance but also because its vocalization performs a political transgression. The perspective of students like Malika and Badr, which is not unified from a gender angle, invites us to appreciate the historically and politically specific manifestations of religious pedagogy instead of presuming its similarities across contexts. Not only do these presumptions reify Islam as homogeneous category but they also prevent us from seeing which faces of the state get amplified at different times throughout students' schooling experience.

The fact that the struggle over the demarcation of orthodoxy and morality plays out in the space of state-controlled education is significant and enriches our study of both lived religion in the contemporary Middle East and the public school as space. The moral aspects of the school evident in the curriculum of Islamic Education and the privileged positioning of the sacred character of Arabic complicate the designation of public education as secular. In the same vein that the state-controlled Ottoman (Fortna 2002) and subsequent Turkish schools (Kaplan 2005, 2006) have strategically deployed morality to strengthen the legitimacy of a centralized state, Moroccan schools directed religious and language training in ways that legitimate monarchical authority and reinforce its nationalist message.

Public school classrooms are different types of spaces than mosques or *madrasas* because they allow us to witness the forging of moral selves in relation to multiple other processes of "becoming": becoming a member of the labor force, a citizen, the member of a social class, a young man and young woman, and so forth.[21] The gendered negotiation of morality is apparent in the special dress code for female students and teachers, in Malika's and other students' take on inheritance rules, and in girls' disagreement with religious experts on the issue of polygamy. In parallel, Badr is the object of the administration's apprehension not because his critique is unique within the school, but because pious young men are stereotyped by the state as potentially violent. More broadly, because objectives of formal schooling can be, and often are, antithetical to each other, their antithesis opens an analytical space where we can notice the fissures in official discourse and people's negotiation of these fissures (Starrett 1998; Herrera and Torres 2006; Adely 2012). Demoralized humanities students, girls and boys, embody, albeit differentially, these fissures within the project of Arabization and, by extension, within the state's self-articulation. Their simultaneous negotiation of morality, social integration, and material empowerment offers a more complex and ultimately richer perspective on piety than can be revealed by scenes of pedagogy located inside the mosque. It is crucial that we do not separate these sides of identity and self-fashioning from the pursuit of moral edification.

Just as public schools are important sites through which to think of learning as a set of diverse experiences of becoming, so does language training bring together the multiple dimensions of persons as they engage with, probe, or transcend the boundaries of normative structures.[22] As we saw, the Moroccan state, like other states in the region and beyond, classifies any unauthorized view of morality as "radical." Interestingly, the threats to orthodoxy that it faces today emerged out of its own foregrounding of Arabic literacy as necessary to moral cultivation. Arabic literacy and access to education through the public school in general turned traditionally powerless political actors—students—into an articulate and confident opposition to the state's moral messages. Nonetheless, possession of these very skills in moral deliberation condemns these students in market, social, and political terms. In short, these students face a situation where the linguistic and moral values of their state education do not coincide with other types of empowerment and fulfillment. Their at once enabled and compromised position prevents us from seeing their dissent as nostalgic for an authentic past or an epiphenomenon of socioeconomic disparity. Nor can we claim that these students define their identity exclusively through moral projects evolving around their engagement with canonical religious texts. Instead, their moral projects emerge out of their relationship with an ambivalent Arabic literacy, systematic and unsystematic religious training, and their myriad other concerns as they encounter the society around them. To be clear, this does not make their piety any less real or less central, but it does mean that their piety does not exhaust their reflexivity about the world around them or their diverse aspirations.

In essence then, the lens that can best capture the moral projects of these young people is one that focuses on the "practical articulation" these students have with multiple institutions in concrete situations (Hammoudi 2009b, 51). Practical articulation allows us to think of unfinished goals, persistent ambitions, and relations of power. After all, no matter how competent and erudite one is, there is always a better speaker of Arabic (the school teacher, the religious scholar, the Ministry of Education) who can claim higher moral expertise and, therefore, authority. Surely, mastering the language of Qur'an or of school Arabic is no less of an ideal to those who have not done so—after all, the appeal of a scriptural language is hardly ever the outcome of its mastery. Rather, the incremental, yet always incomplete, process of learning a language reminds us of the effort rendered by *dārija* and berberophone Moroccan speakers to master Arabic and, crucially, of the difficulties those without literacy face in their struggle to deter the abuses of power. Language training emphasizes approximation, hesitation, blockages, and contingency within all pedagogy, dimensions that unsettle the concepts of mastery and virtuosity. Language training to achieve moral cultivation also privileges a set of questions around learning as ideological inculcation that previous research has sidelined.

Scholarly work of the past decade has paid attention to moral cultivation among the supporters of the Islamic Revival with the aim of parochializing Western liberal notions of autonomy that tend to stigmatize the choices of pious subjects. Inspired by Talal Asad's (1986a) idea of Islam as a "discursive tradition," this body of research defines piety as practices intended to hone morality through the embodiment of sacred texts (Mahmood 2001, 2005). This perspective is valuable, provided that it does not exaggerate incommensurability between liberal and non-liberal religious traditions.[23] Having a relationship to scriptures is significant, but it should not diminish the importance of other engagements with identity. It is by now clear that the students of this chapter operate within the normative terms of a religious horizon defined through a set of texts. Still, their connection to these texts is undercut by many other considerations, among which linguistic disparities, gender tensions, and rampant government corruption are prominent. In light of their multifaceted self-fashioning projects, this text-based normative horizon seems pliable.[24] In the criticism students put forward in their Philosophy course, morality is not separate from a vision of social and professional empowerment. On the contrary, it is this precise dialectic that shapes students' criticism of the state and their embrace of moral and political alternatives. Consequently, centralized and pervasive though it may be, the state's moral agenda is not able to predict the "formation of new structures of interest and conflict" or control "the course of the debate" (Starrett 1998, 11).

The invitation to revisit what happens in and around courses such as Islamic Education has never been as urgent as now when we are in the aftermath or, in some cases, in the midst of the sociopolitical transformations spearheaded in 2011. One of the undeniable messages of these upheavals is the central role played by the inconsistencies fostered through national educational agendas in the disillusionment of youth with the state across the region. Another message sent through the electoral success of "Islamist" parties in the region—including that of PJD in Morocco in November 2011—is how inextricably linked are individual moral projects with imaginations of alternative polities. Despite the ensuing polarization around the concepts of secularism and religiosity, it is obvious that these political imaginations have been multiple and in no way reducible to transparent binary choices. These are challenging circumstances, which nonetheless provide great motivation for those who wish to reinvent analytical approaches to formal schooling that avoid predetermining its capacity to single-handedly shape the ideological horizons of students.

5

Once Upon a Time, There Was a Happy Old Berber Couple

There can be no flourishing of our culture or reform of our educational structure without a genuine modification of our political system. There can be no democratic launch without a radical change in the status of culture.

—Abdellatif Laabi in Kenza Sefriouri, *La revue Souffles: espoirs de revolution culturelle au Maroc* (1966–1973)

I made sure never to miss Mr. Idrissi's senior-year Arab Literature class, admittedly the most enjoyable I ever attended—even counting my own high school years. An amateur actor, Mr. Idrissi was dramatic and enthusiastic, exerting every possible effort to motivate and excite his students. His energy was infectious to the point that both students and anthropologist hung on his every word. During one double session, Mr. Idrissi introduced the class to the topic of modern poetry and specifically to the structure of the modern poem. He asked one of the students to read aloud the introductory passage in the relevant textbook unit.[1] Just as in the Islamic Education class, the teacher urged the student to read with a non-regional accent, for example, to pronounce *thaqāfa* (culture) instead of *taqāfa*. He phrased his remark in the following way: "*Bi-l-lugha al-ʿarabiyya naqūl . . . thaqāfa!*" (In the Arabic language we say . . . thaqāfa). With this statement, the teacher momentarily distanced *dārija* (Moroccan Arabic) from the language of the canon of arabophone poetry taught at school, *fuṣḥā* (Classical Arabic).

139

The introductory textbook passage presented modern poetry as a pro-sodic and thematic shift from classical and neo-classical genres, a shift that reflected significant transformations in cultural production. One of the main exponents of modern Arab poetry, claimed the passage, was Mahmud Darwish. Mr. Idrissi interrupted the reading to ask his students about Darwish's background.[2] They came up with several suggestions: "Mo-rocco, Egypt, Lebanon, Syria?" He gestured "no" with his index finger and clarified: "Mahmud Darwish was from Palestine and is hailed as its na-tional poet. He wrote abundantly about the Palestinian struggle as well as the pain of exile." He reminded his class about Darwish's engaged stance toward the Palestinian-Israeli conflict and cited his renowned po-ems, "*Rita wa-l-bunduqīya*" (Rita and the Rifle) (1967) and "*Ana Yūsif yā abī*" (Oh Father, I Am Yussuf) (1986). While the teacher elaborated on the work of Darwish, a student raised her hand enthusiastically and an-nounced that she knew one of his poems by heart. Mr. Idrissi encouraged her to stand up and recite it. After a few words, he joined the recitation, obviously not able to contain his excitement. The jointly recited poem, written in *fuṣḥā*, was *Ilā ummī* (To My Mother):

Aḥinnu ilā khubzi ummī
Wa qahwatī ummī
Wa lamsatī ummī
Wa takbaru fiya al-ṭufūlatu
Yawman ʿala ṣadri yawmi
Wa aʿshaqu ʿumrī li'annī
Idha muttu
Akhjalu min damʿi ummī

(I long for my mother's bread
My mother's coffee
Her touch
Childhood memories grow up in me
Day after day
And I must be worthy of my life
If I died
to be worthy of my mother's tear)[3]

    (Mahmud Darwish, collection *Āshiq min filasṭīn* (Lover from Palestine) 1966)

As shown by their enthusiastic applause, the class rejoiced in the spontaneous performance of this very emotional poem, which, according to Mr. Idrissi, illustrated the longing for the Palestinian homeland through the longing for the mother figure. Seizing the moment, the teacher reminded students that Lebanese composer and oud player Marcel Khalife had set the poem to music. Some students recognized it and proceeded to sing it in unison.

If asked to point to one single experience during fieldwork that best exemplified the double status of students as "pedagogical objects" and "performative subjects" of the nation (Bhabha 1994, 302), this would be the one. In seeming unison, students voiced the official narrative of Arab-ness promoted by the school. The fact that they performed this Arab-ness via a Mahmud Darwish poem even though they were not sure of the creator's national affiliation makes the scene even more powerful. The scene of collective excitement around the archetypal Arab motherland, Palestine, reflects the regional positioning of Moroccan identity within the larger geographical and cultural landscape of the "Middle East" and the "Arab world." This positioning explicitly elevates *fuṣḥā* into being the fulcrum of a shared ethnicity, which in turn folds Moroccan national culture into the transnational experience of the struggle against European and American imperialism and Zionist expansion. The affinity that students in Mr. Idrissi's class felt with this wider struggle shows the impact of Pan-Arabism on ordinary people, an impact that extends well beyond the tensions and spins of domestic and foreign policy (McDougall 2011). Such an impact should not blind us, however, to the intentional enmeshment of Arab-ness with Moroccan-ness inside the school curriculum. Evidently, the aesthetic dimension of Arabization, by which I mean the stylistic appreciation of arabophone cultural production, is far from peripheral to this everyday process of entrenchment. This dominant aesthetic dimension, which has an ethical and political orientation, aspires to cultivate consent to Pan-Arabism as both internal and foreign policy across generational, regional, class, and gender lines through the production of a shared cultural taste.

Yet, the unity implied by the students singing together in that classroom is misleading. Indeed, even though Arabic poetry at school promotes *fuṣḥā* as an acquired but revered, official but intimate, mother tongue shared among closely aligned nations, a number of students locate their sociocultural, economic, and political subjectivity in other languages and through other images of the motherland. Two students from Mr. Idrissi's class, Bouchra and Moustafa, spent their ten-minute break after class chit-chatting about the Arab Literature course as they leaned against the walls of the crowded hallway. Picking up on Bouchra's casual remark about modern poetry being "beautiful but difficult," I asked her whether she used *fuṣḥā* in everyday life:

BOUCHRA: No, never!

MOUSTAFA: Only as a joke . . .
They both giggled.

BOUCHRA: It's not intimate. But we should, really, because it's our *al-lugha al-umm* (mother tongue).

MOUSTAFA: *Fuṣḥā* is not our mother tongue, *darīja* is!

BOUCHRA [turning toward me]: Hmmm . . . . I have a question. Is our mother tongue the language our mother speaks? What if our parents speak different languages?

CHARIS: Such as?

BOUCHRA: My father is an Arab but my mother is *Shilḥa* (masc. *Schleuh*, a Berber woman from the Atlas Mountains and Sous valley in south Morocco) so she also speaks *tashelḥit* (Berber register of that region). My brother and I understand some but not much.

MOUSTAFA: Both my parents are from the Rif (mountainous region of northern Morocco) but they don't speak *tarifit* (Berber register of that region) at home, only when we go back to our village up north . . .

CHARIS: Do you wish to be fluent in Berber?

BOUCHRA: No, what's the point? It's not practical and it's not the language of the future.

MOUSTAFA: Do you see, Charis? Morocco is [dar.] *ḥmaq* (crazy)! We need to know all these languages, but we don't have a language of identity . . .

BOUCHRA: Why all the drama, Moustafa?

MOUSTAFA: There are tensions and they touch on racism! I speak from personal experience. When I was at primary school, it happened to me a few times that students insulted me about my origins. On the other side, whenever I visit my region, I hear people from the Rif insulting Arabs.

BOUCHRA [addressing me]: I don't agree. Things are no longer that bad. More and more we use multilingualism to show the cultural richness of the country. We don't identify as Arab or Berber, but as Moroccan!

Bouchra and Moustafa's reflections on the mother tongue, Moroccan identity, and the job market illustrate the ways in which pedagogies of nationalism rub against intractable conceptual and experiential fissures. Some students in the public schools adjust the concept of Moroccanness to their personal experience: Bouchra had an Arab father and Berber mother, whereas Moustafa's parents, both Berbers, switched to speaking Berber when they visit their village. Influenced by their background, these students disrupt the singularity of the school's cultural agenda by the statement "*fuṣḥā* is not our mother tongue," a statement that makes their participation in the poetic recitation of Darwish the type of repetition that "does not return as the same" (Bhabha 1994, 312). In short, not everyone who recited *Illa ummī* in class fully identified with and inhabited the Pan-Arab paradigm.

Drawing on intense conversations around cultural production inside class and during breaks, during teacher-training workshops, and at home, this chapter unpacks diverse articulations of Moroccan culture. Currently, a central feature of these articulations is their recognition of plurality within Moroccan identity. These articulations exemplify the recent push and pull around the institutionalization, and therefore the handling, of all Morocco's languages. As shown by Bouchra's optimism around the recent inclusiveness of Moroccan identity, during the last fifteen years discussions on the cultural domination of the Arabic language and culture have become both more visible and more tolerant. There have been consistent efforts to promote *dārija* as the language shared by most Moroccans. Nevertheless, it is the Berber languages and cultures that constitute the key indicator of the national negotiation of pluralism. Berbers have a sizable linguistic presence in Morocco as in other neighboring countries: Algeria, Libya, and Tunisia (Hoffman 2008a). Their closely related languages, which I assemble under the umbrella term "Berber," have three large regional varieties in Morocco: *tashelhit* speakers originate primarily from the Atlas Mountains and southern region of the Sous valley, *tarifit* speakers from the Rif Mountains of the northeast, and *tamazight* speakers from the High Atlas Mountains, roughly at the center of the country. In contemporary Morocco, a speaker of these varieties is known as Amazigh (f. Amazighiyya), Schleuh (f. Shilḥa), and Rifi (f. Riffiya), respectively, names that carry various connotations that become apparent in this chapter.

Whereas for some Moroccans Arabization is the emblem of the anti-colonial struggle, some Berbers consider the policy to be the instrument of their cultural, political, and economic marginalization since independence. Denouncing the term "Berber"—the word historically meant "vandal" and dates back to the end of the Roman Empire—Berber activists have adopted the name "Amazigh" (pl. Imazighen). From the late 1990s onward, royal speeches that recognized Moroccan cultural diversity, both radio and TV channels with programming in the Berber registers, the founding of the *Institut Royal Pour La Culture Amazighe* (Royal Institute for Amazigh Culture, IRCAM) by royal decree in 2001, and the recognition of Berber as a second official language in the constitution that followed the popular unrests in 2011 have been signposts of the state's incorporation of Berbers into the national fold as a recognized minority. The standardization of the Berber languages and their gradual introduction into primary schools as school subjects have further concretized the state's stance.

These measures gesture to the Moroccan state's explicit goal of reinvention by shedding its intolerant past and proving its approximation to democracy along European and Anglo-Saxon liberal representative models. This use of multiculturalism is fascinating not simply because it raises the short-term question of state intentions but also because it implicates public school students in the conundrum of recognition: namely, recognition, which is vital to the experience of identity, applies to all citizens regardless of their differences and yet requires respect for *specific* identities (Taylor 1994). This conundrum, which is inherent in the liberal democratic model, remains unresolved in every modern nation-state, making the Moroccan case comparable with other contexts that negotiate indigenous difference (Povinelli 2002 on Australia), difference through migration (Öyzürek 2005 on Germany, Gilroy 2000 on the United Kingdom, and Prashad 2005 on the United States), or both together.

However, the stories and opinions about multilingualism expressed by high school students, their teachers, and parents underscore the particular challenges and risks of Moroccan multiculturalism. As we see, in the Moroccan context, official multicultural talk produces the appearance of political pluralism at the same time as it depoliticizes the entirety of education through technocratic interventions. This latter move shrinks the domain of public deliberation on education and allows the state to avoid a potentially drastic transformation of its modes of governance. In short, despite or perhaps without good intentions, the strategic national and international channeling of the Berber experience into minority language recognition ensures both the performance of democratization and the maintenance of political oligarchy. What is more, these negotiations over equality and the set-up of democratic institutions are currently taking place within the larger landscape of neoliberal governance. In the realm of education, this governance celebrates multiculturalism insofar as it buoys global competitiveness; at the same time, the state absolves itself of the responsibility to redress the structural inequalities that cause Berber students to stumble. Bouchra's suggestion that the Berber language serves no economic purpose and Moustafa's comment that "we need to know all these languages" infer that the devolution of the burden of social integration and economic participation is placed on berberophone students themselves. These students thus continue to face structural inequalities, inequalities that multicultural policy continues to endow with an ethnicized dimension.

AESTHETIC LACUNAE AND FRINGE POETICS

The public school curriculum promotes Arabic poetry as the epitome of linguistic virtuosity and an object of civilizational pride. It exposes students to Arabic poetry from the first grade in primary school up to their senior year in high school. Whereas the scientific track in high school becomes diversified through the inclusion of prose passages dedicated to historical and social themes, the humanities track remains focused on poetry. The senior-year textbook for the humanities announces that one of its strategic goals is to "reinforce patriotism and the safeguarding of cultural and civilizational identity" (al-Mumtāz fī al-lugha al-'arabiyya, 4).[4] The message is forthright: Arabic poetry in fuṣḥā contributes to the stylistic cultivation of a Moroccan cultural identity that maps neatly onto arabophone Muslim topographies that are charged with an ethical and political orientation. The poems of Mahmud Darwish that so excited Mr. Idrissi's class delve into the predicament of Palestine after the creation of the state of Israel in 1948 and the state's expansion after the 1967 war. Both in and out of class, students and teachers referred to the Palestinian cause on many occasions and expressed declarations of support for displaced and occupied Arab and Muslim Palestinians. The shared language between Darwish and Moroccan students enabled and sealed this regional bond, itself contingent on the naturalization of *fuṣḥā* as the mother tongue and the conception of Palestine as a collective motherland. Hence, by a poetic sleight of hand, *fuṣḥā* became for these Moroccan students an inextricable part of their Arab-ness. As researchers of nationalism might expect, school lessons and in-class conversations largely glossed over the torsions of the Palestinian struggle that eventually undid political Pan-Arabism. They similarly glossed over the intricate nature of Darwish's involvement with the Palestinian Liberation Organization (PLO) and his voiced ambivalence about his status as national poet.[5]

What took place in Mr. Idrissi's class illustrates how modern classrooms have become fertile grounds for the cultivation of cultural homogeneity. This homogeneity is indispensable to nationalism, which, as a product of modernity, necessitates distinct modes of standardization (Gellner 1983). Nationalist narratives tweak historical circumstance to generate teleological stories that forge a cognitive and affective attachment to one's nation (Herzfeld 1986). Although the shared affinity through *fuṣḥā* is not merely the product of political maneuvering, the modern Moroccan state has been especially attentive to the process of turning regional affiliation into an explicit point of identification. As Rebecca Bryant (2004) has shown for Cyprus and Veronique Bénéï (2008) for India, school socialization into nationalism can be efficiently operationalized in moments of conflict. Effective as it may be, though, this routine inculcation of nationalism is "an ever incomplete one" (Bénéï 2008, 2), all the more so for those who express their extracurricular experiences in other languages, stories, and topologies.[6] Nevertheless, monocultural narratives evolve just like the states that institutionalize them. In the current version of the public school curriculum, there are glimpses of a "different presence" in the place of earlier aesthetic lacunae. This different presence is largely Berber. Glimpses of Berber difference are thornier issues than what may initially appear, and the most relevant question to ask about them is not whether school curricula recognize difference or not, but, rather, what constitutes an acceptable version of difference and what are the conditions of its recognition.

The curriculum of the Arab Literature course does not incorporate cultural production expressed in *dārija* or Berber. Although the History textbook refers to Berbers as the indigenous people of North Africa, to my knowledge History classes provide no occasions for the appreciation of Berber culture. This is despite the fact that a Berber aesthetic direction along with its social and moral visions abounds, with poetics being particularly prominent in it. In addition to the oral poetry that accompanies women's everyday rural chores in the mountainside of Taroudant in southwest Morocco (Hoffman 2008a), versified and metered texts of a religious didactic nature in *tashelḥit* date back to the sixteenth century when they featured in what appear to be educational campaigns for the general population (Rausch 2006). Epic poetry in Berber was renowned in the Atlas Mountains at the time of the Protectorate. The *imdyazen* (wandering poets, bards, and comedians who performed and disseminated oral poetry) mastered the art of versification in the partly improvised genre of the *amdyaz* (Jouad 1989). What is remarkable about this latter poetry is that it communicated proto-nationalist Moroccan sentiments against the Christianizing threat of French domination (Wyrtzen 2011). Both in Morocco and in neighboring Algeria, colonial ethnography and, later on, Amazigh activism re-contextualized these poems for their own respective uses under the guise of testimony to a pristine Berber subjectivity and practice (Goodman 2002). However, Moroccan and Algerian nationalist movements did not allow Berber cultural production to shape national culture, a fact which accounts for its omission from state-controlled curricula.

A noticeable exception to the cultural direction of the curriculum is the inclusion of the Moroccan novel written in French, *Il était une fois un vieux couple heureux* (Once Upon a Time, There Was a Happy Old Couple) (2002) in the senior-year curriculum, albeit as part of the French course. This novel by Mohammed Khaïr-Eddine (1941–1995), who was born in Berber-dominated Tafraoute in the southwest of Morocco, unfolds in that rural region. His last and posthumously published novel, it is a slow-paced narrative of the everyday life and ruminations of an old Berber couple reminiscing about the Protectorate. Their thoughts are set against the backdrop of pervasive socioeconomic and cultural changes in the Moroccan countryside after independence. These changes appear all the more irreversible because the old couple is childless and therefore unable to pass on their practices and perspectives to the next generation. This choice of novel and novelist by the Ministry of Education is anything but random, but points to the conditions under which the Berber experience has become part of the multicultural Moroccan identity.

Out of pure coincidence, I happened to sit in one of the initial teacher-training workshops that introduced this novel to senior-year teachers. During the workshop, Mr. Khouaja, the coordinator-inspector for French at the Regional Academy, presented the book to a dozen teachers to help them formulate their lesson plans and set pedagogical objectives. He started the workshop with the disclaimer: "We know very little of this author and his work since he spent much of his adult life in France." Nods around the room indicated agreement around this point. The novel, explained the coordinator, is a "biography of the author's parents," and he thought it would speak to students in class who had ties to the "south." Some of them, he conjectured, might have comparable "memories of their own grandparents." Mr. Khouaja pointed out that there were many "Berber linguistic terms" in the novel that would require translation and deplored the fact that he had no glossary to provide. The main theme for analysis would be the "modes of sustenance in the countryside," especially the preeminent economic role of the weekly *souq* (open market). Another important theme, suggested the coordinator, should be the relationship between *tradition* and *modernity*. Understood as clearly delineated and consecutive stages, *tradition* and *modernity* encapsulated for Mr. Khouaja the struggle over the collective "loss of patrimony" embodied by this old happy rural couple.

One of the younger teachers, who as I later found out was also a doctoral student specializing in Moroccan literature written in French, suggested that yet another theme for investigation could be the relationship between "Berbers and the *Makhzan* (Palace)" during the Protectorate, which, he confidently said, "was equally antagonistic as that with the French colonial power." The coordinator disapproved of this suggestion: "I would advise you to stay away from aspects of the novel that touch on national values. At university one is able to raise such points more easily."

The young teacher retorted, "What is the point of having a novel about Berbers if we can't discuss our national history? It reminds me of history textbooks when I was a student. They mentioned Karl Marx in passing without discussing communism as a political ideology!" The comment evidently crossed a red line because the coordinator censored the intervention with a strict glance that also pointed in my direction, a mumbled phrase about such comments not being productive to a training workshop, and a swift turn to lesson planning suggestions.

Thus, this workshop, guided by the recommendations of the Ministry of Education, molded the novel into a nostalgic depiction of a rural golden age long lost to colonialism, the latter constituting both military repression and technological innovation with its socioeconomic ramifications. Teachers were advised that students should not dwell much on the particulars of the Berber experience, but instead understand it as a southern lifestyle not antagonistic to the government and as symbolic of rural versus urban divisions. Apparent in the coordinator's discouragement of an overt discussion of "Berbers and the *Makhzan*" was the concern that such discussion might poke holes in an official historical narrative that recognized heterogeneity albeit with caveats. Hence by abstracting Berber difference to a wider negotiation of rurality versus urbanization and tradition versus modernity, the Ministry of Education encouraged a view of an overarching Moroccan-ness shaped by the irreversible sweep of history and technology. The problem is that this overarching Moroccan-ness smoothed over or erased several facets of Berber difference (Hoffman 2008a, 16). The novel reflects this erasure in its final pages that allude to the effacement of Berber cultural production. The main character, old Bouchaib, produces collections of religious poetry in Berber. Yet in sharp contrast with the popularity he gains in France through broadcasts of his poems by activist diasporic radio stations and the advocacy work of Berber associations, his poetry never penetrates the Moroccan public sphere (Khaïr-Eddine 2002, 120). The public erasure that the novel describes mirrors the teachers' workshop where the young teacher who resisted the editing built into Ministry recommendations had to self-censure his remarks. His mention of the tenuous relationship between southern Berber tribes and the centralized *Makzhan* administration, as well as the parallel he drew with communism, targeted the most vexed aspects of

Khaïr-Eddine's work in relation to cultural otherness and the political aspirations it bred.

The Ministry's multicultural hide and seek unfolded in a variety of ways inside the classroom. In one of the sessions on the novel that I observed in class, the teacher pushed Berber difference to a state of alterity. I use the term "alterity" as a counterpoint to identity—though not in the strictly Lacanian sense of the splitting of the self—to underscore a degree of othering that begets incompatible difference. During the two-month period she taught the novel, Madame Bensaouda referred to the "south" in generic terms and as if it still belonged to a pre-modern phase of intellectual underdevelopment and doubtful morality. Her focus was on rituals involving local saints, polygamy, the seclusion of women, poverty, and the dangers of illiteracy. In one class she explored the theme of violence and war. She referred to the struggle for independence from the French in the "rebellious south," but did not highlight the twofold Berber resistance to the joint oppression and surveillance by colonial forces and the Moroccan government. Her interpretation also sidelined the political and economic hardships that some regions suffered after independence because of their tense relationship with the central administration and their cultural orientation—traces of which abound in the novel. Instead, what Madame Bensaouda discussed at length was the practice of violence as being endemic to rural mentality and to rural life. She argued that personal vendettas there were as frequent as armed conflict against the European conquerors. In short, the othering of the berberophone south designated the limits of an urban arabophone sensibility taken as shared and as common sense for everyone in the classroom.

When she finally got around to addressing Berber culture in the novel, the teacher accused Khaïr-Eddine of advocating for "divisive regionalism": "There is chauvinism in the work," she claimed, and proceeded to write the words *chauvinisme Berbère* (Berber chaunivism) in the center of the blackboard. She explained the difference between the word "*patriotisme*," which refers to "the appropriate love for one's country," and "*chauvinisme*," which denoted the "excessive preference for one's community." She continued building on the students' French vocabulary by spelling the terms "*fanatisme*" and "*arabophobie*" (fanaticism and arabophobia). Madame Bensaouda did not appear overly concerned by the fact that there were students of southern berberophone background in her class. None of her students raised their hand to contest her assertions, thereby becoming complicit in her discrimination. Their reticence was understandable insofar as Madame Bensaouda endorsed a dominant and official public view, at least in that urban context, which read Berber claims to recognition as antagonistic to the post-independence nation-building project. A way to acknowledge Berbers without poking holes in this project was to posit this dissimilar Berber experience as predominantly rural, backward, and essentially outlived. The novel's folklorish and fairytale title *Once Upon a Time, There Was a Happy Old Couple* encouraged this interpretive maneuver.

With another class of students also studying the novel, a different teacher, Madame Abdelkebir, discussed it in markedly different ways. I attended her wrap-up session on the novel that concluded with student presentations on Khaïr-Eddine's biography, his corpus, and the historical context in which he produced his work. The most memorable part of that session was one student's introduction to the novelist that peeled off the layers of folklorization and lay bare the scathing political critique embroiled in Khaïr-Eddine's artistic vision. This presentation, which admittedly sounded like an academic analysis taken from a website, was remarkable not only for what it expressed in public but, even more importantly, for revealing just how transgressive this expression felt to the student herself:

> Mohammed Khaïr-Eddine was a dissenter from the politics of the Moroccan regime led by Hassan II during the Years of Lead. For this reason, his novels were banned until his death while many of his literary colleagues were persecuted. Khaïr-Eddine witnessed the ordeal of rural to urban migration and of immigration to France where he worked in a factory line. He launched a vehement critique of Moroccan society whose central component was the despotism of types of governance and cultural expression. The main themes of his work are politics, religion, and sexuality, all of which are taboo. The novelist rages against the figures of the family patriarch, the King, and God himself.

Right after she had pronounced the last few words, the student paused, looking uncomfortable, and said to her teacher, "Madame, I am not sure I should go on." Sensing she may have crossed a red line, as did the teacher in the workshop, the student asked for the teacher's confirmation that this dismissal of the cultural pillars of the state (patriarchy, religion, monarchy) was permissible in class, especially in the presence of a foreign researcher. Madame Abdelkebir had not divulged to me any personal details of her background—to this day, I do not know whether she claimed any Berber descent—and had kept her political views to herself. She did, however, reassure the student on that occasion that her commentary was acceptable because this was a class of "literature and fiction." The girl gave her teacher a meek smile of relief and rushed to take her seat. Another student then took the floor to present Khaïr-Eddine's especially incendiary novels *Agadir* (1967), *Le déterreur*" (The Human Ghoul) (1973), and *Légende et vie d'Agounchich* (The Legend and Life of Agounchich) (1984a).

What became apparent in the student presentations was that Khaïr-Eddine's invisibility from the canon of Moroccan literature, his incorporation into the French course, and the recent choice of this specific novel by the Ministry of Education were attempts to coopt a political dissenter of Berber origin. Through this cooptation, the Ministry indirectly acknowledged some of the ripples of the official cultural and historical narrative without allowing them to deconstruct this narrative. It is not surprising that none of the other works of Khaïr-Eddine have made it into the baccalaureate curriculum. Most of his poetic and novelistic production is highly provocative both in linguistic style and in its themes. In relation to his usage of the French language, the author has referred to his writing as "*guérilla linguistique*" (linguistic guerrilla warfare) (Khaïr-Eddine 1998, 9). As for his themes, his poetry and novels are steeped in suffering and display attitudes of violent defiance of cultural and political despotism. For instance, in the novel *Agadir* (1967)—the title is the name of a city in southwest Morocco with a predominant Berber character—the earthquake the city experienced in 1960 levels it and exposes the marginalization of this part of the country by the ruling and economic elites. The city's complete annihilation demands a radical reconfiguration of society, culture, and economy. In the novel *Légende et vie d'Agounchich* (1984) a man from the mountainous Anti-Atlas area embarks on the decimation of another tribe to avenge his sister's rape. His violent trajectory in this predominantly Berber region gives us access to a history of resistance to central authority before the 1935 "penetration of colonialism" (Khaïr-Eddine 1984b).[7] In *Le déterreur* (1973), a man on death row awaits his punishment for digging up and consuming corpses in his hometown after his return from exile. In his own analysis of this novel, Khaïr-Eddine suggests that its protagonist is the ultimate revolutionary symbol "since the true human ghoul exhumes and decimates all that is held sacred in a society in order to make it visible to public view and criticize it. For me, all revolutionaries are human ghouls" (Khaïr-Eddine 1998, 42).

Thus, there is plenty in Khaïr-Eddine's other novels, those not chosen by the Ministry of Education, to suggest that he saw himself as an agitator who deconstructed "the apparent consensus around the fundamental issues of cultural identity, social conformism, language and history" (Touaf 2012, 154). Although some claim that he pursued his radical poetics and politics exclusively through his Berber subjectivity, Khaïr-Eddine also participated in a broader movement of dissent from the post-independence political order. In 1964, Khaïr-Eddine and his high school friend Mustafa Nissabouri published the manifesto *"Poésie toute"* (It's All About Poetry), in which they called for a synthesis of a fringe artistic and political vision that would deconstruct existing cultural and institutional norms (Sefriouri 2013). Subsequently, Khaïr-Eddine joined the core group that founded and funded the French-language literary publication *Souffles* (Breaths) (1966) with its arabophone equivalent *Anfās* (1971). *Souffles* advocated a rethinking of the Moroccan cultural patrimony in ways that would retrieve and honor its Berber and Jewish heritages. It posed "national culture" as an open question and an object of debate and made this debate central to the resolution of the country's socioeconomic and political deadlocks (Laabi 1966).[8] In a special issue devoted to Palestine after the 1967 Six Day War, contributors to *Souffles* acknowledged the centrality of this historical event for the future of the region, yet asked readers to interrogate the unity of Arabism and evaluate how this ideology had obfuscated hierarchy and inequality within different Arab states (Belal 1969). The publication's critique of Pan-Arab populism was quite different from the message conveyed in the Arab Literature class that opens this chapter.

During the entire time it was published, 1966–1972, *Souffles* aligned with Marxist-Leninist attitudes, and its main figures, Abdellatif Laabi and Abraham Serfaty, were members of the radical leftist parties *Ilā al-Amām* (Forward) and 23 *Mars* (March 23) (Sefriouri 2013, 17). The publication became the cultural expression of these political alignments and thus did not fare well in the state of emergency that King Hassan II declared in 1965. During the state of emergency, which followed the dissolution of the Moroccan parliament, the government suppressed insurrections in the Rif region, banned communist parties, harassed all political opposition, and clamped down on demonstrations. It also closed the Institute of Sociology in Rabat in 1970 and refocused school curricula on Arabic philosophy and Islamic thought after a purge of works by Nietzsche, Freud, and Marx that the state deemed inflammatory (Sefriouri 2013, 56).[9] During the teacher-training workshop described earlier, the young teacher alluded to that period by noting its prohibition on discussing national history and the absence of any classroom discussion on communism. In 1972, Laabi and Serfaty were arrested and imprisoned and *Souffles* ceased to exist. Henceforth, the magazine appeared in court as incriminatory evidence of plotting against the state. It is only recently, in line with the rehabilitation of various expressions of dissent by the state, that the publication has become accessible through its digitization by the National Library in Rabat.

Given this context, it is hardly surprising that Khaïr-Eddine has not featured in an official articulation of Moroccan identity and culture in the same way as Darwish. In fact, he was erased from mainstream cultural memory despite his international fame and his association with prominent intellectual figures such as Sartre, Beckett, Césaire, and Senghor. A few, predominantly foreign, analyses of Khaïr-Eddine's work in the 1970s declared that it would be impossible to translate and print novels "as violently blasphemous, pairing God and King in the same reviled figure" (Arnaud 1976, 61) inside Morocco. In the late 1990s, in the introduction to a posthumous compilation of interviews by Khaïr-Eddine, he was characterized as "one of the least known Moroccan novelists. Never has a Moroccan author been more marginalized" (Abboubi in Khaïr-Eddine 1998, 5). This treatment was consistent with the Arabo-Muslim monoculturalism that underlined the nationalist and concomitant Pan-Arab vision of the post-independence state. Hence the contemporary push for the visibility of Khaïr-Eddine is curious. How exactly does it fit with the state's broader institutionalization of multiculturalism?

The inclusion of this specific novel by Khaïr-Eddine suggests that a degree of Berber difference has become essential to the transformation of a formerly illiberal monocultural nation-state into a democratizing multicultural one. However, the Ministry of Education only encourages difference so long as it aligns with common values around patriarchy, monarchy, and religion, values that have long buoyed the rhetoric of the post-independence Moroccan nation-state. Other manifestations of Berber difference run the risk of alterity, invoking an intolerable difference. In a way, then, what we witness inside the classroom is the official production of a "model minority" experience (Prashad 2005). This model minority becomes metonymical of the tailoring of core institutions in relation to ideas of democracy and pluralism, which nonetheless does not entail the drastic transformation of these institutions. What is striking about this metonymization is that it constitutes the multi-stranded outcome of a long struggle among Berbers, the Moroccan state, and extranational actors over the demarcation of difference and the regulation of its handling.

ON THE DEMOCRATIC DISPOSITION
OF MINORITY LANGUAGES

The ascension of King Mohammed VI to the throne in 1999 marked the official end of the state of emergency. In practice, the opening up of the domain of deliberation both institutionally and in the public sphere had been underway since the acceptance of International Monetary Fund loans under structural adjustment agreements in 1987 and the signing of free trade agreements with the European Union and the United States that went into force in 2000 and 2004, respectively. To mark the beginning of a new era in Moroccan history, the state under the new king Mohammed VI engaged in a subtle discrediting of its political and cultural past and professed its reinvention along liberal democratic principles. In theory, these principles would safeguard the non-violent coexistence of diverse practices and values, which, in turn, would define and guarantee liberal democratic ways of relating and governing. The meaning of the concept "liberal" is both geographically and historically contingent, but for the purposes of this discussion it signifies both equality for all in relation to basic rights and liberties and a laissez-faire attitude to socioeconomic opportunity. Specifically, the liberalism that Morocco's international economic patrons pushed for shed any remnants of its rudimentary welfare vision and endorsed the image of nearly unfettered competition. In ideal terms, this competition would be "purged of real conflict" because the type of difference it accommodated would have no social consequences (Povinelli 2002, 16).

Both aspects of this liberal adaptation bear an interesting connection with Berber claims to recognition. This section explores the first aspect: the political will to ensure justice and equality for all. This political will materialized in two key gestures: a commitment to transitional justice manifest through the Truth and Reconciliation Commissions that vocalized the plight of political dissenters during the Years of Lead (Slyomovics 2005) and an investment in recognizing minority claims. In his royal speech delivered on October 17, 2001, Mohammed VI represented Moroccan culture to his subjects-citizens in the following inclusive terms:

> [Morocco has] a plural identity because it is based on varied sources:
> Amazigh, Arab, Sub-Saharan and Andalous, which by their openness to
> other cultures and diverse civilizations and by interacting with them,
> have contributed to refine and enrich our identity. (Mohammed al-Sadis
> al-Alawi, ẓahīr 1-01-299)

This speech recalibrated earlier state rhetoric that had insisted on the exclusive Arabo-Muslim nucleus of Moroccan national culture, and it beckoned toward the institutionalization of a plural national culture.[10] It also announced the establishment of IRCAM as an official response to the advocacy that Amazigh activists had waged since the establishment of the post-independence state. However, the synergy between recognized multilingualism and assurances of liberal democratization emerged most clearly a decade later in the aftermath of the widespread demonstrations of 2011. Along with endorsing more features of constitutional monarchy than ever before, the royally promoted constitutional reforms, approved by the citizenry in a referendum in July 2011, took pivotal steps toward officializing multilingualism by adding the Berber language—labeled *amazighiyya*—as Morocco's second official language and promoting it inside public education and the wider public sphere. Still, the wording in Article 5—"*al-huwīya al-thaqāfiyya al-maghribiyya al-muwāḥada*" (a united Maghribian cultural identity)—did not resonate with the diversity of cultural repertoires and sense of belonging across the Moroccan population (*al-dustūr* 2011, *faṣl* 5). It also elided conspicuous fissures across regional, class, and gender lines. Nevertheless, the constitution's recognition of linguistic minorities was bound to appeal to Morocco's international patrons, given that the UN Committee on the Elimination of Racial Discrimination had outlined the exact terms of this recognition in August 2010.[11]

The constitutional reforms have a performative function, creating the impression of carving out a new avenue for inclusion and consensus. This novelty is illusionary because contemporary rhetoric on minority rights draws on a long semantic appropriation of French colonial and Amazigh activist discourse around the figure of the "democratic Berber." The deployment of multilingualism as an indicator of multiculturalism and democratization has taken a winding path that we could read as a "process of convergence as historical events, overlapping representations, and diverse vested interests come together in a powerful, if historically contingent, accord that is productive of a new common sense" (McAlister 2002, 441).[12] During this process, both official and non-official actors have imbued the categories "ethnicity," "history," and "language" with meanings that have supported their respective desires around representation and participation. What is interesting in our case is that, although different actors have formulated diverse meanings of and functions served by minorities, they all have reproduced the figure of the "democratic Berber"— an image already entrenched in colonial policy that became instrumental to minority rights activism since independence.[13] Thus, in the same way the curriculum has Darwish's mother speaking for the Moroccan Arab identity, it makes Khaïr-Eddine's rural-based, old, compliant Berber couple engender new collective imaginaries around what it means to be Moroccan.

Our knowledge of pre-Arab conquest North Africa is limited, but it is fair to assume that since the Arab conquest (eighth century AC), Berber and Arab populations have mixed substantially through dynastic alliances and Islamization (Willis 2012). Hence the discourse of a divide between Arabs and Berbers emerges as "a patently modern form that has been repeatedly created and recreated" (Silverstein 2004, 45). Because of their Muslim status, Berbers in Morocco were not a subgroup under *dhimmi* law (a pre-national legal provision that ensured the protection of religious minorities subject to special taxation) as was the Jewish community. Understood as distant from and often rebelling against the centralized *Makhzan* government of the heartlands, the Berbers in rural areas [dar.] *bled al-siba* (land of dissidence, the periphery) became the main justification for the French military campaign of pacification in 1912 (Wyrtzen 2011). The ties between the Moroccan experience and the Algerian case are as intricate as they are profound.[14] French ethnology on Algeria during the nineteenth century had already contributed significantly to colonial domination with its racial classification of the occupied population through pseudo-scientific principles of linguistic and physical differentiation. The non-Arab Kabyle Berbers, whom the French assumed to be non-nomadic, less religious, and inherently more democratic than the Arabs, became central to this racial classification through the formulation of a theory of their European descent known as the Kabyle Myth (Ageron 1960; Lorcin 1995).

As both military personnel and French orientalists specializing in Berber language and culture moved from Algeria to Morocco after 1912, they put their experiences to work in their new surroundings. Judging the mixing of Arab and Berber elements in language and practice to be the result of contamination of the authentic Berber nature, colonial officials in Morocco formalized the legal and pedagogical separation of Berber tribes from the urban Arab centers (Hoffman 2008b). On May 16, 1930, the Protectorate administration and King Mohammed V jointly signed the royal decree, later known as the "Berber *zahir*," that removed rural areas from the jurisdiction of Islamic law. In these areas, the decree assigned the adjudication of some legal cases to *'urf* (customary law), with French courts handling other types of legal affairs. Colonial aspirations of adjudicating difference and ensuring the dissemination of French secular values among the Berber population led to the founding of the *Collège Berbère d'Azrou* in 1927. Initially reserved for the sons of local rulers and distinct from other pedagogical structures in the country, the *Collège Berbère* had as its mission the shaping of a francophile Berber constituency that would prevent any resurgence of insurrection in the periphery (Benhlal 2005, 11). Prohibiting the oral and textual use of Arabic and the teaching of Islam, the college hired French and, after the Second World War, Algerian teachers from the region of Tlemcen. The college did not produce the desired allegiance it envisaged, but perceptions about its divisive pedagogical strategy lingered.

The nationalist movement that elevated Mohammed V as the leader of anti-colonialism and national unification campaigned against ethno-linguistic variation and saw Berber claims to difference as counter-national threats.[15] The post-independence government incorporated Berber notables in the royalist party *al-Ḥarakat al-Shaʿbiyya* (The Popular Movement) led by Mahjoubi Aherdan, who was an alumnus of the *Collège Berbère*. This party diffused to a degree the urban Arab focus of *Istiqlāl* politics, but did not resist the Arabization plan that nationalists hailed as the unifying, state-building initiative par excellence. The post-independent state defended its monocultural basis and the translation of Arabization into the distribution of land, resources, and regional governance. It also suppressed any attempt to resignify this monoculturalism.

Berber reactions to their marginalization were multifaceted. Only a year after independence, Crown Prince Moulay Hassan put down a Berber-led insurrection in the southeast Tafilalet region against *Istiqlāl*-appointed governors. In 1959, Abdekrim al-Khattabi led a three-month revolt in the Rif region asking for no less than secession from the newly formed Moroccan nation. The government countered the revolt with heavy aerial and land attacks. Following an assassination attempt against King Hassan II in 1973 orchestrated by General Oufkir, who was of Berber background, activists in the Middle and High Atlas regions led an armed campaign to claim secession for the southeast. The state arrested them and sentenced them to death.

Alongside this armed struggle to secure territorial claims, a civil movement for the recognition of Berber cultural rights grew, beginning with the founding of the *Association Marocaine de la Recherche et de l'Echange Culturelle* (Moroccan Association for Research and Cultural Exchange,

AMREC) in 1967. Its pacifist sociopolitical vision operated under the slogan "L'unité dans la diversité" (Unity in Diversity) and considered Arabic and Islam to be central but not exclusive components of Moroccan identity (Chafik 2005). The civil movement was never monolithic, and the more it grew, the more it diversified. Some activist claims respected the boundaries of the existing state, but envisioned Morocco not as a province of the Middle East but as a self-contained space where communities would negotiate internal differences on equal terms; in turn these activists saw the region as the conglomeration of various Moroccan cultural components, not as a cluster of Arab nation-states. Others agitated for a redrawing of national borders and the creation of another region, the Tamazgha, which would stretch from the Canary Islands to the Siwa Oasis in Egypt (Silverstein 2007, 107).[16] Some activists argued for the joint plight of all minorities across the Arabo-Muslim landscape, reviving rituals that visualized and enacted connections between Berber and Jewish communities in the south or forging actual links with Zionist militants (Silverstein 2012). Some went against the grain of national and regional foreign policy when they declared their support for the U.S. 2003 invasion of Iraq (Silverstein and Crawford 2004, 48).

Sympathy toward Zionism and the state of Israel is especially noteworthy not only because of its daring realignment of interests and affinities but also for its role in deliberately demarcating Berber difference as alterity (Silverstein 2012; Boum 2013). Evidently, these activists saw in Zionism a successful example of a minority community achieving statehood. However, showing support for Israel has always constituted the most transgressive move of opposition to Arab-ness and to a monarchically safeguarded Islam. Ritual revivals that promoted Judeo-Berber culture and some Berber activists' vocal dismissal of the Palestinian struggle as the Pan-Arab prerogative served a similar purpose: they displayed an uncommon moral sensibility among Arabo-Muslim Moroccans. This uncommon moral sensibility needs to be kept in mind when evaluating the encompassing potential of liberalism in general and in Morocco in particular. It is only through noticing the limits of liberal inclusion, even in so-called established democracies, that we can appreciate the relative potency of multiculturalism to fundamentally reconfigure "majority" and "minority" relations (Rawls 1993; Taylor 1994).

Inside the Moroccan school, the state currently fights to prevent the alliance of students with these more far-reaching Berber visions by producing and disseminating a model Berber image through discussion of Khaïr-Eddine's novel. It invites teachers to promote this image as the emblem of difference within the non-threatening fold of rurality and tradition. This way, Berber Moroccans become at school "the impossible object of an authentic self-identity" (Povinelli 2002, 5) that can redeem but must not crumble national and state foundations. Markedly, this version of difference sidelines claims to territorial change and to the diverse regional alignments we saw earlier. It brings to the fore culture not as a lived, ongoing relationship to the present, but domesticated as patrimony and folklore.

The limitations on Moroccan multilingualism cum multiculturalism evident in curricular content intersect other marked and unmarked gestures of governance outside the school walls. Despite considerable government investment in liberalizing the public sphere, the state at times has curtailed the use of both *dārija* and Berber either through legal persecution or through the indirect financial bleeding of endeavors deemed as threatening to the state's official cultural politics.[17] Still, the state strategy of direct coercion has been replaced by the cooptation of artists and cultural producers who were previously antagonistic to official cultural rhetoric. Some of these former antagonists have become model dissenters and culture brokers whose inclusion into circles of power, through visibility and financing, has symbolized the accomplishment of multiculturalism. This inclusion may have been well intended, but the hitch is that it has only been possible as long as these model dissenters stop demanding drastic institutional reform—such as secularism, the abolition of the monarchy, or territorial changes—and upsetting presumed to be "common" sensibilities around these three issues.

HANDLING MULTICULTURALISM

Multiculturalism poses a serious challenge to the universalist aspect of liberalism as the recognition and equality of all citizens irrespective of identity. What is more worrying than this general philosophical and legal quandary is the strategic deployment of a culturalist imaginary to un-hinge linguistic and cultural difference from concrete claims it could made to political change. In this vein, an emphasis on culture as a bounded ethno-linguistic bloc becomes the instrument of mitigation of the chal-lenges difference has and still poses to the idea of the nation and the com-position of the state (Grillo 2007). This culturalist policy does not pass the test of everyday experience in Morocco. In fact, it is in some tension with how ordinary people understand the growing presence of Berber language and culture in the public sphere.

In Morocco, the shift from the suppression of Amazigh activism in the 1970s to state involvement in shaping a model minority experience through the creation of IRCAM is the most visible instance of the state's official direction on multiculturalism. Since my fieldwork began in 2007, various interlocutors in various contexts kept mentioning to me the name of IR-CAM again and again. Their intense interest in IRCAM made me keen to visit its headquarters and experience its atmosphere and ambience. The institution's connection to royal patronage is hard to miss. IRCAM, which boasts an estimated annual budget of USD 100 million, had its first offices in a building owned by the Group Ominum North Africa, the largest Moroccan enterprise controlled by the royal family (Silverstein and Craw-ford 2004, 233). The current IRCAM headquarters building is a glass and steel edifice, architecturally impressive and luxurious, whose walls are adorned with numerous portraits of Kind Mohammed VI. It is a state-of-the-art research facility in the high-end neighborhood of Rabat. When I visited the headquarters, I was welcomed by layers of security guards, admissions offices, and secretarial staff. On my way out, I struggled with the heavy load of books the center generously offered me, a load that testi-fied to IRCAM's significant role in the production of school and adult literacy manuals as well as historical and sociological studies.

After my brief visit, I rushed to the home of a family for lunch. This family did not trace any Berber connections in its immediate genealogy. The children of the family went to public school and lived in a lower class urban neighborhood close to a medium-sized *souq* (open market). I went straight to the kitchen to show the mother, Bouteina, and the children of the family my new book acquisitions and to share my impressions of

IRCAM. Bouteina browsed through the teaching manual for IRCAM's standardized Berber (called *Tamazight*) for first graders. She found the symbols of the language utterly incomprehensible. Her children made an effort to read out each symbol according to the book's instructions and, unable to do so, burst into laughter. Bouteina teasingly encouraged her children to learn Berber by going to the *souq*, because "it is known that a *Schleuḥ* vendor only gives you a good price if you speak their language." Her children reminded me not to buy anything from the Berber [dar.] *mul l-ḥanūt* (store owner) next to their apartment, warning me that he is expensive and "not very nice."

Bouteina continued her introduction to Berber culture with the assertion that "in Morocco, there is racism between the two [Arabs and Berbers]." Her statement immediately brought to mind the comments of Moustafa, the student I spoke to after the Arab Literature class, who had also raised the issue of racism. Yet, contrary to what Moustafa had claimed, Bouteina addressed the racism Berbers displayed against Arabs in the *souq* and the street. She described the Berbers as [dar.] *qbiḥ* (mean), although some, she said, were nice people. She singled out the Berbers of Khenifra (a province in the Atlas Mountains in central Morocco) as particularly immoral and as tolerant of female prostitution. She described their communities as having [dar.] *"māshī saḥḥa māshī īmān"* (neither health nor faith). These latter comments echoed Madame Bensaouda's analysis of the Berber south as the epitome of backwardness and of questionable moral dispositions. By making prostitution and lack of religious faith the indicators of this transgression, Bouteina placed Berbers outside the sensibilities of many Arabo-Muslim Moroccans and of people residing in the urban centers. Nevertheless, Bouteina concluded, "The Berbers are better than us because they have learned Arabic, while we have not learned their language. In my heart, I do want to learn this language, I want to be able to understand what they say between them." Clearly, her wish to learn the Berber language did not connect to an aesthetic appreciation of it, but stemmed from her skepticism of the honesty of Berber exchange practices and her wish to be able to curtail Berber merchants' alleged dishonesty.

The conversation finished there, and we made no more reference to this topic until a few weeks later. On my return to the family's home, Bouteina delighted in narrating to me the story of her most recent visit to Rabat. After convincing her husband to drive her there, they first set off to visit the university where she had studied Arabic Literature for a year before she got married. She was very nostalgic about seeing her department, but to her disappointment she found the building old and decrepit and the classrooms in bad condition. Driving back from the university, her eye caught the IRCAM building, and she got very curious. Despite her husband's reluctance, they stopped, walked around the building, and eventually entered it. More than anything, she was surprised by the building's shape: for her, its diagonal rooftop represented the ambition of the Berber language to "reach for the skies." She added, "The Berber language is *maline* (cunning)." She noticed that the staff "from parking personnel up to the director," did not speak to her in *dārija* and considered this to be discriminatory "since Arab administrations accept all kinds of people." Although she was obviously impressed by the IRCAM project, she stressed her conviction that the effort will not succeed: "You know, they will never reach Arabic because Arabic is rich, it is a complete language, you can see the harmony of the alphabet; instead, you have the circles and triangles of this Berber alphabet, it is not as beautiful, is it?" Despite her stylistic comments about Arabic, which were evidence of her political convictions, this visit had unsettled Bouteina's conviction in the inferiority of Berber to Arabic. I reminded her that the king, whom she ardently supported as the embodiment of both political and religious authority, had sponsored IR-CAM and the ascension of Berber language and culture. In response, she evaluated these royal intentions as follows:

> There is a competition between the two [Arabs and Berber]. The King recognized the Berber languages to avoid big clashes, because even though things seem calm at some point they may explode.... He didn't want violence or any potential claim to autonomy, or else there would be two kingdoms, and who would be the King of the Berbers?

Bouteina's assessment of the political objectives of IRCAM suggests that the liberal recognition of Berber alterity made "thinking otherwise" possible only within certain parameters, a key one being the maintenance of monarchical authority.[18] Her emphasis on language as the space of multicultural encounters highlights the recasting of multilingualism as the safest manifestation of difference.

There are a number of reasons why linguistics has become central to the work of IRCAM. It was colonial ethnology that first mapped ethnic distinction onto linguistic differentiation more so than onto physical appearance and custom (Hoffman and Gilson Miller 2010). Then, in the precarious position that Berber difference occupied within the context of post-independence, a plea for linguistic recognition appeared more benign than their claims for self-determination. Eventually, language claims also played into the agenda of the transnational advocacy of minority rights in the country through the concepts of endangered "minority" and "indigenous" languages. Along similar lines, multilingualism in educational planning fostered international institutional hopes of countering the challenges faced by berberophone students entering public education (Wagner 1993; UNESCO 2011).[19] Last, but not least, linguistics proved most effective as a form of advocacy because it did not antagonize the territorial integrity of the post-independence nation or its modes of governance. For all these reasons, but primarily the last one, linguistics became the metaphorical "territory in which the fight had to be launched" (Rachik 2006, 30).

The especially intense debate that erupted in the 1970s over which register best communicated a Moroccan Berber experience made clear the directive role of the monarchical state in minority language promotion. Pioneering intellectuals of Amazigh-ness such as Mohammed Chafik understood Moroccan culture as a conglomeration of both *dārija* and Berber articulations, positing these as languages of popular rather than high culture and considering them to be indigenous registers: "The Moroccan Arabic idioms offer an illustration of the way in which a compromise is made between a Berber substratum and exogenous influences" (Rachik 2006, 38). Ahmed Boukous (1995), the current rector of IRCAM, made use of Bourdieu's (1991) understanding of the dialect as a politically failed language to advocate for official support for a standardized register called *Tamazight*. To this end, facilitating terminological innovation, standardization, and the transition from orality to textual production became IRCAM's main research endeavors. IRCAM opted to promote *tifinagh*, an ancient script that bears no resemblance to Arabic, with the justification that the script was historically accurate. However, there were important political reasons to use this script. On the one hand, its use sidelined accusations of collusion with formerly imperial agendas that would have arisen had French script been used. Simultaneously, it assuaged the fears of too much appropriation by an Islamic rhetoric of inclusion had the Arabic script been used. On the other hand, *tifinagh* is a largely unfamiliar and rather obscure script that makes learning for both amazighophone and arabophone speakers an arduous and protracted practice. Despite this last consideration, the chosen script seemed useful precisely because it circumvented a thorny discussion around the sanctity of Arabic: namely, the *tifinagh* script distanced ever further the potential de-association of arabophonie from Islam, which could have had serious implications for the religious-dynastic legitimacy of its monarchy.[20]

The paradox of Amazigh advocacy as IRCAM promoted it is that it both made multilingualism coterminous with sociopolitical democratization and subsumed this process into a technocratic linguistic enterprise. What is more, it did so under royal patronage, which claimed to stand outside the realm of institutional politics. In "A New Life for Tamazight, a New Horizon for Morocco," Boukous (2003) presents the empowerment of Amazigh culture and the official *Tamazight* register as a comprehensive social and political vision:

> Such a project, as well as the recognition of linguistic diversity that it entails, is homage to forms of expression and to linguistic practices where the norm is worked by those very people that are called to obey it, and not imposed by those who are charged with the task of forcing it into the social fabric. From this fact, it [*Tamazight*] constitutes a step towards new conceptions of collective life that are democratic and modern . . . . It should help us enter the linguistic and cultural pluralism that defines life in today's world and tear the iron chains imposed on us by those nostalgic of a unique paradigm in thought, culture and in the practice of politics. (Boukous 2003, 3)

According to such claims, the equalizing impact of standardizing the *Tamazight* version would both result in individual economic and social empowerment for the underprivileged and extend to broader political transformation from below. The "iron chains of nostalgia" and "the unique paradigms" in thought that Boukous invokes refer to the policy of Arabization and its cultural oppression. His message is in equal parts ambitious and ambiguous. For one, the representational nature of Boukous's politics of representation is tenuous; the conceptualization of cultural plurality by urban intellectuals and activists may mean very little to Berber speakers who occupy different positions economically, socially, and regionally. Yet it is his plea for sweeping political change that is especially incongruous with the fact that IRCAM owes its existence to, and consequently has a vested interest in, the maintenance of the monarchical regime. Bouteina's political evaluation of Berber visibility ("Who would be the King of Berbers?") reveals how Moroccans who identify as Arabo-Muslim perceive the uses and limits of official multiculturalism.

Increasingly since the decade of the 2000s, both Morocco's official supporters—the foreign governments and the international press that praised its resilience and efficacy of governance—and its challengers, who hailed it as a chameleon-like authoritarian entity with a voracious appetite (Tozy 2008), have depicted the Moroccan state as exceptional. Nonetheless the evolution of this state does not appear all that exceptional if we take into consideration the basic mechanisms of neoliberal governance on a global scale. A research center and lobby, IRCAM epitomizes the neoliberal enterprise: even though in the past Amazigh activists had been shrewd enough to deploy language rights as an avenue to recognition and participation in socioeconomic and political life, currently the teaching of language, and language rights alike, is a technocratic intervention seemingly autonomous from the operations of an elected government. By institutionalizing multilingualism as an indicator of multiculturalism and taking its control away from the regulatory powers of parliament, the Moroccan state—in this instance, the Palace and its authority over the government—has sundered the democratizing potential of multiculturalism at the very moment it adopted the most visible insignia of a burgeoning democracy.

The founding of IRCAM reveals a modus operandi that can also apply to the institutional reforms introduced in Morocco after the popular unrest of 2011. What Beatrice Hibou (2011) calls "anti-politics" for the Moroccan context—but is essentially a central feature of neoliberalism everywhere—entails foregrounding technocratic expertise and advancing a public understanding of reform as neutral and apolitical. This discourse first qualifies politics as a quintessentially divisive and self-interested activity. Next, technocrats, members of the business elite or civil society, take over domains of governance such as educational restructuring. Their actions precede and in fact make insignificant the public deliberation that would happen through channels of political representation. This trend is in line with global principles of "good governance" that consider technocratic intervention as a nonaligned buffer to the potential economic excesses and mistakes of the state.[21] The technocratic trend liberates elected state officials—members of councils or the parliament—from the task and risk of matching public demand with policy. What is specific about the Moroccan case is that both technocratic decision making and civil society tie in with the Palace in some way or the other. This makes the horizon of resistance appear particularly fuzzy to oppositional actors, who are aware that a change in state institutions cannot result in the meaningful transformation of governance. How do these institutional blockages practically affect Moroccan students, both amazighophone and arabophone, as they steer through multilingualism in curricular and extracurricular spheres?

SCHOOL BERBER AND BERBERS AT SCHOOL

Vijya Prashad's assessment of the neoliberal configuration of multiculturalism in the United States—"to feel the effects of race pride without the means to live proudly is small comfort" (2005, 197)—applies uncannily closely to the Berber case. This congruence is not coincidental. The latest Moroccan constitution (2011) established standardized *Tamazight* as the second official language, but in the same article strongly encouraged mastery of foreign languages with a view to increasing interaction with and integration into what it called the global *"mujtama' al-ma'rifa"* (knowledge society) (*al-dustūr* 2011, al-faṣl 5). This juxtaposition of languages is important because it makes visible the dissonance between the concept of a heritage minority language that protects indigenous identities and the concept of a global language that provides "competitive advantage in the global market place" (Mitchell 2003, 387). Significantly, although both concepts are subject to globalized norms of multicultural nationhood that agencies such as UNESCO support, the concept of a global language encourages us to see language as a coveted commodity in the neoliberal landscape of global interaction (Neela Das 2011). The fact that the constitutional delineation of Morocco's languages does not reflect the political economy of the country, which reserves little space for monolingual *dārija* or *fuṣḥā* speakers and even less for monolingual berberophone speakers, affects the latter students in two ways: it makes their language synecdochic to nationalist cultural and political redemption at the same time as it leaves them doubly removed from the arena of economic competition in relation to all graduates of the public school. Bouchra's and Moustafa's weariness at the beginning of the chapter about fluency in Berber ("What's the point?," "We need to learn all these languages") reflects their perception of institutionalized multilingualism as a technique of governance. This technique makes minority speakers responsible for their access to economic and social resources despite the historical structural inequalities of their position.

The belief that transcription, standardization, and systematic dissemination through media and formal schooling can elevate a disenfranchised language into an agent of empowerment was as fundamental to the Arabization policies of the 1960s and 1970s as it has been to the endeavors of Amazigh activism. Since its founding in 2001, IRCAM aspired to unite the assemblage of Berber languages into the official register *Tamazight*. In the space of a decade, street and shop signage in urban centers began to display standardized *Tamazight*, and television broadcasting offered newsreels in this version of Berber. The ambition was to turn *Tamazight* into a "language of education, recognized and promoted" (Rachik 2006, 19). Indeed, the *Commission Spéciale Education et Formation* (Special Commission for Education and Training, COSEF) announced that, as of 2005, 960 primary schools around the country, about 20 percent of the total number, had introduced the instruction of *Tamazight* for three hours per week.

Yet berberophone and arabophone school participants, researchers, and non-IRCAM affiliated Amazigh activists were skeptical of this initiative. One contention was that *Tamazight* was a subject and not a language of instruction. If so, the policy had little potential to facilitate learning for berberophone students who already struggled to cope with Arabic and French on their entry to formal education (Errihani 2006; 2008).[22] In this light, the introduction of *Tamazight* appeared more like cultural training for urban Moroccan students of arabophone background. This cultural training is problematic not only because of its superficial nature but also because it adds to the linguistic and general workload of public school students throughout the country. Skepticism extended to the modes of implementation of the course because teacher training for *Tamazight* instruction was minimal and the adoption of the language in the curriculum remained optional (Aissati et al. 2011).

Inside urban high schools, school participants of Berber background approached the process of standardization of Berber with caution. Some of the teachers I worked with closely had a long history of activism within the branches of the Amazigh movement. Even though a number of them found the position of IRCAM as a cultural broker to be fruitful for their advocacy, others saw the cooptation of an activist agenda by the king as harmful to their cause's more forceful lines of contestation. Overwhelmingly, however, teachers worried about the dire condition of the already multilingual Arabized school (with Arabic and French) that would only deteriorate through the addition of one more language. These concerns increased when contemplating the fate of rural public school students (see Figure 5.1). Madame Amelal, who was of Berber descent and a teacher of history for the senior year, described her concern in the following terms: "Now we will train them in the Berber language and cut them off completely from the rest of the country." The teacher referred to the measure as "the IRCAM *ẓahīr*," an intertextual reference that hinted at the French Protectorate's Berber *ẓahīr*. The reference implied that the state engaged in a divisive agenda that would segregate schooling for the rural berberophone areas. Her view resonated with fears that IRCAM's pedagogical agenda works as an extension of, not a deviation from, earlier state policies toward Berbers. Generally, interlocutors like Madame Amelal assigned standardized *Tamazight* instruction to a sphere of power broking that was little concerned with the improvement of student lives.

FIGURE 5.1

Photo of village school in Ighazoun-n-Imoulass in the Saghro Mountains in southern Morocco. Berber writing on the wall, in the *tifinagh* alphabet, says *zg thamfit ayd ittawi oughanim tanoumi* (The cane straightens from a very young age). Courtesy of Baudouin Dupret.

Despite their relative indifference and sometimes aversion to this pedagogical agenda, school participants of Berber origin shared their cultural and linguistic knowledge with their peers inside and outside the school walls. The networks in which this cultural knowledge was distributed relied on the regional varieties of Berber rather than the newly standardized version of IRCAM. Although classroom conversation rarely addressed students' regional backgrounds, such backgrounds were a common object of discussion during breaks. Often, it was student attempts to classify me within a Moroccan geo-landscape that triggered these conversations. In their rhetorical and relational move to bring me into the national fold, students speculated about my possible origins from the Rif. This classification often opened up discussion about north versus south distinctions, observations on the various *dārija* and Berber accents, exchanges over customs and family structures, and conversations about regional physical characteristics. What stood out during these conversations was that the use of the term "Amazigh" was very rare and that regional origins did not always coincide with linguistic skills. In fact, some students who identified as Berber did not speak the regional variety of their area, especially if they had grown up in a predominantly arabophone town. Others spoke it fluently and attached great importance to the language. Classmates raised and debated hotly the topic of language mastery; such debate was especially intense among students who shared a regional background. For instance, Lahiane, a student from the Rif, teasingly yet repeatedly reprimanded his friend Yassine from the same region for not speaking *tarifit*. Likewise, Salma, a student from the Sous region, had begun teaching *tashelḥit* to her fellow student Marouane during their daily bus ride home. This peer pressure demonstrates that there was a strong desire for the survival of local varieties of Berber, even within an urban arabophone environment that privileged Arabic and foreign languages.

Berberophone teachers and inspectors also operationalized regional language networks at school. I would have not noticed these networks had I not fortuitously tapped into one in my effort to access the public school system. The first inspector who offered to facilitate my research inside the schools was from the berberophone Khenifra region. He pledged to introduce me to a few school principals with whom he was on close terms. What he did not mention at first, but what became clear during these introductory visits, was that his personal contacts were mainly with school principals from his region. During these visits, regional affiliation was openly held as the justification for the mutual support between inspector and principal. They sealed this affiliation by conducting their conversations in their shared Berber dialect. Similarly, most of the teachers with whom this inspector worked closely and whom he urged me to approach had ties to one of the numerous activist Amazigh cultural associations in urban centers and rural areas alike.

The discretion that students, teachers and inspectors showed in code switching between *dārija* and Berber as they navigated the urban school landscape connects with the terms of negotiation of multiculturalism in self-avowed multicultural societies. When Ernest Gellner and Charles

Micaud refer to such discretion as "an acknowledgement and defense of difference that does not necessarily underscore or advertise its idiosyncrasies" (1972, 11), they considerably underplay the extent to which such discretion is a necessity. For example, when the young teacher at the training workshop and the student presenting on Khaïr-Eddine failed to exercise this discretion, they crossed a red line. Multicultural societies implicate their minorities into paradoxes of recognition whereby they are both asked to perform their difference in public only to pledge allegiance to the same patriotic ideal of the mainstream. Before Berber languages were officially recognized, state-sponsored cultural festival displayed and positioned difference within Moroccan society. As Deborah Kapchan (2008) has discussed about the Festival of Sacred Music in the city of Fes and Aomar Boum (2012) has shown for the Gnawa Festival in the town of Essaouira, the festivalization of difference creates a space where different religious and ethnic minorities momentarily perform their coexistence based on the contemporary rhetoric on toleration. Yet this occasion is matched by the demand that minorities do not mark their difference in other spaces, including at school.[23]

One thing to keep in mind is that exercising linguistic discretion as the partial erasure of Berber difference was possible for the school participants I knew precisely because they had lived in a predominantly arabophone town and had steered their way through the Arabized public educational system. In other words, their experience had made them versatile in this linguistic negotiation for the sake of academic and other socioeconomic endeavors. Their position was starkly dissimilar from that of other Moroccan youth who had not benefited from continuous exposure to Arabic and French. Persistently high rates of rural illiteracy and of school dropouts, as well as the gender disparity that undercuts Berber monolingualism, require our consideration of the political economy of institutionalized *Tamazight*. Even though dissecting the linguistic landscape between rural and urban is reductive, it is undeniable that rural Morocco, with a sizable number of monolingual berberophone speakers, suffers disproportionally in educational and economic terms (Crawford 2005, 183). Hoffman (2008a) has insightfully shown that the fissure between claims to heritage and these structural inequalities place Berber women in especially precarious positions. Both state and Amazigh activists often hold these women as emblematic of the preservation of their "local specificity" at the expense of their immersion into economic spheres that demand communication in *dārija, fuṣḥā*, and French (Hoffman 2008a, 7). Therefore, introducing standardized *Tamazight* into public education may well testify to a public and official wish to present Morocco as fostering equality, but it also maintains entrenched socioeconomic hierarchies by adding one more linguistic obligation to the already linguistically overloaded public school curriculum. This overload is experienced by arabophone students throughout the country, but even more so by berberophone students of the urban centers and most certainly of the rural contexts.

Has the dream of multiculturalism as the foundation for the redistribution of privilege failed, or was this dream—as neoliberalism has shaped it—never meant to ensure this redistribution? Comparative analysis of the post-Nixon United States and the Moroccan state since the 1980s suggests that the type of multiculturalism that inhered in conceptions of the neoliberal state made consent to its modes of governance possible in more and less democratic contexts alike. Hence celebrating multiculturalism as an indicator of equal economic and political opportunity is more than just premature, for that would assume that the correlation is deferred in Morocco, but is in fact misguided.[24] The neoliberal Moroccan state did not alleviate but actually made use of cultural difference in three ways: it instituted multiculturalism as a formal acknowledgment of diversity, a smoother term for difference that glossed over important distinctions between and within the various cultures; it claimed cultural blindness as a strategy to promote the idea of individual merit in ascension and success; and it held certain groups of Berbers as examples for imitation over others and as justification for the latter's inability to respond to seemingly equal state opportunities.

The similarities between the U.S. use of multiculturalism and the case of Berber speakers are hard to ignore (Prashad 2005). Given the close encounter between the two states through diplomacy, direct investment, and development funding, it is fair to assume that the pluralistic state of Mohammed VI adopted the necessary ideological rhetoric that would support U.S.-led neoliberal change. This ideological rhetoric of multiculturalism is necessary to attain consent within liberal democracies, but it is perhaps more crucial to the legitimization of democratizing, more cynically called façade, democracies in the eyes of the international community.[25]

DISPERSED REGIONS AND REIFIED STATES

The Moroccan state appropriated some of the claims of the Amazigh activist movement to enact educational reforms that could validate the experience of berberophone Moroccans and could reconfigure the linguistic and cultural landscape of Moroccan society. The trouble is that this validation entailed a number of limitations on the demarcation of acceptable difference. It is not uncommon for minorities to face the impossible choice between representing a pristine state of difference while not antagonizing majority values (Povinelli 2002). In moments of controversy, these majority values can and do resurface as better and as universal. What is most dangerous about this multicultural imaginary is not that it tweaks difference so that it becomes digestible, but that it "defers the problems that capital, post-colonialism, and human diasporas pose to national identity in the late 20th and early 21st centuries" (2002, 29). The Moroccan example constitutes a prominent case of this deferral because the state's negotiation of liberal principles has legitimized political arrangements that differ considerably from those of representative democracies. In fact, the ultimate condition for the recognition of difference is loyalty to the monarchical institution. This conjunction raises pressing questions for how we can approach the tenuous association of multiculturalism with democracy in the neoliberal period.

How are Darwish's poetry and Khaïr-Eddine's novel bound up in the encounter between the policy of Arabization and its dissenters? This chapter portrayed the public school through the lens of Moroccans of Berber origin who are marginalized by the monocultural nationalist discourse of Arabization. Their marginalization exists alongside the other frustrations that undercut the educational experience of students. Thus whereas the students who sympathize with transnational Muslim movements pull the Arabo-Muslim ideal away from the state and into a new direction, students of Berber origin resist the idea that national belonging hinges on Arabic—be it *fuṣḥā* or *dārija*. Some may even tie their argument to an aspiration for drastic territorial transformations or profound political reform just like some Amazigh activists. However, conversations on multilingualism and critiques about the constructedness of national and regional identity can do little to redress socioeconomic hierarchy. For multilingualism to act as catalyst for more sweeping changes, it needs to expose and resist the process through which the language of cultural rights is redirected to thwart the very redistribution of political or material privilege it promises to achieve.

PART III

6

Desires in Languages

Linguistic ethics [...] consists in following the resurgence of an "I" coming back to rebuild an ephemeral structure in which the constituting struggle of language and society would be spelled out.

—Julia Kristeva, *Desire in Language: A Semiotic Approach to Literature and Art*

In a badly lit, run-down, and unheated locker room, the girls in the senior-year Humanities track were getting ready for gym class. While changing into a tracksuit, adjusting her *ḥijāb* (veil), teasing her best friend about her dreadful volleyball skills, and singing the latest tune she heard on the radio, Khadija reported the newest developments of her online romance with Tarek. A student in the year below, Tarek spoke with Khadija online without being aware of her offline identity. I now understood why her girlfriends called her Camelia: it was her MSN (instant messaging service) pseudonym. Khadija assured me that after spending long hours chatting with Tarek she had learned French *"par amour"* (out of love).[1] Her statement elicited great laughter among the group as Khadija cleverly played on the ambiguous meaning of the expression *"par amour"* as both love for the French language and love for Tarek. Her close friend Meryem teased her about the stratagems she used to engage in online chatting on her family's only computer despite the explicit prohibition of its use and the vigilant monitoring of her two brothers and parents. There was really nothing surprising about this locker room scene of peer sociality and romantic awakening, but for the fact that it was the first time that these girls, with whom I had spent considerable time in and out of class, told me about their use of French for flirting. As they headed out for gym class, I asked Meryem if she also flirted online and, if so, whether she did it in French. She replied,

> Of course! It is true that French is our means of seduction! It is *classe* (classy, bourgeois). . . . In my opinion, media, you know like TV, the internet, mobile phones, have played a big part in this. . . . Also, if we choose *fuṣḥā* (Classical Arabic), we are reminded of earlier times before satellite TV and foreign films, or of our parents, who used to exchange handwritten love letters . . . do you see the difference?

On that day, these students gave me access to a part of their lives I had heretofore neglected: romance. Even though boys and girls learn together in Moroccan public schools, parents and teachers strongly discourage, if not prohibit, expressions and demonstrations of romance in public, particularly for girls. Therefore, for many young people, courtship is primarily a linguistic activity consisting of online chats. Ever since that locker room exchange, I began to think of romance as a parallel to schooling. Romance and its desired outcome, marriage, signal a passage into adulthood in comparable ways to earning a Baccalaureate degree and securing a stable income. In the broader context of an official emphasis on women's education and professional advancement in Morocco (Newcomb 2006; 2009), schooling enhances female students' marriage prospects by suggesting the possibility of two income-earning members in a nuclear household. Unfortunately, as opportunities for both sexes for steady employment and to create a family have dwindled because of economic uncertainty, school and marriage appear as two sides of the same neoliberal coin as this coin has fashioned social relations.

In addition to being implicated in societal change and the political economy of Morocco, romance traverses alternative spheres of language learning. For instance, Khadija confessed that she learnt more French through flirting online than at school. Hence literacy acquired in school becomes the precondition for negotiations of identity and relationships outside the sphere of professionalization and even in the absence of success in the former. French plays a multipart role in these negotiations. Far from equipping arabophone public school students to succeed on an equal basis in the job market, French-language skills nonetheless appear instrumental to their dreams of love and future happiness. Significantly, these dreams in turn mold French in shapes that can accommodate their specific needs. The "flows and forms" (Gaonkar and Povinelli 2003, 395) of the French linguistic sign outside school walls designate the desires and fears that both reside in and transfigure language practice.

Romance in French evokes closely associated feelings of desire and fear in the classed, gendered, and generational negotiations of identity and modernity. On one level, romance breeds the desire for love as basis for marriage, a relatively recent and predominantly urban bourgeois aspiration, given that it supersedes the definition of marriage as an arranged alliance between families or tribal groups. Meryem's allusion to classiness, which points to both refinement and social status, best captures this modern bourgeois spirit. Although the families of public school students endorse this love-based vision of marriage, they worry about the repercussions of romance for the reputation and situation of young women. This is evident in Khadija's having to maneuver to gain access to the family computer and chat with Tarek, even though her brothers, as she confided with some indignation, "spent the whole day in the *cybers* (internet cafés) and chat rooms." Yet, while this chapter is especially mindful of the specific experience of young women with romance, it is not my intention to claim a stark and stable gender hierarchy between male and female students. For a number of reasons, the most significant of which being the enmeshment of gender attitudes in other structural positions, ambiguity around proper gender behavior in a romantic context is as prominent as are idealized and hegemonic ideas about such behavior. Furthermore, anxiety about romantic behavior relates to broader issues around integration and fulfillment that affect the subjectivity of both genders. On another level, Meryem's comments on her parents' courtship practices highlight the distance she felt from the youthful romance of earlier generations. Although it is very likely that Meryem's parents, who attended a largely francophone public school system, spoke more and better French than she did, she nevertheless imagined them flirting through handwritten letters in *fuṣḥā*.

Young students today interact in a "commodified romantic culture" (Lukose 2009, 134) that requires access to national and satellite television, mobiles phones, and the internet, as well as a fair amount of technological savvy. These media bear the imprint of modernity doubly understood as technological innovation and global connectedness. Ethnographic explorations of media consumption in the Middle East, Africa, and elsewhere have highlighted the metonymical character of romance in deliberations over the effects of neoliberalism on subjectivity, effects that extend well beyond young adulthood.[2] In what follows, we see high school students engage with courtship through the consumption of global TV formats, movies, and online sites. How they interact with media offers great insight into the function and meaning of the dominant language of romance, French, in perceptions around and performances of Moroccan identity. More specifically, flirting in French becomes an indicator of widespread ambivalence over their embeddedness in social strata that are partly steeped in and partly cut off from global flows. As a result, in some contexts, flirting in French emerges as practically problematic, culturally inauthentic, and morally threatening, whereas in others it seems like the key to the flourishing of desire and intimacy.

The issues around romance in French and the youth consumption of media may at first appear frivolous in relation to other dilemmas around the current situation of organized education, development, or neoliberalism. However, romance in French endows individual and collective tensions around identity with affective actuality. It raises questions around identity by merging language learning, the concept of nativeness, and gender roles and has done so for some time, as testified by the post-colonial literature in Morocco and the wider Mahgrib. The comparison of literary articulations of romance with scenes of media consumption corrects a number of misconceptions about current experiences. This chapter's ethnographic data give weight to the transformative quality of the passing of time that decidedly pluralizes the experience of post-colonialism. Its ancillary goal is to bridge the cultural dilemmas that pertain to language practice with the material concerns of societies immersed in the current circulation of global capital. There have been calls to dampen the triumphant hymns of post-colonial, which are also post-modern, bricolages in thought and practice (Dirlik 1994; Hall 1996). Interestingly, most of these critiques have drawn on the literary canon of the so-called Third World production. How can ethnography, which observes subjectivity in motion, take its turn and serve as testimony of the differential meanings and shapes of linguistic practice?

For the students I observed, romance in French did not make use of the same French they learned at school. Not only did their online vocabulary use more slang but also their communication was inattentive to formal grammar, spelling, and syntax rules. Moreover, it was incessantly mixed with Morocco's other languages, both those that the public school sanctioned (French and *fuṣḥā*) and those that it marginalized (*dārija* and Berber). Online writing codes brought these languages into novel patterns of circulation, steering linguistic innovation by sidelining *fuṣḥā* as a potential language of intimacy and by shedding the shackles of written monolingualism. Although this steering did not enable the students to erase the material and semiotic landscape of official linguistic hierarchy, it displaced the school as the arbiter of literacy and contested the school's injunction about what constitutes "good French." Put another way, students showed that this cyber code, which I intentionally refuse to name as either *dārija* or French, related not to school languages as a copy to an original, but rather "as copy is to copy" (Butler 1990, 31). The sensibilities and conundrums of these Moroccan young people as speakers and potential lovers revealed, through this code, "unknown regions in the vast universe of language" (Kristeva 1989, 30).[3]

The invitation to legitimize desire and its cultural products in the midst of power relations is not the same as the technological determinism that has permeated analyses of youth media practices. One of the distinct abilities of anthropologic attention is to "reopen the problem of mediation" (Mazzarella 2004) as context and time specific, which in turn ensures that we do not conflate recommendation with analysis. Surely, diverse media have their own potentialities that encourage certain modes of identification and types of interaction. Online romance offers experiences precluded by formal schooling, experiences that we need to seriously explore. However, the potentialities of the medium become germane only in relation to other negotiations with the school, the state, and the market. An attention to youth investment in online literacy and sociality encourages explorative, but not prescriptive, ruminations on the future of learning in Morocco, a future that may well lie outside the public school.

LESSONS IN MODERN ROMANCE

Most students I knew spent their leisure time, as well as a good chunk of their homework time, watching TV. They did so in their family living room with their siblings, parents, grandparents, and other relatives and with friends and guests. Male students could linger outdoors after school or after completing private tutorials in the evenings, but the majority did not have enough pocket money to socialize in cafés or movie theatres. Rules about hanging out in public were stricter for female students. Hence going to school and watching TV framed the everyday and in a way that constituted corresponding pedagogical sites for identity and sociality. A central motivation for watching TV was the wish for exposure to romance and the related themes of sexuality, love, and marriage. Images and stories of romance abounded on screen, but their consumption involved much more than a thirst for instruction through vicarious experience. It was also guided by an intergenerational effort to produce some consensus on youth behavior and, through this effort, get a grasp on the possibilities of successful moral and social integration. The visual products I will unpack in the following pages are the live singing contest *Studio 2M* and the teen-flic feature film *Marock*. In these visual products, the use of French inflected images of affluence, new patterns of mobility in public space, and global connectedness. It also refracted fears around the moral and social risk involved in premarital love affairs and uncontrolled sexuality, a risk that is considerably higher for young women. It is precisely the ambiguity of mediation as both intimate and distant (Mazzarella 2004, 346) that made these programs fertile ground for the intergenerational broaching of the vexed topics of sexuality and romance.

2M is the second national channel after *al-Maghrib*. It was founded twenty years ago as a privately owned subscription channel, but has been accessible free of charge to the general public since the late 1990s. Although both *al-Maghrib* and *2M* are essentially national channels, their design and content differ drastically. *2M* broadcasts more diverse programming, and the technical quality of its image is noticeably more sophisticated. I often heard students complaining about how boring *al-Maghrib* was because its programming is mainly political, in contrast with *2M*, which offers a wide variety of programs closer to their interests.

A typical 2M day at the time of my fieldwork included two to three Egyptian melodramas and Mexican telenovelas spread out during the morning, afternoon, and early evening; consecutive news broadcasts in *fuṣḥā*, French, and *Tamazight*, cooking programs in *dārija*; occasionally, Moroccan series or feature films; and American sitcoms at night.

There was no satellite connection in my host family's home. The children of the family, whose ages spanned from 11 to 22, turned the TV on during their lunch break (from 12:00–2:00 p.m.) and then after their return from school until bedtime. They combined homework, meals, and chats with watching the youth shows that attracted them: the afternoon music program *Haute fréquence* (High Frequency) featuring Moroccan, European, and American popular music videos and, on Sundays, the live show with the double title *Ajyāl-Générations* (Generations) that featured up-and-coming artists, young journalists, and a live audience. Whenever American sitcoms were aired at night, some members of the family tried to watch these programs, which were dubbed in French without Arabic translation, while the rest of the family chatted over them. The assumption was that 2M bought these series from France and could not afford to dub them in Arabic, so broadcasted them as is.

The more I watched TV, the more I found the consistent presence of untranslated French on 2M astonishing, to the point that I initially assumed that the channel was a jointly funded French-Moroccan venture.[4] My host family corrected me: "No, 2M is 100 percent Moroccan. The news broadcast in French is for the *richards* (the rich) here in Morocco who may not know Arabic well enough to understand the news." Though not surprised by the untranslated French broadcasting, the family commented incessantly on French speaking while watching various 2M programs. Their responses suggested that 2M's subtle promotion of the celebratory message *"vive la différence"* (long live difference) (Jerad 2007, 60) evoked a range of desires as well as positions of uncertainty and exclusion. The most vivid expressions of this ambivalence around French speaking involved programs that focused on Moroccan youth.

June was an especially fun month for Moroccan youth because that is when 2M broadcasted its month-long singing contest *Studio 2M*. A Dutch entertainment company Endemol owns the copyright for the original format of the program, but the show became famous to Moroccan audiences through its Lebanese version *Star Academy* broadcast by the LBC channel: this Lebanese version is itself a version of *Star Académie* of France that appears on TF1. The Moroccan version is an adaptation of all the above, yet the format is also reminiscent of a local variety show broadcast on national TV in the 1980s. This local variety show presented different regions of Morocco through their typical dances and songs with guest artists performing in front of a live audience (Davis and Davis 1995). The *Studio 2M* singing context, which first aired in 2004 and has been broadcast every June since, recruits young candidates between 18 and 28 from throughout Morocco; during my fieldwork, it was the most popular show among Moroccan youth in the summer season. Throughout the week, ten-minute trailers kept the audience up to date with the progress of each contestant, and the weekly contest called "Prime" aired live on Saturday night. Rumor had it that the Casablanca studio that hosts the contest occupies more than 1,200 square meters, the largest in Africa. During the three years that I spent June in Morocco, the Saturday-night *Studio 2M* "Prime" was a social event that regularly brought families and friends together in front of the TV. In addition, big outdoor screens were set up, allowing large audiences to enjoy the program and support their local contestant.

In June 2007, the show had one male and one female presenter, Chakib Lahssaini and Meryem Said. They were young, attractive, and fashionably dressed. Chakib Lahssaini, a Moroccan born in France, addressed the audience, jury, and contestants in French while Meryem Said spoke to them in *dārija*. The two presenters did not translate each other's words but instead kept the show going through code switching. The 2007 judges were choreographer Christie Caro, oud player and composer Said Chraibi, tenor Ahmed Ghazir, and songwriter and composer Malek. These judges, some of whom were Moroccans living in the diaspora, expressed themselves in different languages: some addressed contestants in French, others communicated in *dārija* infused with French terms, and one used *fuṣḥā* exclusively. In 2007, no contestant, presenter, or judge used Berber in either song or speech. This linguistic oscillation extended to the contestants themselves and to their choice of song.

I watched the first "Prime" episode of the season with senior-year student Nidale and her family, who lived just around the corner from me. In this episode, a male contestant, also a high school student at the time, performed the song, "*Ya bint al-nās*" (Hey, You Good Girl) by legendary Moroccan singer Abdelhadi Bel Khiyat, in *dārija*. A true classic, the song is the love confession of a poor young man to his loved one. The expression "*bint al-nās*" literally means "girl of the people," but it denotes a girl who is well bred both in terms of moral decency and affluence.[5] Nidale's whole family sang along enthusiastically. Parents and children singled out this contestant and expressed the conviction that he would win. They called him [dar.] *dkī* (smart) because he understood "what the audience wanted." They approved of the song as typically Moroccan and of its depiction of romantic love: it is essentially a marriage proposal to a decent young woman from a poorer but steadfast young man. The judges were equally excited and told the contestant, "You sang a song close to our hearts."

In stark contrast, another male contestant, a 19-year-old young man from Marrakech, provoked the hostility of Nidale's family. In his introductory video, aired just before his first live appearance, he spoke only in French, played tennis, and claimed that his ambition was to "*faire bouger les choses*" (shake things up) by introducing a rock dimension to the show. He sang a Jim Morrison song. Nidale and her siblings did not have a problem with his choice of an English song because they were well versed in American and British pop and rock repertoires. They did, however, mind that their on-screen peer introduced himself in French. Feigning indifference, Nidale's elder brother Simo asked, "Is he even Moroccan?" and in the next breath added, "Tennis is a sport for the rich, isn't it?" The young people in the living room seemed tantalized by the fact that the contestant showed himself on TV walking down the street next to a girl who was obviously his girlfriend. Most often, contestants appeared in their family living room surrounded by relatives or with classmates and friends of the same sex. One of Nidale's sisters, Kawtar, muttered [dar.] "*ḥchūma*" (shameful) while fixing her gaze on the girl on screen. Considered a positive attribute for any decent, educated person, and particularly for a young woman, feeling and showing shame imply an attitude of modesty and obedience to elders and non-kin (Newcomb 2006, 11).[6] Kawtar's admonishment criticized the on-screen couple for having no modesty about the public display of their bond and invited them to display such a quality, *tḥasham* (to feel and show abashment). Reactions of both fascination and shock to the contestant's triangle of activities—speaking French outside school, playing tennis, and dating in public—were palpable in the living room.

Another contestant who triggered discomfort at home represented a recurring category in the contest, the diasporic Moroccan. This contestant was a female Belgian university student of Moroccan origin. Her introductory video presented her at her Western-style country house outside of Brussels hanging out with her family, and at her part-time job as waitress in a restaurant. At work, she wore tight jeans and a fitted T-shirt. Nidale's mother was scornful of the girl's outfit and the ease with which she spoke to the camera while in such a "demeaning job." Nidale remarked, "If I was on TV and my family saw me like this, I would die of shame. But then again, the concept of *ḥchūma* is just Moroccan, right?" Her comment appeared conciliatory, but in essence distanced this female contestant from a native image of female decency. Indeed, according to the standards of Nidale's family, a female waitress in a restaurant would not qualify as a *bint al-nās* and would only tenuously qualify as Moroccan. Her mother agreed with Nidale by nodding her head. Emboldened by her mother's consent, Nidale derisively addressed the contestant on the TV screen: [dar.] *"Yalla, sīrī fī Belgīkā!"* (Go on, go back to Belgium). Her siblings chuckled.

In some ways, *Studio 2M*, a global TV format adapted to local content, is the celebration of a multivocal Moroccan culture that expands well beyond Morocco's national borders. The two male contestants are different versions of the modern Moroccan young man: the one epitomizing continuity with a Moroccan artistic past and the other opening up new avenues for global involvement through anglophone music forms. Behind this juxtaposition, however, lie diverse social positions that Simo was sensitive to, as evident in his comment, "Tennis is a sport for the rich, isn't it?" In addition, the two contestants pointed to competing versions of female morality through, on the one hand, the song the first one chose, *"Ya bint al-nās,"* and, on the other hand, the second contestant openly walking alongside his girlfriend. Nidale and her siblings could not identify with the second contestant and his girlfriend and thus placed them in unattainable and condemnable linguistic, material, and moral realms. They discarded the diasporic female contestant as foreign because her sartorial choices, mediated exposure, and language skills set her apart from their own under-standing of respectable female Moroccan-ness. A more cynical reading of the editing of the show would consider the choice of songs and contestants to be an intentional provocation of social sensibilities around sexuality, material privilege, and the differences of Moroccan diasporic life. In either case, the show presented an occasion for the youth in this living room to reflect with their family on their own position and behavior. In this col-lective attempt to achieve intergenerational consensus around gendered youth identity, the family members condemned practices that appeared problematic and alien to them. They equally wrestled with emerging de-sires that the circulation of these images engendered. Tellingly, they kept watching the show day after day and week after week. The terms *bint al-nās* and *ḥshūma* demarcated the lines of youth morality and indicated the desire and risks involved in sexuality, predominantly female sexuality.

The opposition of these *dārija* terms to the untranslated, non-accented, and fluent French in 2M broadcasting deserves attention. *Studio 2M* ap-pears simultaneously on the *2M Monde* satellite channel and thus reaches Moroccan expatriates who are no longer assumed to speak *dārija* or *fuṣḥā*. But if this linguistic choice targets a global Moroccan community, it does so at the expense of the non-elite in-country audience for whom this type of French impeded comprehension. For my host family *Studio 2M* was an uncertain, if not distorted, reflection of Moroccan youth culture. Viewed from those who were consuming it, *Studio 2M* was multilingual but not of the right kind of languages. Its arrangement of multilingualism silenced this youth and discouraged rather than invited their identification with contestants.[7] Nidale and her siblings attributed foreignness to elements that appeared incongruent with their own experience.

That this youth-oriented show became the opportunity for a commen-tary on the sociocultural and moral set-up of Moroccan society is not unique to contemporary Morocco. Media products, be it a singing contest like *Studio 2M*, the Egyptian popular music that fascinated young Bedou-ins (Abu-Lughod 1993, 506), the Mexican telenovelas that captured Hausa youth (Larkin 1997), and Iraqi pop videos that young men in Aleppo avidly watched (Borneman 2011), are occasions for negotiating the boundaries of sociocultural normativity, of which gender and sexuality are vital components. Interestingly, these practices of consumption unsettle the assumed binarism between non-Western local versus Western global culture. For example, the youth in my host family consumed Mexican telenovelas, Egyptian *musalsalāt* (soap operas), and Indian Bollywood films. Because all these shows dealt with romantic love, the mother of the family used their plots as an occasion to instruct her children— especially her daughters—on the dos and don'ts of gendered behavior. For this mother, who conflated the visibility of young women on stage with speaking French and with moral transgression, *Studio 2M* was especially hazardous: "It's like a disease," she once admitted to me, "with all these boys and girls singing love songs to each other and then perhaps falling in love with each other, saying *je t'aime* (I love you) on camera!" In her critique of the show, she communicated the risk of transgressive public intimacy through the French expression "*je t'aime*." As I often heard at school, some mothers forbade both their daughters and sons from watching the show.

The most forceful dramatization of ambivalence about the linguistic, material, and moral boundaries of romance during my fieldwork was the Moroccan teen flic *Marock*, its title a playful synthesis of "Maroc" and "Rock." The first feature film of Layla Marrakchi, a Moroccan director living in France, *Marock* recounts the audacious romantic affair of two affluent high school students attending the famous *Lycée Lyautey*, the French Mission school of Casablanca. These are the type of students my host family called "*les richards*" (the rich). The film couple is a Muslim student Ghita (Morjana Alaoui) and Jewish student Youri (Matthieu Boujenah). Ghita and Youri explore intimacy in circumstances and contexts that differ drastically from those of the youth I lived with: they smoke hashish, wear provocative clothes, engage in premarital sex and drunk driving, and flaunt religious conventions by not fasting during Ramadan and by dating each other. Although Youri's tragic death in a car crash brings this transgression to a halt, the film does not display a moralistic stance toward the couple's rebellious attitudes and actions. The female protagonist Ghita remains defiant toward her parents, her older brother, and the rest of Moroccan society.

The specter of France in the scenes of *La Mission* class life and in Ghita's impending trip abroad after taking the Baccalaureate exam is impossible to miss. The young characters speak fluent and perfectly accented French both with each other and with their parents, reserving *dārija* for their servants and their chauffeurs. Intriguingly, both protagonists and their surrounding cast of young relatives, schoolmates, and friends display an acute awareness of their separation from the youth of other social strata. On discovering that she does not have the money to study abroad and must therefore attend a public Moroccan university, one of the female characters expresses her dread in these terms: "Can you picture me here at university with people from the Moroccan school? Damn, they hate us over there; I don't even speak good Arabic!" (*Marock* 2007). Admittedly, the range of other cultural references that display these young people's embeddedness in Euro-American commodities and habits goes beyond French. The couple and their friends listen to American and British bands (The Auteurs, David Bowie, Army of Lovers, Grant National), wear baseball caps and T-shirts brought by relatives in the United States, and discuss the latest powdered recreational drug that youth consume in London and Paris (Edwards 2007, 291).

Nidale obsessed about the film for some time, speculating about its plot and deploring not having seen it. Passing by the *souq* (open market) one day, I caught sight of a copy of the film and decided to buy it for her so that we would watch it together with her siblings. During the first five minutes of the film, we were all very impressed by the affluence we saw on screen in the villas, cars, and outfits of these "other" Moroccan students. As the plot unfolded, however, the everyday practices of the students on the film appeared entirely alien to Nidale and her siblings: those other students had chauffeurs who picked them up from school, multiple servants, and private tutors who taught them at home in preparation for the Baccalaureate exam. As the on-screen youth continued to engage in the pleasures and trials of first love and nights out spent clubbing and partying, the young people in the living room tried hard to understand the French spoken in the film and were shaken by the moral laxity of their more privileged counterparts. They interrupted the movie frequently to inquire incredulously about the nativeness of the on-screen characters—"Are these Moroccans?"—just like they had done with some contestants on *Studio 2M*. After a half-hour, they got so disengaged from the film that they started to chat over it, and some even left the living room. During the only explicit sex scene between one male student and a prostitute, one of the sisters, Kawtar, sprang from the sofa to stop the video with a nervous giggle. By doing so, she displayed the *ḥshūma* (abashment) she considered appropriate to her sex, age, and social position.[8]

Romance and intimacy in both *Studio 2M* and *Marock* may seem trivial in light of the economic marginalization and social uncertainty the youth I knew faced as students of the Arabized public school and members of a non-affluent family with few connections in professional spheres. Yet if we choose to credit the desires and anxieties evoked by TV and film romance as real and serious, then romance turns into an entry point to this youth's molding of mediated images into potential identities (Masquelier 2009, 207). What drives the circulation of cultural forms such as *Studio 2M* and *Marock*, and what are the effects of their consumption? In a process similar to the Egyptian *infitāh* (economic liberalization) of the 1980s and its promotion of an urban bourgeois consumerist lifestyle, the neoliberal reshaping of the Moroccan economy, which also generated the *2M* TV channel, has come with its own propositions for situating language, morality, and culture within the country.[9] These propositions theoretically involve everyone, but in reality are very elitist. Certainly, some version of French connects diasporic, elite, and less affluent youth to these broader formulations of modernity and youthfulness. Yet their respective multilingual skills allow them blatantly different degrees of access and mobility to the stage of *Studio 2M*, the night clubs featured in *Marock*, and the flights the diasporic contestant and the *Marock* characters took to travel to Europe. Female students have more formal restrictions of access than their male counterparts, but essentially young men cannot navigate these spheres either without the necessary cash or connections. Thus, aspects of linguistic aptitude such as accent and non-academic fluency signal stratification within the category of young Moroccan.

The uncertainty around romance in French and the awareness of its social price, expressed through references to *ḥshūma*, are significant angles through which the youth in my host family and students like Nidale interpreted these programs. These feelings are easy to miss lest we juxtapose the production of media to its reception and to other facets of lived culture mediated in turn through parents, the school, and so forth.[10] Student reactions to the activities of the *Studio 2M* contestants—working in a bar, playing tennis—and toward those of the characters in *Marock*—clubbing, drinking, having sex—are a mixture of fascination and alienation, as seen in these comments: "Tennis is a sport for the rich, isn't it?" and "If I was on TV and my family saw me like this, I would die of shame." The young audience's misrecognition of other Moroccans, "Are they Moroccan?," is simultaneously a questioning of self-perception: "Am I Moroccan?" This introspective question points to dividing lines within Moroccan society even if as it takes its cues from the repertoire of globalization. Given this concern with internal hierarchy, the normative criticism of "Western" encroachment on local realities is inadequate because it forgets that centers and peripheries of a geographical, economic, or gendered character within countries are as important as those between countries (Abu-Lughod 1993).[11] This leads to an interesting comparison between these scenes of media consumption of romance in French and post-colonial literature and theory that delved into language, self, and the Other.

THE FOREIGN LANGUAGE OF THE INTIMATE OTHER

Because language was instrumental to the French colonial mission and to the nationalist agendas that superseded it, colonial and post-colonial literature and its literary analysis made language training, especially in French, central to the fashioning of subjective identity in relation questions of nativeness and foreignness. This body of work has posited language as a catalyst for a retrospective examination of the self, which often caused authors to clash with normative assumptions around origin by birth and national belonging.[12] Their elite participation in the collective experience of colonialism and post-colonialism often enflamed this already destabilizing retrospective gaze. For many authors, the discursive and visual universe of love and romance concretized these negotiations with identity, bringing to the fore their affective intensity. However, the perseverance of this cluster of themes—romance, language training, identity—in the scene of media consumption just described is as poignant as it is vulnerable to misrecognitions of internal hierarchy and of the passing of time.

The term "post-colonialism" can function as a descriptor of both literary and ethnographic experiences only to the degree that we keep testing its resonance with diverse groups of people. Ethnographic data, which show little tendency to coherence, highlight the instability of cultural identity and the schismic nature of all processes of identification. Watching and commenting on TV programs and films reveals the specific engagement of some young Moroccans with the world. Although their imaginaries grind against the history of colonization, they are not static and, significantly, are in interaction with mutable institutions such as the Arabized school, the state, and mass media. Because temporality and location are integral to the work of fantasy and to feelings of exclusion, we should insist on disentangling the different stakes of identification for differentially positioned interlocutors. Shohat expresses this call for specificity in her questioning of Algerian identity after colonialism: "Does the 'post' indicate the perspective and location of the ex-colonized (Algerian), the ex-colonizer (French), the ex-colonizer settler (Pied Noir), or the displaced hybrid of the First world metropolitan (Algerian in France)?" (1992, 103). Her question is as clear as it can get, but our extended exposure to literature and literary criticism around the disorders of colonialism has habituated us to see colonialism and post-colonialism as singular experiences and consequently not pay enough attention to the nuances within and between them.

Romance, language, and identity are key themes in Abdelkebir Khatibi's francophone novel *Amour bilingue* (Love in Two Languages) (1992). The novel chronicles the love affair between an immigrant Maghribian man and a foreign woman, an affair that acts as a metaphor for the immigrant man's reflections on himself conducted in multiple languages. The foreign lover, from whom the Maghribian man eventually separates, is the site for the exploration of distance and intimacy through contact with another culture. Throughout the novel, the narrator, who occupies both the "I" and the "he" of the text, communicates the urgent need to define his identity through language: "*Une parole m'interpelle*" (a spoken word summons me) (1992, 47). The novel begins by postulating the French language as foreign and the *he* of the text as struggling in exile with comprehension: for example, *mot* (word) sounds a lot like *mort* (death) to the easily confused ear of the foreigner (1992, 10). All the while, classical Arabic as the language of God, the narrator's paternal line, and his own name undermine his efforts to express himself in French. Classical Arabic is in tension with another woman, the figure of his mother, who is portrayed as illiterate. Even though the narrator's mother must have spoken either *dārija* or Berber, both infused with religious expressions in Classical Arabic, her distance from writing signals her marginalization. The final position of the francophone Maghribian immigrant is one of in-betweenness, a position that keeps its distance from both linguistic signs, French and Arabic. This distance shatters the utopian hope to belong. This in-between position evokes feelings of fear and loss, but eventually turns into empowerment through multiplicity: *"La bi-langue...Elle serait ma troisième oreille"* (The bi-language? . . . It would become my third ear) (1992, 11). Generalizing this post-colonial story of a migrant romance to an existential experience, Khatibi's *bi-langue* aspires to describe the conditions of all speaking at all times. Put another way, the author advocates for dissociating identity from any one unique register.

In his essay, *"Le monolinguisme de l'autre ou la prothèse d'origine"* (The Monolingualism of the Other, or the Prosthesis of Origin) (1996), Jacques Derrida complicates Khatibi's universalizing call to multiplicity through his own perspective as a pied-noir Algerian Jew. The text, set up as a response to *Amour bilingue,* unfolds Derrida's own complex positioning toward the French language: *"Oui, je n'ai qu'une langue, or ce n'est pas la mienne"* (Yes, I only have one language, but it is not mine) (1996, 15).[13] The romance here is between individual and language, and the goal of the work is to prove that linguistic affiliation does not signify inclusion. In an attack on the concept of the mother tongue, Derrida recalls his own schooling, an exemplary point of contact between Algeria and France: "It was first of all an educational thing, something that happens to you 'at school'" (1996, 65). He first engages with the politics of marginalization of Arabic and Berber in his childhood. Tracing their erasure as languages of instruction, Derrida shows how the hegemony of French imperialism triumphed through the classification of *fuṣḥā* as an optional foreign language and through the non-classification of *dārija* and Berber. Nonetheless, Derrida interrupts his deconstructive analysis to present a highly emotional narrative performance. After undoing language as a basis for identification, he goes on to display a powerful quasi-erotic attachment to the French language. He presents his passion for linguistic purity, his exaggerated desire for a perfect command of the language, and his resentment of his own regional accent. The deconstructive work is at its epitome here, where Derrida exposes all the artificial connections between language and self and lets them interact in complicated ways. This confession of love for French ends in a suggestion that any language, including one's own language, is approachable only through the zeal of possession.

The arabophone novel, Mohamed al-Achaari's *al-qaws wa-l farāsha* (The Arch and the Butterfly) (2010), also delves into the forging of identity through love and marriage, the post-colonial nation, and migration. This triangle in turn feeds into the themes of religious radicalization and the consequences of the unfettered circulation of global capital in Morocco.[14] The novel features two types of romance: the arranged marriage between the main character al-Firsiwi and his first wife Rabia, and his passionate love affairs with other Moroccan women during and after his marriage. His unfulfilling conjugal bond with Rabia encapsulates al-Firsiwi's overwhelming regret both as an individual and as a member of a generation of leftist dissidents who by the 1990s had compromised politically, socially, and morally (Laachir 2013). Having a German mother also causes al-Firsiwi to straddle the thin line between nativeness and foreignness. Achaari describes the German mother's union with his Berber father in an unusual way: the foreign woman comes to Morocco in an effort to recapture her own ancestral story that dates back to the presence of German troops during the French Protectorate. In fact, she stakes her claims to the Volubilis ruins located near Meknes, because her ancestors served in that area. More predictably, after marriage she becomes the emblem of her husband's moral transgression and material greed. Her eventual suicide turns the tables on Western domination as this foreign woman is crushed under the ruthless forces of turbulent and unspoken social histories. The works just described explore romance as experience and as metonym, endowing individual and collective tensions of identity with affective actuality. Although their narrators are no longer young, the works are filled with memories of childhood and adolescence.

Similar anxieties and desires around identity manifest themselves in the activity of watching *Studio 2M* and *Marock*. This similarity is both undeniable and decidedly partial. Indeed, the zeal of possession has salience for the youth audience of *Studio 2M* and *Marock* despite their own awareness of the violent imposition of the French language in Morocco.

What is distinct about their experience is that through their formal pedagogy they endure another form and another moment of symbolic violence, which implicates them in a new set of contradictions around questions of nativeness and foreignness. Both in literature and the family living room, romance is the prism of youthful aspirations for social mobility, access to a global scene of economic and cultural circulation, and moral experimentation. Their shared frustration with French training is, however, deceptive because the Moroccan students of the Arabized school respond to their difficulties with comprehension and translation and not to the burden of their fluency as do francophone writers. Equally, the symbolism of the French language that students struggle with was set in motion by colonialism, but is not only the product of colonialism, nor does it address the French as its only Other. These students' attribution of foreignness relates to their Moroccan peers and reflects this youth audience's own sense of marginalization within Moroccan society. The Arabized public school is central to their dilemma given that it has become a place of rapprochement with Arabic as the language of identity and community. Conflations of literary works with empirical material run the risk of neglecting the fact that the languages that traverse the post-independent society do so unequally (Pandolfo 2008). Equally problematic is the elision of the passing of time, which prevents us from tracing the evolution of modernist European imperialism into contemporary relationships of symbolic and economic domination.

The female figure looms perilously in both contexts, the novels and the TV shows and movies, as either the excess of rootedness—Khatibi's mother becomes a negative image of locality through her illiteracy, whereas the "*bint al-nās*" in the song represents valued qualities—or as the excess of distance: the figure of the foreign lover in Khatibi, the foreign wife in al-Achaari, and the diasporic Belgian contestant in *Studio 2M*. Derrida remembers his mother as a questionable mediator of a mother tongue, yet her own voice remains conspicuously absent.[15] Al-Achaari gives his Moroccan female characters a voice and the ability to claim their sexuality outside marital bonds. However, he makes it clear that such behavior is the result of their elite status, diasporic experience, or capacity for secrecy.[16] In all these works, women become metonymic of moral normativity even when the purpose of their presence is to contest the naturalness of these perceptions. The young Moroccan women on screen in *Studio 2M* and *Marock* dare to experiment with the terms of their visibility, but they do so either through the safety of mediation, their foreignness, or material privilege. As for the young Moroccan women in the living room, they face another set of parameters when dealing with seduction, claiming love, and aspiring to social integration as they negotiate these from their specific position as non-elite women with a predominantly arabophone education.

This social stratification within gender relations, as it intersects education and moral norms, risks getting lost in the universalizing contentions of literature and literary criticism in the post-colonial moment. Literary criticism is especially guilty of ignoring this stratification. An heir to postmodern and poststructuralist thought, this type of criticism sees the system of language as an allegory for social structure. Following the allegory, it turns the political frames of colonialism and post-colonialism into the enabling mechanisms of enunciation, which become themselves vulnerable to subversion. This gesture is useful for an understanding of resistance as more than a rational, calculated, clear-cut rejection of the "content of another culture" (Bhabha 1994, 110). Along these lines, anthropology and post-colonial criticism seem complementary endeavors because they treat culture "as an uneven, incomplete production of meaning and value, often composed of incommensurable demands and practices, produced in the act of social survival" (1994, 172). Yet the ambition to foreground this unevenness can only go so far in post-colonial criticism, given that it does not sufficiently acknowledge that its material is the textual production of elite figures.[17] The opinions of the youth audience of *Studio 2M* and *Marock* push this conversation in two directions: by shifting the drama of misrecognition within Moroccan society, these opinions remind us of the diverse internal power struggles that affect the process of decolonization. Equally, they force us to recognize the inseparability of cultural dilemmas from the workings of neo-imperialism within global market integration.[18]

Returning to the students of the Arabized school who spend their leisure time fantasizing about romance, albeit in an inconvenient manner and an atmosphere of uncertainty, we see that their post-colonialism is distinctive. It expresses a discomfort that, although set in motion by colonialism, manifests within a contemporary vision of social integration and global access to material and symbolic prestige. To a degree, this vision colludes with the consumerist intentions of artifacts such as *Studio 2M*, artifacts that pass as celebratory calls for global connectedness but actually play into the hands of global capitalism by turning more people into consumers. Nonetheless, this process is not unidirectional. Aspirations of love "of the right kind" push the youth of this living room and other students of the Arabized public school to adopt French for the purposes of courtship. Away from the classroom, the schoolyard, or the family living room, young people—especially girls—adjust their linguistic practices to prevalent ideas about modern romance, experimenting with language, sexuality, and class along the way.

ON CYBER LOVE

As seen above, high school students juggle contradictory ideals of morality and premarital romantic love, which shape romantic norms for both sexes in relation to their social level and linguistic skills. These norms are particular to their urban position and their educational experience. Equally specific are the creative ways in which they deal with such contradictions so that they can both experience the pleasure of romance and protect themselves from the social indictment of moral transgression. This indictment is harsher for young women who aspire to have "a good match" in the future, but it does not leave young men unscathed. Widespread experimentation with romantic norms throws French into types of circulation that differ from those of an elite lifestyle or from diasporic hybridity. This experimentation is subtle and complex, but the undeniable popularity of online romance suggests that the impact of technological change inheres in these "subtle social shifts" (Carey, 2005, 443) at the intersection of the virtual and actual that emerge from a synthesis of user motivations and the allowances of virtual sociality.

Zakaria was one of my most frequent desk mates in the senior-year scientific track. He dreamed of being an actor, but his parents had categorically opposed this aspiration, insisting that he pursue a degree in engineering. He was utterly indifferent to the prospect. In fact, everything suggested that he was going to fail the Bac, but Zakaria did not seem to care. Instead, he spent his time writing short plays in *dārija* that he performed in front of his classmates and teachers whenever they gave him the chance. He was a talented comedian and singer, skills that he cultivated daily while nursing his vision of enrolling in an art or music school in the future. During many of our back-row discussions, Zakaria confided that he felt alienated from his classmates. Contrary to everyone else who wanted to "leave Morocco and make big money," Zakaria insisted that he adored his country and wished to live there forever. He was particularly proud of the "Moroccan way of life," which he often made the topic of his plays, comedies that dramatized aspects of the everyday in the working-class neighborhoods of his town. His plays' message, which he often directed at his classmates, was that they should "be themselves and feel proud about that." Zakaria was famous at school for his hilarious impersonation of an Arabic-inflected French accent, a sign of someone who wishes to feign sophistication and affluence.

One day the picture I had formed of Zakaria was thrown completely off balance. We were spending a break together, along with his best friend Redouane, when Zakaria sprang up from the bench where we were sitting and rushed off to speak to a girl from another class. As Redouane informed me, he had spoken to her on the online MSN messenger service and had suggested a *connexion* with her, by which he meant starting an offline courtship. After speaking to her in person, he came back disappointed and also surprised that he had been rejected. She refused his suggestion with the vague excuse, "*Je ne peux pas*" (I cannot), without further elaboration. I could not stop myself from interrupting, even though I knew I was being inconsiderate, and asked, "She said that in French?" "Yes," replied Redouane, rolling his eyes, "because whoever flirts in French is cool. We are Moroccan, but as soon as we start flirting, we say things like *je voudrais créer une connexion avec toi, je t'aime*, and so forth" (I would like to date you, I love you). The air was heavy with rejection and Zakaria sulked and stared at his shoes. To cheer him up, Redouane started recounting his own adventures with online dating. Zakaria's spirits picked up: the two had some flirting wisdom to share. They were very keen to have online romances, but were reluctant to give out their phone numbers. Zakaria explained that he did not wish for his mother to check his cell phone and read the texts from girls who wrote "*je t'aime*" (I love you). I wondered

how many girls did that. He smugly replied. "Many." He then explained
that he had *copines* (girlfriends) all over Morocco, as well as abroad,
though the latter were not serious, just "good experience." I asked what
language they communicated in, and he said that it depended on the girl.
For example, if she is *classe* (classy, bourgeois) they will speak in French
and may even use some English. "What are the signs that she is *classe?*"
I inquired. "Well, if she contacts you on MSN by saying *ça va* (how are
you), this is a good start!"

Many such high school romances were purely virtual, and often one of
the two parties had no intention of pursuing it offline. The language of
these romances entered the same arena of experimentation; students who
would not otherwise express themselves in French commit to doing so for
the sake of flirting. Male students I met maintained that it was the girls
who demanded that flirting take place in French or at least that there be a
mixture of French and *dārija*. Many of the girls I spoke to confirmed that
this was the case. Fati was one of these girls. Fati had repeated the junior
year three times, with French being one of the subjects she had failed
twice. Yet whenever she discussed her romantic adventures with me, she
would infuse her vocabulary with French: "*le mec*" (a guy), "*une nana*" or
"*une meuf*" (a chick), and "*reprendre la relation*" (to get back together with
someone). She was very popular with boys her own age and with university students. During that period, she had a secret admirer who sent her
text messages every night. She showed me the latest one: "*Bone nuit, tu fait
parti de me reves*" (Goodnight, I'll dream of you). When I protested that
the spelling of the message was incorrect (normally one would write *Bonne
nuit, tu fais partie de me rêves*), Fati got irritated with me for missing the
point:

> FATI: Never mind the spelling! This is MSN French, not school French. I
> only chat in French. If someone contacts me on MSN by saying *salām*
> (hello), I will block him immediately because he is *sha'bī* (from a
> working-class background)!"
>
> CHARIS: OK, but how about the rest of the conversation?
>
> FATI: I use a mix of *dārija* and French, but the most crucial aspect of MSN
> flirting is to understand if someone is classy and modern. If someone
> writes [dar.] *kanbghik ḥabiba* (I love you darling) I don't like it at all;
> it's *sha'bī* (common, working class)! (cringing)

CHARIS: What if he used English to chat you up?

FATI: Hmm, arrogant! But if he's a foreigner, that's fine.

The use of French in online romance by both male and female students does not align with their educational experience in *fuṣḥā* and everyday communication in *dārija*. Evidently, mediated images of francophonie as a vector for intimacy on *Studio 2M* and the film *Marock* traversed other spheres of sociality. Zakaria and Fati were open about their view that using French online reflected an urban bourgeois perspective by referring to *classiness* and by condemning monolingual arabophone chatting as common and working class. The fact that none of the two had mastered academic French and that Zakaria satirized Moroccans who faked fluency in French suggests that these students did not feel more at home with French than with *dārija* or Berber. Thus they were not in the same position as the characters of the film *Marock*.

Dārija does not lack vocabulary to discuss flirting or sex. In fact, its repertoire is rich and ranges from a euphemistic to a cruder lexicon. The latter is rarely used at school and is generally believed to be part of a lower class masculine register, *lughat al-shāriʿ* (street slang). One day, the same group of girls I had hung out with in the locker room decided to give me a tutorial in the more explicit vocabulary in *dārija*. They insisted that I use my notebook to record the different words and their meanings. Even though we were in an empty classroom, the girls laughed hysterically and somewhat nervously at our collective breaching of a taboo topic. Yet they meticulously named body parts and types of sexual acts. Their tutorial led to musings on what would happen on their wedding night. Khadija, one of the most outspoken of the group, declared, "I'm really scared of the first wedding night!" Another girl, Houda, rolled her eyes, turned to me, and said: *"Elle ne veut pas; moi je veux"* (She does not want to; I do). Houda had never spoken to me in French before. I did not probe Houda's language choice, but asked them if they all chatted with boys online. They excitedly admitted that this is how they spent most of their time at home, especially when their parents were not present. They mentioned that it was only online where they could truly "unveil"—they used the "*dévoiler.*" The girls were not referring to the *ḥijāb* (veil) per se—only half of them actually donned the veil—but rather to interacting with boys in a more open way than was allowed in the public sphere.

The balancing act that these girls strived to accomplish by limiting their romantic explorations to the online sphere is captured by an adjective they often used: "*ouvertes*" (open). The term itself is indicative of the widespread ambivalence about modern youth attitudes and values. On some occasions, the term has the positive connotation of being open to the world, to new ideas, and to novel lifestyles. This meaning applies to both men and women; for instance, somebody could boast about how open he or she is. In other contexts, the term "*ouvert(e)*" is gendered and refers to girls who are immodest; for example, those who frequent cafés, cinemas, or discos and have boyfriends. This use of openness is derogatory: mothers would often admonish their daughters against that behavior. The group of female friends who gave me a tutorial could not and did not want to risk the impression of being open in the negative sense. However, they were interested in discovering the emotional intensity of love and in entertaining the possibility of sexuality that underpins romance. This is where the metaphor of unveiling and the use of French conspired to produce a protected space for experimentation.

The metaphor of unveiling, an act akin to gendered intimacy because a veiled girl would unveil herself only in front of her relatives and husband, is particularly apt for virtual romance. Intriguingly, it is only after veiling in a pseudonym and in another language that the girls felt they could unveil to their virtual interlocutors. As suggested by the girls, virtual romance offered the opportunity to elude family control and public surveillance. Therefore, whereas Zakaria and Fati highlighted the use of online French as an act of social passing in material terms, the girls in question revealed that online French encouraged intimacy through this very linguistic distance. In other words, they could be *ouvertes* in the good sense of appearing modern and willing to converse with young men, but not *ouvertes* in the negative sense of interacting with non-kin men offline. This balance had a linguistic manifestation: as Fati mentioned, saying "*je t'aime*" in French felt safer than saying "*kanbghik.*" Actually, "*je t'aime*" is not the most accurate translation of "*kanbghik,*" which literally means "*je te veux*" (I want you). One hypothesis is that saying *kanbghik* felt too transgressive because of a corporal dimension that evoked inhibition in girls. By choosing "*je t'aime*," the girls avoided the embarrassment of expressing such intimacy in *dārija*, the language of the home and their parents. The dominant use of "*je t'aime*" rather than "*kanbghik*" seemed to respond to the same dynamic of anonymity or the use of pseudonyms in online chatting. Namely, it was a translation of the self as the partial protection that could allow for openness. Glaringly absent was the use of the third choice: the *fuṣḥā* word, *uḥebu* (I love). The verb *aḥaba* is more refined than *kanbhigk* and highlights the emotional side of romance (*ḥub* means love in both *fuṣḥā and dārija*). Despite this refinement, *aḥaba* carries the imprint of school lessons, religious texts, and the specters of parental love letters. French therefore did not constitute for them the language of interiority and intimacy, but rather the language of concealment through which the girls could articulate intimacy.

These online practices permitted a degree of social testing and gendered access to intimacy that families, formal schooling, and the public sphere discouraged. The students I observed were aware that virtual sociality did not escape real-world coercion nor did it operate on an entirely different logic (Boutieri 2014, 41). As is also the case with Moroccan girls in the Netherlands who use specific online sites to broach taboo topics, Khadija and Houda knew that the pleasure of online anonymity has as its backdrop the limitations of pursuing and discussing these experiences offline (Brouwer 2006). For many of these young women at school who wanted to protect themselves from accusations of openness, the online evasion of public surveillance was temporary and decidedly virtual. Their opportunistic appropriation of urban bourgeois romance was unacceptable to their families and social circles: they were "caught between several worlds whose borders the new media technologies can cross" (Abu-Lughod 1989, 47), but that they themselves could not. Opportunities for this evasion diminished even further for those who did not have literacy in either French or Arabic, itself a gendered and classed phenomenon, and for those without access to a computer or mobile phone. What is more, this evasion reified French as the language of social privilege and openness to the world. Students of more privileged backgrounds would make use of their French fluency on MSN to exclude, that is, to deter potential interlocutors who they thought were beneath them. They did so by using more sophisticated terms or the latest French argot. Hence in addition to offering an opportunity for the expression of desire, flirting in French performed its own segregation against those who could not appear classy enough online.

These are important counterweights to the triumphant and premature interpretations of the liberating and equalizing nature of cyberspace, interpretations that reached a level of frenzy during the period of the Arab Uprisings. Cyberspace and social media are not novel cultural products, but rather the most recent instantiation of the relationship between technology and sociocultural arrangements (Spitulnik 1993). Certainly the internet has several new affordances (Buckingham 2008), including the preservation of anonymity, the possibility for instant connection, and its content-generating capacity for users. But it is the motivations that undergird the use of such potentialities rather than the technological features themselves that define virtual intimacy. The architecture of the medium can encourage particular forms of female sexuality as much as it can sustain principles of particular forms of female modesty. It can intensify the transnational networks of communities as much as it can encourage a rootedness to the most conventional ideas of the nation as territorial boundedness (Bernal 2005; Aouragh 2012). What is more, anonymity and intimacy are equally features of non-digital practices. For instance, downtown Cairo cinema audiences have used the unsupervised space of movie theatres more so than the films themselves to engage in playful moral and political behavior deemed improper elsewhere (Armbrust 1998).

Instead of forcing virtual intimacy into the straitjacket of sociopolitical transformation, it may be more productive to examine how cyber intimacy in French exceeds the pragmatic and political considerations that undergird French speaking at school and in the job market. Though not without ambiguity, young people's desire for intimacy unsettles neat correlations between linguistic and social stratification and defers or even tricks them. What is worthy of our attention is the recirculation of school languages in forms that differ markedly from those that grammar books, school examinations, and job interviews dictate. The next section traces how French appears and circulates in cyberspace.

DISAGGREGATING (SCHOOL) LANGUAGE
TO FORGE (YOUTH) LANGUAGES

When I pointed out the spelling mistakes in the text message she had received, "*bone nuit, tu fait parti de me reves*," Fati was quick to correct me: "Never mind the spelling! This is MSN French, not school French!" In her dismissal of grammatical accuracy, Fati suggested that French was not only part of a flirting code but also a feature of a technology that reconfigured the use and shape of languages as they were taught at school. As mentioned earlier, this online code required academic mastery of French but not nearly to the degree that school did, and it placed different value on formal grammatical features. Intrigued by the role of MSN in language use, I finally created an account to the delight of many of the students I observed. Some of them were online every evening on their own computer or their family computer or, more likely, in one of the growing number of *cybers* (internet cafes) around town. Through my online conversations with students, I managed to understand the MSN linguistic code more quickly than I anticipated. I attributed this swiftness to two factors that are emblematic of the code. First, MSN communication makes ample use of French words (more so than face-to-face interactions); hence I felt at ease mixing my *dārija* with French whenever I ran out of vocabulary. Second, the rules of transcription for both Arabic and French are lenient enough so that I was not self-conscious about any incorrect spelling. I sensed that similar concerns made students more comfortable with using their multilingual skills online. As illustration, I had the following conversation with Ilham, a senior-year humanities student, on the day she passed her Baccalaureate exam:[19]

> ILHAM: - *J'ai eu mon bac* (I passed the *BAC*)!
>
> ILHAM: *rani farhana bzaf* (I'm very happy)!
>
> CHARIS: *habiba mabrouk, très heureuse pour toi* (congratulations dear; I'm very happy for you)!!!!
>
> ILHAM: *merci hbiba je sait* [*sic*] (thank you dear, I know)
>
> ILHAM: :) *Bouteina njhat* (Bouteina succeeded)
>
> CHARIS: *besa7* (Really)?
>
> ILHAM: wé (yeah)

CHARIS: *shno 3ndha* comme moyen (what's her average)?

ILHAM: *man3raf, 3ndha ghir* la reponse (I don't know; she only has the reply)

CHARIS: *makein mushkil lmuhim huwa* le bac (that's ok; the important thing is the BAC)!

ILHAM: *iwa . . . koi 2 9* (so . . . what's new)?

CHARIS: *shnu* (what)?

ILHAM: *quoi de neuf . . . tou7chtek! tou . . . dans quel lye mtn* (what's new . . . I missed you! where are you . . . in which lycée are you right now)?

CHARIS: *ana daba fi X* (I'm now in high school X)

ILHAM: *ah oui, mazyane tema . . .* (ah yes, it's nice there)

ILHAM: *b3da chwia nn* (it's a little far, isn't it)?

CHARIS: *nn mashi bezaf* (no, not very)

ILHAM: *darou le bac en meme temps que nous yak* (they sat the BAC at the same time as we did, didn't they)?

CHARIS: *wé* (yeah)

At first I interpreted this mode of communication as online code switching between French and *dārija*. With time, though, I have come to see this transcription and communication as a new code based on its own rules and serving its own distinct functions. I refuse to give this code a name, but consider it specific to Morocco despite the fact that it shares features with online writing codes across the arabophone world. The code is flexible, but follows some basic principles. I provide here a brief and non-systematic presentation of its main elements. Linguists may find this presentation simplistic while non-specialists may find it superfluous; my specific objective is to showcase the effects of this new linguistic form on the social status of Morocco's languages, particularly on French and *dārija*.

The code is an evolution of cell phone writing used for sending text messages. Because cell phones did not initially allow for an Arabic alphabet, Latin transliteration of Arabic was essential. Like any effort to transliterate into another alphabet, especially between two alphabets that differ so considerably, ambiguities inherent in oral communication created a wide range of methods for word transcription. There evolved a few principles for consonant transcription: for example, the letter *shin* is scripted with a *ch* and *sh*, and the letter *kha* is scripted with a *kh*. Vocalization, however, is more individual: for instance, the word *country* can be scripted as *blad*, *bled*, or *bld*. The use of numbers, so easily accessible on both cell phone and computer keyboard, compensates for more pronounced differences in alphabet: hence, the letter *ḥa* becomes 7, ʿ*ayn* becomes 3, and *qaf* becomes 9. The correspondence between number and letter does not have a phonetic connection but a visual one: the two symbols look like each other. Putting together all these principles in one expression, the online version of the expression *kanḥamaq ʿlīh* (I'm crazy about him) becomes *kan7maq 3lih*.

The transcription of French words also makes use of numbers, but the difference is that these numbers have a phonetic affinity with the words: for example, the proposition *de* becomes 2 because it sounds like the number two in French, and *neuf* (new) becomes 9 because it sounds like the number nine. French is the more common choice for certain words such as *oui* or *wé* for affirmation and *non* or *nn* for negation. The use of French words during online chatting oscillates between an orthographic and a phonetic transcription. The phonetic transcription simplifies spelling and overcomes issues of orthography, an important indicator of linguistic competence in pedagogical and professional environments. Generally, the malleability of the code at the hands of each writer distinguishes it from the languages of the school and the job market. It is hard to claim standardization for the code because online interlocutors create ongoing modifications just by virtue of using it. Recently, some of my online interlocutors have started incorporating English terms into the code, a practice that was more rare back in 2007 or 2008 when only English words such as "ok," "hi," or "bye bye" were used.

The effects of this online writing technique, which is an assemblage of languages the online writing technique had previously disaggregated, are worthy of attention. As far as French is concerned, the code fabricates a type of French as the language of private interaction, a language that is available to more than the elite. In contrast with the inadequate training in French provided by the public school, the keyboard serves as an instrument of inclusion because it resignifies multiple symbols of the Latin keyboard for the purpose of communication. This temporary sidelining of language mastery is antithetical to offline social stratification, a stratification that is tangible for students of the public school. As is the case with the adoption of French for flirting, the code cannot take credit for the disappearance of social distinctions; yet the social passing it permits—a balancing act of linguistic and cultural capital—has considerably more chances to succeed than in face-to-face communication where issues of accent and appearance come into play. I take this passing as significant, not only because it is another indication that students are acute commentators on social stratification but also because it is evidence of what Tsing calls "the necessity and power of the guise" (1993, 253). In short, by proving that they can use French for their own intimate purposes, students reify the prominence of French in their social space. However, they also expose the fluidity of the very linguistic parameters that relegate them to less-than-fluent speakers. The online code cannot replace academic or professional French, but it invites us to consider the fact that what Fati called MSN French is no less "correct" than school French, therefore turning school French into a temporal and political specification of French.

The code also re-spatializes spoken *dārija*. Through its relocation to the digital space, a space of modernity, spoken *dārija*—what Fati called *shaʿabī* and Zakaria thought of as strictly local—acquires a renewed significance in the negotiation of identity and sociality in contemporary society. In fact, the code affects the circulation of transcribed *dārija* on other digital media and offline: bands use it to transcribe their song titles or lyrics on the back covers of their CDs or online, and commercial advertising disseminates the code well beyond young consumers. Linguistic mixing is already a feature of spoken *dārija*, but this mixing is more extensive and more individually inventive on the internet than in face-to-face communications. What is most important to emphasize is that use of the code may be the only instance where these students have the power to steer their own communicative practices and the threads of knowledge production and dissemination. When I asked them how they learned to write in the code, the students were unable to explain it, but would instead suggest, "If you're young, you know how to do it" or "If you use the internet, you know how to do it." From this angle, the literacy that students acquire at school and the sociality encouraged through being at school become platforms for a whole range of other activities. In this case, the consumption of culture suggests an individual and collective anticipation of innovation and subversion.

In *The Practice of Everyday Life* (1984), Michel de Certeau turns away from an analysis of underlying structural frameworks and opted for a model of sociality that functions like individual sentences do for an established vocabulary and syntax.[20] By favoring the moment of enunciation, De Certeau privileges not only speaking itself but a vast range of actions that describe the world otherwise: "reader's practices, practices related to urban spaces, utilizations of everyday rituals, re-uses and functions of memory" (1984, xv). These practices manage to opportunistically reconfigure culture, which develops "in an atmosphere of tension, and often violence, for which it provides symbolic balances, contracts of compatibility and compromises, all more or less temporary" (1984, xvii). In a similar way, writing in the new online code is a practice of consumption (of French signs) turned creation. Given that the linguistic landscape of schooling is in flux, this code has the potential to be a culture-making gesture that can even envisage the replacement of the Arabic of the school with *dārija* or relativizing ideas of linguistic mastery altogether. Its eventual sociopolitical impact is unknown, but it is not unbelievable that such writing in code will become a more formal position, "taken also because it seeks itself in the circumstances created by opposition and by social and political hegemonies" (Hammoudi 2006, 275). This way, we can see the ramifications of this code as more than a parody of dominant language ideologies, though we should not exclude the element of parody from it.

Reflections on anticipation and creativity on the code's potential take us back to the school, the institution charged with the formal task of directing cultural identification. High school students engage in a multitude of projects of self-definition far beyond the school walls. They rehearse literacy and sociality in different spheres and reconfigure their position toward cultural production and social status even if they cannot ensure their social integration. Colonialism may be the series of events that set all these practices in motion. Yet for the youth in question colonialism is not the central referent of their practice. Contrary to the novels they are required to read, some cultural items do not relate to colonialism as something that needs transgressing. In fact, those cultural items are "visions of this less anxious creativity" (Appiah 1991, 357). The creativity that students display is a critical counterweight to their frustration at scientific innovation and the production of knowledge. Certainly, their creative online code cannot be a space-clearing gesture and instead must deal with the fact that French is deeply embedded in social stratification, that computers were inventions of the global north, and that they demand foreign-language skills. Their creativity also takes its cue from exposure to the global market of images and identities. Nevertheless, this less sanctioned online circulation of linguistic signs unsettles even further the cultural prerogatives of the policy of Arabization. It exposes the school's porousness and dethrones it as the locus of knowledge dissemination. As individual investment in formal schooling throughout Morocco and across the region withers and digital learning and sociality flourish, new concepts and patterns of learning emerge in the broader process of youth socialization.

7

Out of Class, into the Street

On my way home yesterday, I decided to walk along the main avenue. It was dusk, I guess it was around 7 p.m. The avenue was full with demonstrators, you know, the unemployed ones. There were so many of them, even women! One of them was pregnant. Some of the demonstrators clashed with the police and others ran away to seek refuge in the side streets. I got really scared. I thought, what if a policeman mistakes me for one of them and arrests me or, even worse, hits me? I started walking faster but not too fast, trying to look like I minded my own business. Suddenly I stopped because a crowd blocked the sidewalk. Passers-by had gathered around an injured guy. He had been stricken on the head and there was blood all over his face, he just lay there semi-conscious. . . .
I made my way through the crowd to get closer even though it was risky to stand on the street. As soon as I saw him, tears came to my eyes, the people next to me were shaking their heads, everyone was really upset. . . . And then we heard this man screaming just a few steps away. We all turned around. He was holding his two-year-old son by the hand cautioning him: "Do you see? This is why I'll never take you to school! You're better off selling fruit in the market; you're better off riding a bicycle! As a matter of fact, I will get you a bicycle first thing tomorrow and you can start practicing!" The man was clearly shaken by the scene, and I swear to God he was being serious, but he made me want to laugh. I wanted to laugh and cry at once.

Gesticulating wildly, the shock of the scene still imprinted on her face, Omama narrated this incident to a group of us while we stood in the schoolyard for the morning assembly on a sunny day in 2008

FIGURE 7.1

Photo of an urban high school classroom. Photograph by author.

(see Figure 7.1). The national anthem burst through the loudspeakers and shut down her recounting. I distinctly remember finding this instance especially uncanny and smiling mirthlessly as I turned to face the flag. The rest of the group was silent. Stories like Omama's were told so frequently that nobody was especially surprised to hear them, though their disappointment and unease were palpable in their silence. The unemployed graduates in these demonstrations epitomized these students' greatest fear: the failure to achieve financial independence, a respectable social standing, even marriage and a family. I often heard parents trying to dissuade their children from attending or even observing these demonstrations for fear that they might lose all motivation to go to school. Contact with the unemployed graduates was unavoidable, however, not least because many families had at least one member who, after studying at school or university, was facing long-term unemployment, the euphemism for which is the adjective [dar.] *gils f-dār* (sitting at home). Since the late 1980s, the presence of unemployed graduates rallying outside government institutions and along central avenues has been an integral part of the urban landscape. Their organization, the *Association Nationale des Diplômés Chômeurs au Maroc* (National Association of Moroccan Unemployed Graduates, ANDCM), founded in 1991, has grown to have a nationwide presence with more than 100 branches (Badimon and Bogaert 2014, 182).

There is a connection between this association and the youth-led movement *Ḥarakat ʿIshrīn Fibrāir* (February 20 Movement; named for the date of its first demonstration in 2011) that steered popular revolts during 2011–2012 (Fernandez-Molina 2011; Desrues 2012). Even though the February 20 Movement incorporated more social groups than just the unemployed graduates and more explicitly correlated socioeconomic marginalization with the structures of authoritarianism, the message it articulated had been long preceded by the claims of these graduates. The tenuous pact, which I intentionally do not call an agreement, which the authoritarian post-independence state had struck with its citizens-subjects, had relied on the generalized provision of skills and jobs for the public sector. The founding of the Arabized public school was crucial to this pact, even though in reality this school has all along been embedded in cultural domination by France and a socioeconomic hierarchy with divisions over the Berber population, between urban and rural contexts, and across class and gender lines. As neoliberal economic policies and politics aggravated this delicate balance among cultures and groups and enlarged all the fissures between them, this fragile arrangement appeared especially hollow and the types of coercion it required felt even more unbearable.

Many observers of Morocco glossed the Arab Uprising slogan "*Shughl, Karāma, ʿAdāla ijtimāiyya*" (Work, Dignity, Social justice) as the common claims of a demographically oversized young population across the Middle East and North Africa. What they overlooked is that language policy and linguistic hierarchies were crucial to this popular contestation. The February 20 Movement made *dārija* (Moroccan Arabic) central to its disaffection and resistance to authority. It associated authority both with royal and governmental edicts in *fuṣḥā* (Classical Arabic) and with elite symbolic and material capital contingent on francophonie. The Moroccan state fully understood the strong connections between the Movement's demands and language politics. The new constitution, drafted by a consultative commission that the king appointed and ratified via referendum on July 1, 2011, revised the government's stance toward Morocco's languages. It reinstated *fuṣḥā* as the official language of the country, but it established *amazighiyya* (Berber) as the second official language, guaranteeing its dissemination through public education. The constitution did not address Moroccan Arabic, but presented Morocco's "Arab and Berber languages" in the plural as constituents of a singular, authentic patrimony and as resources for the future (*al-dustūr 2011, faṣl 5*).

For the Moroccan students of the Arabized school, these constitutional reforms will not amount to much so long as the cultural politics of formal education and the job market remain unaltered. In Omama's story, the father's cynical attitude about schooling ("you're better off riding a bicycle") and her own affective response to his comments—both laughing and crying—testify to their joint abandonment of the ideal of public education and their belief in the state as the promoter of individual fulfillment. Therefore, the material and symbolic emptiness of the public school, which the students, teachers, and parents who featured in this book endlessly conferred about and negotiated, becomes a clear illustration of the broader emptiness of the experience of citizenship that drove widespread upheaval in Morocco and elsewhere in the region. In this sense, the February 20 Movement encapsulates the temporary consensus that linked the demands of the unemployed graduates with those of other disenfranchised and critical sections of the population in order to address the socioeconomic, political, and cultural exclusions of the Moroccan state and society.

I left the unpacking of the public school's emptiness to the conclusion of this book for methodological and theoretical reasons. The timing and mode of my own discovery of the hollowness of the public school as an institution made it a finding for me rather than a hypothesis. In writing this book, I purposefully let the images and feelings around this hollowness emerge out of the discussions, appraisals, and practices of school participants, replicating the way this phenomenon concretized for me through fieldwork. This book is thus structured to set up a process of discovery of this hollowness for the reader—allowing discovery to emerge from experience—which is itself deeply interwoven with my overarching interpretation of the much talked about demise of Moroccan public schools. Contrary to international and government articulations, the serious challenges the public school faces do not emerge as the logistical consequence of earlier structural planning, but rather as the largely unforeseen outcome of people's responses to the state's ambivalent and unfair pedagogical agenda. Placing school participants at the center of this negotiation over learning means making their version central to an investigation of the experience of education in Morocco and possibly elsewhere in the region. It is undeniable that public schools lack basic amenities, as well as learning equipment. It is equally irrefutable that certain pedagogical methods and school subjects need substantial recalibration to respond to emerging modes of sociality in both formal and informal arenas. As school participants insist, however, the cultural and linguistic tensions that undercut the Arabized public school present the greatest barrier to learning and to managing the transition from school to society.

It is through the responses of school participants that the Moroccan school appears not to be failing, but to be decentered—a qualitative difference that holds vast theoretical implications. The struggles staged inside the public school reflect wider strains in the country's cultural politics after colonization and up to today's advanced implementation of neoliberalism. These strains illuminate the fact that the school has not functioned as a mechanism for the social integration of Moroccan youth nor, for that matter, as an instrument for their ideological subjugation. These reflections drive my drastic reassessment of Morocco's educational crisis, as well as of public education in the global south and north, an extension that undergirds my critique of our modernist attachments to specific ideas about the meaning of "education" and "schools." This critique necessitates two moves identified throughout the book: a readjustment of the historical and geographical scale along which we evaluate Moroccan educational experience, which in turn calls for merging the ideational and material facets of this experience, and a scrutiny of formulations of education, schools, and the state that have hitherto pushed to the side both the modernist foundations of the concepts themselves and our conventional approach to them.

THOUGHTS ON SCALE AND DISPERSAL

Arabization was the pillar of a nationalist agenda of sociocultural engineering in the post-independence era. It captured a linguistic operation—the transformation and expansion of *fuṣḥā*—and made it the central mediator of this agenda. Making an arabophone education available to all Moroccans was a modern goal par excellence because of its explicit link to development theory—Arabic would communicate burgeoning domains of experience on Morocco's road to technological progress—and for its political motivation—Arabic would ensure the legitimacy of the monarchical state through the micro-disciplining of knowledge, communication, and identity. As we saw, the inherent and emergent contradictions of this linguistic operation intersect contemporary student experience and wider public evaluations of literacy, knowledge, and skills across generations. Inside the school, the form and role of *fuṣḥā*, always in a dialectical relationship with Morocco's other languages, are the subject of heated deliberations over students' social position, cultural identity, moral stance, and political perspective. These deliberations are complex because they take place along the dividing lines of discipline orientation (scientific versus humanities), generation (teachers, coordinators, and parents versus students), class (elite versus non-elite), and gender (Muslim men versus women, modern men versus modern women). At the interstices of these lines, which often appear messy and elusive, lies important insight into the predicament of Morocco, as well as other postcolonial nation-states, during advanced neoliberalism.

As competition for the most promising academic disciplines and friction over the language of the most valuable subjects show, the Arabized school is the battleground between the older schemata of hierarchy of French colonialism and Moroccan nationalism, and new versions of socioeconomic organization within development initiatives and global market integration. In this battle, the ideologies of language that supported nation-state building and the preservation of the monarchical state confront the accelerated commodification of all language. The process is inseparable from the re-spatialization of capital, nominally flexible and open but essentially imbalanced, within and outside Morocco. What is both remarkable and discouraging is that neither nationalist campaigns nor the transformation of the economy through the outsourced sectors of real estate, tourism, communication technology, and banking have alleviated the injustices of the colonial arrangement of material and cultural privilege. The most undeniable change in the domain of formal schooling is, in fact, discursive. Official discourse instrumentalizes and depoliticizes formal schooling through a focus on the purportedly pragmatic benefits of some (language) skills over others. Students, teachers, coordinators and inspectors of education, translators of school subjects, and parents continually contest this depoliticization. They have done so for some time now inside classrooms, teacher assemblies, their living rooms, on cyberspace, and in the street. Their labor has heralded, overlapped with, and will outlast the more publicized events of the Arab Uprisings.

The deliberations over the role of schooling in the individual's integration into society and in promoting the common good that take place inside and around the high schools featured in this book indicate that the challenges these lower and middle class students face are not new. Moreover, they are not caused by Morocco's recent, more intensive immersion in global economic activity and increasing interconnection with global prerogatives around knowledge and skills. On the contrary, school participants rescale the phenomenon of the hollow school to be the consequence of local cultural politics conceived by colonial planning, inconsistently appropriated by the post-independence state, and repositioned in development initiatives and neoliberal reform through an intentional sidelining of historical memory. Their rescaling of the rhetoric of dispersal—a rhetoric that attributes the educational crisis to global transformations—is itself an act of resistance, because interrogating the continuity in transition and the methods of exclusion that transitions keep intact leads to contesting official gestures of scale-making. Rescaling unsettles the *post* of colonialism and elucidates the links between post-colonialism, development, and neoliberalism. In fact, lived experience adjusts periodization in both a chronological and qualitative fashion: as the lexical marker "post" and the labels "post-colonialism," "development," and "neoliberalism" materialize more rhetorically than experientially, they prompt us to tackle post-colonial dilemmas and development problems in a single terrain of analysis.

The temporal and epistemological convergence of the twilight of European imperialism with the emergence of the international development model means that the consequences of the colonial experience, as well as the lingering attachments between former centers and peripheries, have swiftly morphed into other, yet related, patterns of organization and sociality. This collusion means that both post-colonial studies and critical development research face the similar task of deconstructing the modernist ideologies of universalism and positivism that supported and justified both endeavors of domination.[1] Yet the merging of their respective insights has been both peripheral and unsystematic. This segregation, and thus the discontinuity within the critique of modernism, has both disciplinary and wider institutional explanations (Hall 1996; Kandiyoti 2002). Because of this segregation, the field of post-colonial studies has largely taken on the work of exploring the domain of the inter-penetration of cultures and efforts at cultural identification during and after the colonial encounter (Said 1987; Spivak 1988; Bhabha 1990, 1994, among others). Meanwhile the field has paid less heed to how cultural identification overlaps with systems of material inequality that persist within international development and in the unfolding of global market integration.[2]

In turn, critical development studies have underplayed colonialism more than is appropriate and embraced the thematic emphases of development practice instead of probing its omissions. Scholars such as Arturo Escobar identify development as "a historically singular experience, the creation of a domain of thought and action" (1995, 10) even while unearthing the orientalism of development visions (1988, 429). From the perspective of the Moroccan public school, reading development as a break with colonialism is unconvincing: the dissolution of the colonial system is less real once we pay ethnographic attention to how colonial ideas (and ideals) persist and operate within Morocco's contemporary institutions and become part of students' self-perception and efforts at self-fashioning. This long *durée* perspective clarifies how the symbol of the *ingénieur*—the francophone academic orientation that embodies colonial, nationalist, and neoliberal visions of progress—has ensured social stratification and the domination of French over Arabic inside the ostensibly equalizing public school. Similarly, the deployment of the "democratic Berber" by colonial military campaigns through to present-day overtures to liberal pluralism undercuts the self-congratulatory lauding of the tolerant Moroccan state.

Even scholarship that has resisted the epistemological distinction from colonialism that gave birth to both development practice and research has mostly missed the opportunity to capture experience along both cultural and material lines. In a field whose application depended mostly on economists, lawyers, and statisticians, researchers of society and culture often pursued their critical interventions within the issues favored by those dominant disciplinary perspectives.[3] Thus development research both within multilateral agencies and academia has habitually underplayed the cultural underpinning of schooling in the global south and hence underestimated the inescapably political nature of "learning" and "competence." When development research touches on education, it places its emphasis on education's measurable aspects such as enrollment and dropout rates, infrastructure, and test scores. The pragmatism of this focus is not just elliptic but is actually mistaken: it does not recognize that what harms students is not the quantitative presence of multiple languages, but the qualitative relationship between different languages that impedes student access to material comfort, a position in society, and self-confidence. The anthropology of education and linguistic anthropology have been more attentive to the juncture of the material and cultural value of skills and resources, linguistic and not (Hornberger 1998). Still it is deplorable, but not coincidental, that these educational and linguistic experts have rarely been invited to sit at the table of development policy making. This sidelining is further evidence of the intentional demotion of certain lines of inquiry by the big players of change, whose oversimplifying positivism fuels domestic and international policy to this day.

Yet change also hinges on the bargaining over what constitutes reality. Part of the reason why repetitive and expensive campaigns of educational reform have not panned out nationally or internationally is that they have ignored the complex motivations that drive learning processes at school and elsewhere. Joining cultural politics with the political economy of contemporary Morocco through the prism of Arabization—as language ideology and policy—I merged the material concerns of high school students with the processes of cultural identification they engage in, arguing that the two are inextricably linked in their lives. Students may resent the fact that Arabic cannot lead to social integration and scientific innovation within Moroccan society, yet they remain morally and affectively close to this language to the extent that they fail to recognize French-speaking Moroccans as true Moroccans. Along similar lines, Berber students may feel adamant about the relevance of Berber to them, but strongly oppose the possibility of their further marginalization in Moroccan society and job market through minority language schooling. Furthermore, although a lack of competence in academic French may lead to feelings of social exclusion, the same students flirt and chat online in French as a tactic of alleviating such feelings, even if provisionally. By so doing, what constitutes weakness and marginalization in one sphere turns into opportunity and innovation in another.

The segregation of learning along post-colonial and developmental axes and the assumption that both colonialism and development constitute separate world-making gestures have legitimized the discursive authority of both these modernist paradigms. This legitimization applies even more to the concept that leads the current phase of transition in Morocco—"globalization"—as the cultural side of and also euphemism for global market integration. How useful is the concept for the elucidation of Morocco's cultural politics? In "The Global Situation," Anna Tsing (2000) warns us not to repeat our earlier wholehearted acceptance of modernization as world transformation in our analysis of globalization. She advises us to reassess earlier attempts at defining globalization that treated it as a dynamic of circulation and flow capable of remaking the world. Instead of foregrounding circulation and flow, Tsing advocates for paying attention to the effects of multiplicity and dispersal in the specific settings where the scale-making forces of the global—finance, international institutions, technology—negotiate their parameters. Hence instead of accepting globalization as the new scale by which to measure success and progress, we can question its intentional deployment by the mechanisms of the nation-state. These mechanisms interact with the global in intricate ways that require critical investigation.

For the Moroccan students I knew, the Moroccan state has become elusive and peripheral in some domains of learning—evidenced by its inability to shepherd transitions into the job market and its spectral presence inside private educational institutions—while remaining central in other domains, such as religious pedagogy. This occasional invisibility does not testify to the retrenchment of the state, but instead facilitates certain aspects of state operation, such as its participation in the circulation of global capital. Needless to say, this type of participation does not always relate organically to formal processes of attaining consensus and participation (Greenhouse 2005, 360). Hence, on one level, school participants who engage with educational privatization extend the neoliberal rhetoric of self-management and contribute to the wider acceptance of unequal structural positions. On another level, privatization delegitimizes the Moroccan state's main instrument of ideological legitimation, the Arabic language, as a shared and unifying register among all Moroccans. In spaces where the state attempts to represent all society through Arabo-Muslim symbolism, it faces vigorous competition from other actors such as Islamic movements and transnational Amazigh advocacy. Evidently then, global neoliberal transformation, despite a prevalent rhetoric of externality, takes place within the localized interaction between the Moroccan state and its citizens. The two sides are not demarcated as sharply as the terms imply, but are both affected by globalist dreams.

Engulfed in their intricacies yet maintaining a critical distance from the scale-making assertions of modernity and globalization, this book has traced the precise exclusions that prevent Moroccan students from the types of access they desire. The most vexing of these exclusions concerns the marginalization of Arabic from the contemporary Moroccan job market. This marginalization, I repeat, echoes colonial intentions, national divisions, and neoliberal visions of the labor force. It is obvious that these intentions, appropriations, and conflicts traverse but also extend beyond the classroom. How does this decentering of the experience of knowledge and skills affect the way we understand education and schooling, respectively?

LIVING AND LEARNING

Throughout my research on Moroccan public schools—from reading, to fieldwork, to sharing and discussing my work, and to completing this monograph—I stumbled with a sense of unease on the "disconnect" I saw between my reflections and the anthropology and sociology of education. I initially attributed my resistance to cross-cultural comparison to dramatic disparities of location. These disparities, I told myself, accounted for the fact that categories meaningful to school students in the United States, such as inner city, immigration, race, and so on, were only tenuously relevant to the Moroccan case. I have since changed my mind. Comparison between schools in different contexts feels strained not because of geographic distance, but because of the erroneous but deeply engrained belief that "schools" are known for what they are and what they do: they enculturate youth in the political and economic objectives of their societies and governments. The theoretical extension of this belief is that researchers of "education" respond to the invitation to fill in the details of local particularity from observing local "schools." What happens if we pry open all of these beliefs? Drawing on groundbreaking propositions in the anthropology of education, of the Middle East, and of the state, I argue against the presumptions that education is what happens at school and that the school is the instrument of the state. The first presumption supposes that education reins in sociohistorical and cultural arbitrariness, whereas the second places school and state in the same empirical reality. The stakes of this re-theorization are indeed great for the Moroccan school, which, according to conventional understandings of schooling and education, can only be read as either or both a geohistorical peculiarity and modernist failure.

Hervé Varenne has formulated two potent criticisms of the anthropology of education. The first concerns the conflation of the terms "education" and "school" in the anthropological study of American schools (2008, 356). Urging us to disentangle the school from the occurrence of education, Varenne temporarily places the school outside the equation in order to correlate education with cultural transformation (2008, 363). The conflation of education with enculturation—namely, a process of disciplining and controlling contingency—lies at the heart of an anthropological bias toward the dynamics of reproduction and order. This bias automatically links the school to methods of control. The anthropological legacy of deeming initiation rituals and informal apprenticeship as enculturation has lent support to this conflation (Van Gennep 2004). As a result, culture became predominantly that which one has to learn for the sake of participation, continuity, and order. Yet what if culture is not just what you predominantly teach and learn but also other activities such as "paying attention, investigating, deliberating, setting up" (Varenne 2008, 362)? As Varenne asks, through the prism of these other activities, could we relocate education at the intersection of order and disorder?[4]

> Anthropologists, and not only anthropologists "of" education, fail to notice the central place of, precisely, *education as the other aspect of culture.* Arguably, anthropology should claim education along with culture as its core concepts to the extent that one cannot hope to understand cultural evolution without also understanding education. (Varenne 2008, 363; emphasis added)

Extricating education from the school and drawing it nearer cultural transformation allow us to escape the impossible choice between idealism and conservatism around learning. By looking at education as synonymous with cultural transformation we no longer need to consider it as either teleologically empowering (Dewey 1916; Freire 1986) or quintessentially suppressive (Althusser 1984; Bourdieu and Passeron 1990). If education, in the sense of diverse, continuous attempts to deal with cultural change, leads to some people's emancipation—as Fatima Agnaou (2004) shows in the case of adult literacy classes for Moroccan women—it can also be conservative and meaningless for others, as happens among the inner-city crack dealers of New York studied by Philippe Bourgois (1996). In both cases, education has very little to do with the space of the school. For Agnaou, women's literacy is an indicator of the broader negotiation of women's rights between the emerging Moroccan civil society and international organizations, whereas for Bourgois education is a facet of the institutionalization of racism through urban marginalization.[5] I do not intend to draw attention to the undoubtedly significant informal learning practices here. My loftier goal is to enlarge the term "education" enough so that it cannot be theorized solely through the experience of schooling or through any single institution for that matter. This conceptual separation enables us—in our double capacity as researchers of education and teachers—to admit and eventually disengage from our own idealization of the school. We can and should eventually recognize that both conservatism and idealism with regard to the school emerge from our deepest faith in the school as the center of any civilizational process. In sum, if we release our control of the categories "education" and "school," we can allow our interlocutors to better articulate how they intellectually and practically grasp the relationship between the two.

The high school students whose stories inspired and structured this book straddle arbitrariness and contingency as intensely as they experience a systematic shaping of subjectivity and collective life by Morocco, France, the United States, and other nations. They do develop a certain "habitus"—that is, a set of internalized dispositions—as a result of official intentions and their own positioning with regard to these intentions (Bourdieu 1977). Still, the shifting ground on which they perform this habitus and exchange it for privilege does not allow them to be unreflexive and nonresponsive to ideology, be it linguistic or not. In fact, the deeper their embodiment of certain tenets of the Arabized school, such as a formulation of Muslim identity through literacy, the more forceful their critique and search for alternative modes of being and acting.[6] What is more, the changes these students grapple with in this larger recalibration of a valuable labor force and of the educated person are not entirely in the hands of their state or any another state. They represent instead a convergence of external and internal dynamics. These dynamics enhance the Moroccan state's grip on the students' future at the same time as they weaken this state's fiction as a tangible center on which students can project the symbols and practices of citizenship. Student online creativity in the margins of Morocco's official languages, a creativity that is both calculated and unwitting, does not do away with the oppression of an unequal linguistic educational system. It does, however, destabilize this system's naturalness by claiming that the "standard" or "correct" languages of textbooks and exams are only versions of a language among other possibilities.

This theoretical shift has serious political implications for the study of North Africa and the Middle East. Responding to the attribution of terrorist violence by U.S. political and public discourse to the backward and illiberal schooling of a vaguely defined Muslim world, scholars have exposed what they called an American Protestant idealism bent on the centrality of school-based education. They have urged their audience, whose members were increasingly international and mostly unfamiliar with the region, to see students of the Muslim world as witnesses and actors in situations that are larger and more influential than their schoolrooms and schoolbooks:

> We imagine that of all public social institutions the school is the arena par excellence in which unformed potentials of our children are given shape as they are molded into members of our nation, bearers of our culture and tradition, and the laborers who will build our future. . . . By linking hatred, incitement, and murder to schoolbooks, rather than, say, to the daily experiences of children and adults living under foreign military occupation or dreadful repressive monarchies or to family backgrounds, social and economic structure, the public sphere more generally or the self-interest of local political leaders, an explicit set of claims is beings made about the content of schoolbooks and curricula. (Doumato and Starrett 2007, 2–4)

Directed at every researcher of education in the region and beyond, these remarks serve as a cautionary note against the dangers of educational idealism. They also implicitly reconfigure the school as a public space that resists a generic definition and exists only as the tangibly used, imagined, invested category of social action by different people. Through this opening up of categories, we can reenable cross-cultural comparison. Significantly, this comparison does not need to use the school as its object, but can and should emerge from other dimensions of life that may or may not relate to classrooms.[7]

These thoughts bring me back to Omama's account of the father of a young boy rejecting the idea of schooling because of the symbolic and physical violence that unemployed graduates suffer at the hands of the very state that has encouraged them to study. The perspective of this cynical father and Omama's implicit validation of this cynicism outline the relationship between the school and the state. This book has focused on the way language ideologies work in student life as young Moroccans plan their professional and social futures. It insisted that the challenges of public education in Morocco inhere in the tense negotiation between post-independence language policy and cultural politics and current student aspirations. Instead of looking for sociocultural reproduction within the institutional mechanisms of concealment and stratification, it has construed learning as the series of multi-referential and to some extent unpredictable endeavors of school participants (students, teachers, parents) to fulfill these aspirations. Their endeavors do advance certain aspects of state policy, such as the value of French and science, while they reverse official discourses on meritocracy and the significance of academic performance. School participants' acute awareness of these discrepancies and their abandonment of the public school contradicted the idea of schooling as successful economic entrapment—a dimension of schooling that the inspirational works of Foley (1990), Devine (1996), and Luykx (1999) tend to foreground.

Because it cannot answer the urgent question of social integration, the Arabized Moroccan school becomes an empty signifier: it becomes hollow. Students, parents, and teachers strive to adopt the insignia of this empty signifier, the Bac or a university degree, but no longer imbue it with meaning. As for the school's moral and political inculcation, it is equally incomplete. The high school students I met were at an age and stage in their life when the contradictory messages of schooling had become apparent. At this point, moral cultivation may have influenced students as to what kind of Muslims they want to be, but has not convinced them that the state is the authority that encapsulates the ethical messages they should embody and honor in their everyday life. Equally, the persuasive power of Arabization's curricula is at best partial for students whose private and social lives incorporate Berber language and culture. As Gregory Starrett aptly argues about schooling in Muslim societies, despite our deepest faith, "the content of schooling is not at the heart of either civilizational process or of civilizational struggle" (Starrett 2007, 228). This argument is strongly reminiscent of Varenne's theoretical proposition.

This scholarly consensus becomes even stronger when one recognizes the ontological distinction between school and state. In essence, the school is a tangible space with a set of operations that to a degree direct the experience of a group of people, students, for a set amount of time. These operations and experience can be the object of empirical observation. We cannot claim the same for the state, despite our frequent and insistent use of the state as an entity in the singular. Even in the case of Morocco, where the state borrows the anthropomorphic image of the monarch and where the monarchical circle dominates both the political scene and the sphere of economy as a major stakeholder, it is impossible to determine its contours. In fact, the state is most approachable, suggests Michel Trouillot

(2001), in the effects of its ideological operations. In this case, state and school do not belong in the same epistemological realm. Thus the school cannot mirror or serve the state in literal terms, but it can and does root the state in the lives of students, education professionals, and parents, as well as in the work of scholars.

It is precisely because it performs such an important operation that the school's demise presents strong proof of the fissures in the fiction that the state is a universal and eternal mode of organization. What the modern school has done for the modern state—that is, map out social life onto biological development and structure individual and collective time—is no longer a taken-for-granted or even a necessarily desirable function. Thus systems of subordination may work well for some time, but times change, bringing into their orbit potentially unchartered types of learning and yet unformed languages. Alternative ideas around learning that students warmly embrace in cyberspace and offline strengthen the suspicion that the school, as well as the state, appears to students as anachronistic and in need of radical recalibration. The incongruence of the symbol of the state with the re-spatialization of activity and subjectivity on a global scale furthers the dissolution of its fiction.

In light of the acknowledgment that these modernist fictions have provided the prisms through which we have long shaped our analysis of learning, our interpretation of educational "crisis" can only stand if we change the meaning of crisis from "disaster" to that of "turning point." The latter interpretation introduces the need for "judgment," which also happens to be the original meaning of the Greek word "krisis" (Mazawi 2014). In this reworked framework, crisis talk serves at least two antithetical intentions. On the one hand, it supports the strategic shaming of earlier visions of learning and knowledge, a shaming that well serves agents of neoliberal reform. On the other hand, crisis talk may signal the withering of modernity's fictions in which the ideals of the public school and the nation-state have featured centrally. This second type of crisis talk and the breakdown it points to are much deeper than the skepticism people express toward the state's ideological agendas, among them Arabization. It represents a breakdown of the consciousness of how to be in a collectivity and face an (always) uncertain future together. This second type of crisis talk is as liberating as it is unsettling, because it requires all of us—Moroccan students, educational professionals, and researchers alike—to push our imagination to envisage drastically otherwise the future shape of collective organization and redistributive justice in Morocco, as well as in the rest of the region. The events of the Arab Uprisings, which have explicitly and implicitly postulated schools as a metonym for the urgent need for drastic socioeconomic, political, and cultural transformation, have motivated us to move faster in this direction.

NOTES

1. SCHOOLS IN CRISIS

1. These acts copied the self-immolation of Mohammed Bouazizi in the city of Sidi Bouzid that spearheaded the Tunisian revolution and subsequently other uprisings in the region. The following Moroccan episode is telling: in January 2012, a group of unemployed graduates occupied the ground floor of the Ministry of Education in Rabat. Several of these graduates, all men, expressed their despair at police intervention by showering themselves in gasoline and setting themselves on fire. Passersby filmed and then disseminated on YouTube fuzzy and shaky videos of one of the protesters succumbing to the flames and five others getting severely injured.

2. For earlier studies of Moroccan youth, see Adam (1963); Bennani-Chraïbi (1994); Bourquia et al. (1995); and Cohen (2004).

3. One can get a taste of this in the articles by Thomas Friedman, foreign affairs op-ed columnist for the *New York Times* and three-time Pulitzer Prize winner. In an article drawing on his experience in Yemen titled "It's All About Schools," Friedman suggests that the introduction of modern education and critical thinking can be the most effective solution to Muslim terrorism: "So here is my new rule of thumb: For every Predator missile we fire at an al-Qaeda target here, we should help Yemen build 50 new modern schools that teach science and math and critical thinking—to boys and girls" (Friedman 2010). For similar views about the importance of a particular type of training in the region, see the Arab Human Development Report on Knowledge (2005) and the Arab Knowledge Report (2009).

4. Very little of the content of this World Bank Report is new. Critics of development discourse have illustrated how reports of this kind acquire authority through a diagnosis of challenges based on a specific theorization of the domains of education, economy, and development (Escobar 1988; 1995; Ferguson 1993; Mitchell 2002). The same reports routinely veil international involvement in the unfolding of sociopolitical and economic events in the analyzed countries. In the report in question, the ambiguity around the feasibility of comparisons among the MENA countries is, as Fida Adely aptly argues, "not unusual for this genre of reports, but can be decidedly misleading" (2009, 110).

5. A comparison between "The Road Not Traveled" report and the comments of then-minister of education, Ahmed Akhchichine, reveals significant convergence. In an interview, Akhchichine stated, "We need to reinvent the economic model. The ideal is that buildings should be the responsibility of local actors, the material and organization are the responsibility of the Ministry, and that the management is private. We could have schools based on this tripartite model" (2008, 39).

6. There are sixteen Académies Régionales de l'Education et de la Formation (Regional Academies for Education and Training) of the Ministry of Education across Morocco's seventy-two provinces. In addition to their monitoring function, the regional academies are officially responsible for 30 percent of curricular content to ensure its adaptability to the pedagogical needs of the different regions of the country.

7. Various endeavors to expand and standardize the Arabic language date back to the first century (Muslim calendar: AC), which is equivalent to the seventh century BC. However, it would be wrong to group these endeavors with the decolonizing initiative of Arabization that took place across the Maghrib and, to some degree, the rest of the region. Those earlier endeavors were underpinned by different understandings of culture and of the way culture related to "a people."

8. Policies of Arabization were integral to the educational systems of many states in the region as they emerged from their respective experiences of European colonialism (Colonna 1975; Massialas and Jarrar 1991; Sbaiti 2010). The particularities of both colonial and nationalist agendas in each context preclude analytical generalization, not least because the delineation of inclusion and exclusion of a people that needed Arabizing was distinctive in each case (Wien 2011). These particularities encourage us to consider under which circumstances and on whose terms this colossal project of translation was put to work in specific settings.

9. For a thorough examination of the concept of language ideology, see Kroskrity (1993); Woolard and Schieffelin (1994); and Ahearn (2001).

10. For in-depth reviews of these works, see Berger (2002); Harrison (2003); Bensmaïa (2009); and Allen (2011).

11. Although a central pillar of the decolonizing agendas of Morocco, Tunisia, and Algeria, the policy of Arabization was implemented differently in the countries. For a thorough dissection of the three different implementations, see Granguillaume (1983).

12. Even though the term al-ʿarabiyya al-muʿāṣira (Modern Arabic) exists, I rarely encountered it at school, in everyday life, or in the media. Sociolinguists of Arabic sometimes refer to the language of the media as al-ʿarabiyya al-ṣaḥāfiyya (journalistic Arabic). This term is equally misleading because the register of media varies depending on the topic, the targeted audience, and the background of the author.

13. In this book I have sidelined Spanish, a language with a strong presence in north Morocco but of minor importance in the geographical location where I predominantly lived and worked.

2. STUDY *ANTIGONE* TO BECOME A SCIENTIST!

1. As of 2004, the Moroccan educational system offers six years of primary and six years of secondary education. A Pedagogical Reform by the *Commission Spéciale Education et Formation* (Special Commission Education and Training, COSEF), founded by the

Palace in 1998, introduced continuous monitoring, integration of regional and national examination grades into one score, and reorganized courses into disciplinary tracks.

2. Other branches of this track are *al-ʿUlūm al-Riāḍiyya* or *Sciences Mathématiques* (Mathematics), *al-ʿUlūm al-Iqtiṣādiyya wa-l-Tadbīr* or *Economie et Gestion* (Economics and Management), *al-ʿUlūm wa-l-Tiknūlūjiyāt al-Kahrubāʾiyya* or *La Technologie Électronique* (Electronics), and *al-ʿUlūm wa-l-Tiknūlūjiyāt al-Mīkānīkiyya* or *La Mécanique* (Mechanics).

3. This track has four branches: *al-ʿUlūm al-Sharīʿiyya* or *Sciences Religieuses* (Religious Sciences), *al-Lugha al-ʿArabiyya* or *l'Arabe* (Arabic Language), *al-Adab wa-l-ʿUlūm al-Insāniyya* or *Sciences Humaines* (Humanities), and *al-Funūn al-Taṭbiqiyya* or *Arts Appliqués* (Applied Arts).

4. Course material for Humanities, Social Sciences, and Islamic Studies is in French, but instruction is given in a mixture of Arabic and French. Students of law pursue either arabophone or francophone studies.

5. The Baccalaureate cycle extends over two years. In the Experimental Sciences class, the subjects of French, Arabic, Islamic Education, History, and Geography are assessed in the first-year examination, whereas the subjects of English, Philosophy, Geology, and Biology, Physics, Chemistry, and Mathematics are part of the second-year examination.

6. The letter *g* here transcribes a Moroccan Arabic consonant that corresponds to the initial letter of the English word *gas*.

7. This corporatized view of the language is standard in the contemporary marketplace, which is steeped in French globalized enterprises. Recent reports maintain there are about 750 branches of French companies providing more than 120.000 jobs inside Morocco (Zejly and Achehbar 2014).

8. F.A.R and FAR 4 Ever refer to the football team *Forces Armées Royales* (Royal Army Forces) Rabat. The Italian words *tifosi* (football fans) and *ultras* (hardcore fans) refer to Italian football.

9. Scholars of sub-Saharan francophone Africa have forwarded similar arguments (see Decock 1970).

10. See Heggoy (1973) and Sraieb (1993) for Algeria and Tunisia, respectively. Despite the presence of organized non-religious education in Tunisia since the 1880s, only 1.25 percent of Tunisian Muslims were enrolled in "modern educational institutions" by 1930. This figure increased to 12 percent in 1949 and 19 percent in 1953 (Sraieb 1993, 249).

11. I am referring to the division of Morocco into north and central regions controlled by Spain and France respectively, between 1912 and 1956 and not to the Sahara in the south, which Spain controlled between 1888 and 1975.

12. Senegal, Indochina, Algeria, and the Protectorates of Morocco and Tunisia differed considerably in their negotiation of assimilationist versus associationist agendas of cultural contact. For more on this topic, see Lewis (1962); Colonna (1975); and Shepard (2006).

13. A comparison between nineteenth-century educational planning in France (Watson 1966) and early twentieth-century planning in Morocco (Segalla 2009) shows that educational policies for working-class French students in the metropolis were recycled as colonial policies for Muslim students. The curriculum for both working-class French children and Moroccan students intended French to be used as an instrumental language, namely an economic tool.

14. The free school was a private nationalist initiative. The free schools of Morocco, Tunisia, and Algeria varied considerably in their orientation and curriculum.

15. By the term *salafiyya*, I refer to the religious reformist movement of Morocco as it developed at the turn of the twentieth century. The movement drew from the intellectual guidance of figures such as Jamal al-Din al-Afghani (1838–1897), Mohammed Abduh (1849–1905), and Rashid Rida (1865–1935). It sought to eradicate other expressions of faith, such as sufism, and reshape Islam so that it could better withstand the Western challenge (Geertz 1968; Burke 1972).

16. From the point of view of my left-leaning interlocutors, the policy did not represent Hassan II's cultural convictions. Rather, Arabization was the king's plan to counter the popularity of the French-inspired, secular, leftist opposition through the widespread promotion of Arabo-Muslim culture.

17. In 1999, the Charter for Education and Training (*Charte de l'Education et de Formation*), which was essentially an agenda of reform announced by the royally appointed High Council for Education, made reference to the integration of Arabic in scientific disciplines at the university level. However, to this day, there has been no change in the institutional position of French in the sciences in higher education (Belfkih 2000).

18. The prices of private tuition and revision classes were accurate at the time of my fieldwork 2007–2009 and for the two cities in which I conducted fieldwork. At the time of writing this chapter, the currency equivalence between MAD and USD is approximately 1=0.1.

19. The public educational system positions teachers on a salary scale according to the grade they teach, their academic skills and credentials, and their experience. As teachers informed me, high school educators enter on scale ten, which starts with a yearly salary of 4,000MAD. This is supplemented by "hardship" costs if the position is in a rural area, which could reach an additional 2,000MAD per year. After eight years of service these teachers could earn up to 6,000MAD. After twenty years of service, their salary could reach the amount of 12,000MAD.

20. Foreign textbooks cost about 300MAD each, in contrast with public school textbooks, whose cost ranges from 48MAD to 56MAD.

21. Access to private education declined after independence but rose in the 1980s when even Mission schools, formerly public, became private (Moatassime 1992, 27).

22. According to Hammoudi (2009b), Bourdieu's conservatism towards processes of enculturation seems to have evolved out of his understanding of tradition within what he saw as an unchanging Kabyle society. Bourdieu shifted from an ethnological to sociological analysis in his investigation of the effects of colonialism on Algerian workers who immigrated to the city. After engaging with the urban context, Bourdieu correlated the mode of adaptation to a capitalist economy with a triangular division of the population into social classes—a theoretical move that Hammoudi (2009b) contests. The two works of Pierre Bourdieu that are most relevant to this discussion are *Sociologie de l'Algérie* (1958) and *The Algerians* (1962).

23. Bourdieu similarly argues, "Teachers constitute the most finished products of the system of production, which it is, inter alia, their task to produce" (1991, 197).

24. In the essay "Social Space and the Genesis of Classes," Bourdieu expresses skepticism toward the Marxist conflation of "theoretical class," which "allows one to explain and predict the practices and properties of the things classified," with "empirical class"

or "a group mobilized for struggle" (1991, 231). Although the first definition only exists in sociological lexicons in the sense of a probability, the two come together in practice under the summoning of representatives who "feel authorized to speak in its name" (1991, 251). However, Bourdieu insists on the idea of triangular social stratification in his work on public education in France, a society that was explicitly class conscious in those triangular terms (Bourdieu and Passeron 1990).

3. PARADOX AND PASSION IN THE TOWER OF BABEL

1. These courses are part of the Bac 1 or otherwise known as the regional examination.

2. English translations of Arabic and French passages from the Translation course and textbook are mine unless otherwise indicated.

3. This is not an exclusively francophone view of Arabic. Dickins, Harvey, and Higgins argue that in scientific texts it is "less likely to be a problem translating into English than into Arabic since the terms of such new objects and processes typically originate in English" (2002, 152).

4. No scientific textbook of the Moroccan curriculum is devoid of the presence of French. Small glossaries at the end of each unit and short dictionaries in the final pages of each book provide French translations of Arabic terminology, but they preserve the Arabic terminology as the original term.

5. On these occasions, *tarjama* takes on the additional meaning of "biography" in the North African literary tradition: "an account of the subject's name and ancestry, date of birth (and death, if applicable), a catalog of teachers . . . a bibliography of works written by the subject" (Reynolds and Brustad 2001, 42).

6. Caliph al-Maamun (830 AC) founded *Bayt al-Ḥikma*, a renowned translators' academy aimed at the coordination of such work for the benefit of linguistic unification across the empire.

7. The fez (Turkish rendering of the Arabic work *tabush*) refers to a felt hat made of red kilim fabric that originated in the Arab Andalusian region.

8. For a study of scientific translation from English into Sanskrit, Urdu, and Hindi in India, see Dodson (2005).

9. Barthes' structuralism was open ended and gradually shed much of its systematicity (Sontag 1993). Yet even in his most structuralist essay "Myth Today," Barthes sanctions the Saussurian theory of language as system only insofar as doing so allows him to discuss the limits of the arbitrariness of signification in "mythical language," which is his label for language in society. In fact, it appears that Barthes' distinction between what he calls "first-order language" and "myth," which he designates as "second-order language," emerges out of his Marxian desire for reconciliation between "reality and men . . . object and knowledge" (1993, 149). In many ways Barthes' mythology is comparable to that of linguistic anthropologists who take the extra-linguistic domain as central to the definition of both materiality and signification. Barthes' claim that "the specific study of forms does not in any way contradict the necessary principles of totality and history" (1993, 95) is not far from Woolard's and Schieffelin's argument that ideologies of language "envision and enact links of language to group and personal identity, to aesthetics, to morality, and to epistemology" (1994, 55).

10. Barthes calls myth a "meta-language," which means "a second language in which one speaks about the first" (1993, 100). Recent explorations of translation (Jaffé 1999;

Venuti 2000) similarly posit translation as both a linguistic and metalinguistic activity. In this sense, any act of translation can be considered an act of mythologizing.

11. Intriguingly, Barthes qualifies the naturalization of history as the particular mythological gesture of the French bourgeoisie: "The status of the bourgeoisie is particular, historical: man as represented by it, is universal, eternal. The bourgeois class has precisely built its power on technical, scientific progress, on an unlimited transformation of nature: bourgeois ideology yields in return an unchangeable nature" (1993, 130). Barthes indicates the bourgeois foundations of the imperial project through his central example of a *Paris-Match* magazine cover of an African soldier saluting the French flag. The example is poignant, because both bourgeois and colonial ideology are contingent on a universalization of a version of culture as transformed nature.

12. Although the Qur'an mentions both Babel and the Tower in the *"surat al-baqara"* (The Cow) and the *"surat ghāfir"* (The Forgiver), respectively, the two do not feature together in a parable similar to that of the Judeo-Christian tradition.

13. Niloofar Haeri has located the same idea in the early twentieth-century Egyptian press: "Now we have no recourse but to seek *al-ʿulūm al-ʿasriyya* (contemporary sciences) from Western peoples, because our truths and valuable possessions are dispersed in their lands and protected in their homes. In this search, we are demanding a stolen right and a lost good, which the spirit of our ancestors is crying for bringing back and utilizing" (2003, 85).

14. Persian words formed the basis for pharmacology, mineralogy, and botany and Greek words the basis of philosophical, medical, and logical notions (Versteegh 1997, 62).

15. Given the extent of translation that had to take place in the scientific domain, the academies resorted to a range of methods, including morphological and phonological integration of foreign words (*talfasa* from *television*) and direct borrowing of foreign terms by either phonetic inscription or the insertion of Latin into the Arabic text (such as *laser*) (Versteegh 1997, 179–181).

16. I am referring to the Bureau for Coordination and Unification of the Institute for Studies and Research on Arabization founded in 1961 and to the *Congrès de l'Arabisation* (Arabization Congress) in Algiers founded in 1973.

17. Noam Chomsky's training focused on philosophy and linguistics. However, as a student, he worked closely with Zellig Harris, a linguist interested in establishing a mathematical method to analyze language data.

18. Lakdhar-Ghazal sees dialecticism as a source of semantic instability. He also claims that although Turkish and Persian terms could have contributed to the modernization of Arabic, these languages were not deemed prestigious enough to serve as templates or lexical pools (1976, 45). Interestingly, Kemal Ataturk's Turkish language reform of 1928 reversed this language ideology. This reform strove for the purification of Turkish from its backward Arabic and Persian elements (Lewis 1999; Çolak 2003).

19. In these works, including Jean Jacques Rousseau's *On the Origin of Language* and Johann Gottfried Herder's *"Essay on the Origin of Language,"* oriental languages are expressions of pure emotion, itself the direct result of their primitive nature. This emotion hinders their capacity for abstraction and scientific reasoning: "The genesis of oriental languages, the oldest known, absolutely refutes the assumption of a didactic progression in their development. These languages are not at all systematic or rational" (Rousseau 1986, 152). Conversely, French is not poetically gifted but is a "prose of sound reason" (1986, 152).

20. It is telling that even Chomsky, who seeks for a level of language that reveals "the basic properties of thought and conception" (1971, 2), remains skeptical of the ability to sever structural from semantic processes: "The syntactic and semantic structure of natural languages evidently offers many mysteries, both of fact and of principle" (1971, 123).

21. Prof. Merzouki's patriotic indignation is reminiscent of Moroccan intellectual Abdelfattah Kilito's revolt against the submission of modern Arab literary expression to a Western original: "The reader of an Arabic text soon connects it, directly or indirectly, to a European text. He is necessarily a comparatist, or we could say a translator" (2008, 16).

22. The intensity, as well as the divergence of opinion among these translators, agrees with yet also complicates Talal Asad's skepticism toward the work of anthropology as a "translation of cultures" (1986b, 141), a skepticism he primarily addresses toward Ernest Gellner and secondarily toward British social anthropology. Asad is sensitive to the immersion of anthropological translation in systems of inequality. The languages of the Third World that researchers study are more prone to forcible transformation than the languages in which anthropologists take field notes or write monographs—which Asad assumes is English. His criticism is very relevant here, especially because Asad illustrates his argument through the predicament of "modern Arabic," a language that had to "undergo a transformation (lexical, grammatical, semantic) that is far more radical than anything to be identified in European languages—a transformation that has pushed it to approximate to the latter more closely than in the past" (1986b, 158). However, what the translators of this chapter communicate is more complex. Language inequality and the power relations that undercut the work of translation do not play out solely between academia and its subjects. Instead, in Morocco, issues of translation become the constant object of debate and practice, thus turning the anthropological interpretation into one among many strands of the struggle over communicative and creative parity.

4. INHERITANCE, HERITAGE, AND THE DISINHERITED: SACRED ARABIC

1. Following Talal Asad (1986a) and Gregory Starrett (1998), I define this orthodoxy not as a "body of opinion" about right and wrong practices and attitudes, but rather, as a "particular relationship to authority" (Starrett 1998, 8).

2. I borrow the term "scripturalism" from Clifford Geertz's description of a religious transformation that took place in Morocco during the nineteenth century and reached its apogee in the 1920s and 1930s. This transformation entailed a retrospective look into Muslim-ness vis-à-vis the social impact of European intervention. This retrospection resulted in a renewed emphasis on the main texts of the Islamic faith (Qur'an, hadith, Islamic law, and the acceptable commentaries around them) as the only sources of religious authority.

3. This academic trajectory, under the patronage of Hassan II in 1973, constituted a revival of traditional religious institutions. The Ministry of Education renewed the shape and direction of these institutions through introducing foreign languages and sport. In this trajectory the student progresses from al-taʿlīm al-asāsī (primary) to al-taʿlīm al-thānawī (secondary) education and can then compete for entry into higher education institutions.

4. Since 2002, the Ministry of Habous and Islamic Affairs has run these schools with the help of a committee of educational experts and a council of ʿulamā' (religious scholars). The Ministry manages 494 al-madāres al-ʿatīqa (traditional schools) and 10,183

al-katātīb al-qurʾāniyya (Qurʾanic schools). This Ministry also administers the *Dar al-Hadīth al-Hassaniyya*, a higher education institution for Islamic Studies founded by Hassan II in 1964.

5. *Tarbiya Islāmiyya* is not a core course for any Baccalaureate track except *al-taʿalīm al-asīl*.

6. *ʿĪd al-fiṭr* or *ʿīd al-ṣaghīr* marks the end of Ramadan. *ʿĪd al-aḍha* or *ʿīd al-kabīr* celebrates the willingness of Ibrahim to sacrifice his son Ismael as dictated by God. *Al-mawlid* marks the commemoration of the birth of Prophet Mohammed.

7. The hybridity of moral education inside formal schooling is by no means exclusive to our time or the non-Western world. For example, for an analysis of moral education dilemmas in late nineteenth-century France, see Zeldin (1970); Ozouf (1982); and Stock-Morton (1988).

8. The unit titles in Arabic are *"usūl al-maʿrifa al-islāmiyya," "al-tafakkur fī al-kawn wa athāruhu fī tarsīkh al-īmān," "al-wiḥda al-ḥuqūqiyya,"* and *"al-wiḥda al-ijtimāʿiyya"* (*Tarbiya Islāmiyya* Bac 2, 2010, 9).

9. "The Qurʾan describes itself as a scripture that God ʿsent down' to the Prophet . . . and, in Arabic, this word conveys immediately, and in itself, the concept that the origin of the Qurʾan is from above and that Muhammad is merely a recipient. God is the one to speak in the Qurʾan" (Abdel Haleem 2004, xv). An elaboration of the different ideologies around scriptural languages in the Judaic and Judeo-Christian traditions is beyond the scope of this book. Nevertheless, it is worth noting that ongoing theological investigation into the idea of an Adamic language, the origin of all languages, led some Church fathers to formulate proto-nationalist ideologies (Olender 1992; 1997).

10. In his introduction to his English translation of the Qurʾan, Mohammed Abdel Haleem formulates this latter view as follows: "Arabic grammar was developed to serve the Qurʾan, the study of Arabic phonetics was pursued in order to determine the exact pronunciation of Qurʾanic words, the science of Arabic rhetoric was developed in order to describe the features of the inimitable style of the Qurʾan, the art of Arabic calligraphy was cultivated through writing down the Qurʾan" (2004, ix). Abdel Haleem presents the language as a more neutral medium whose harmonization with historical social time has allowed it to develop and transform so as to respond to emerging realities.

11. These clarifications complicate and enrich two threads of sociolinguistic research. On the one side, Charles Ferguson's (1959) fruitful reflections on "diglossia" tend to naturalize the distance between low and high variants in Arabic and understate the fluidity between the two registers. On the other side, sociolinguists who helpfully historicized Arabic language ideologies have generally favored an analysis of intellectuals and their works. While informative, these cannot be assumed to represent the lived experience of other speakers.

12. The Arabic language became the "core ingredient and the most prominent manifestation of nationalism" (Suleiman 1994, 3) and of anti-colonial and modernizing campaigns during the late nineteenth and twentieth centuries across the region. The singularity of the term "Arabic" notwithstanding, this language assumed a number of meanings, at times foregrounding its ethnic angle—largely the work of Christian minorities and secularist figures—and at others appealing to the continuity of an Arabo-Islamic civilization, which was usually the mission of reformist Muslim scholars and nationalists who shared their perspective.

13. The same traits informed rearticulations of Islam across the region. In Turkey, the biography of Hayrettin Karaman, key advocate of the religiously oriented imam-hatip schools, highlights his insistence on Arabic literacy as the key element in moral cultivation. To this purpose, he wrote a number of Arabic textbooks and Turkish-Arabic dictionaries (Özgür 2011).

14. During the formative years of the anti-colonial campaign, the nationalist press defended the monarchical privilege with rigor: "The King is there for us; he incarnates continuity, permanence and the nation" (Aouchar 1990).

15. Some of these dynamics informed political institutions in the Jordanian, Saudi Arabian, and Syrian states (Anderson 2005; al-Rasheed 1996; and Wedeen 1999).

16. As did the Alawite campaign, the Hashemite dynasty controlled the writing of history in Jordan thus ensuring that history schoolbooks characterized the Jordanian nation as "radiating out from and dependent upon the Hashemite Kings" (Anderson 2001, 5).

17. This is an extract from the *Hymne Chérifien*, the anthem of the Kingdom of Morocco. Léo Morgan composed the anthem before independence, but Ali Squali Husseini wrote new lyrics for it in 1970. The singing of the national anthem concludes each morning assembly.

18. These groups referenced the Qur'an in order to defame the King as *"al-ṭāghūt"* (the impious tyrant) and bore the brunt of state repression (Slyomovics 2005, 169).

19. It is remarkable that even secular supporters of Arabization I spoke with found no better ally to their advocacy than the PJD. They published their views in the PJD-affiliated press and interacted with party members inside associations for the protection of the Arabic language.

20. By complicating Jack Goody's (1968) idea of a society that achieved literacy by using learning practices through recitation, Brinkley Messick invites us to understand this type of religious learning as "a fully realized type of civilizational literacy in Muslim societies" (1993, 24). This is an important reformulation of both pedagogy and literacy so long as it does not exaggerate the impact of literacy in the redefinition of socio-political and moral hierarchies.

21. Scholars of Islam have insisted that contemporary religious subjectivity emerges out of a complex interaction with distinctly modern institutions, such as the bureaucratic state and novel modes of communication (see Wagner and Lotfi 1980; Zeghal 1999; Hefner and Zaman 2007; Kadi and Billeh 2007). This scholarship has worked hard to dispel bias toward religious institutions such as the *madrasa* within the post-9/11 landscape. Its exploration of the content and pedagogical methods of moral cultivation has encouraged many to revisit widely held positions about the mechanical, non-rational, and demagogical nature of traditional or religious education (Boyle 2004). However, its ethnographic focus has provided an incomplete picture of the moral projects of young people today, most of whom spend their day in public school classrooms.

22. An excellent illustration of this analytical stance is Ayala Fader's (2009) account of the socialization of Hasidic Jewish girls in Brooklyn.

23. In his review of Marcel Mauss's concept of disciplinary practices, which was the precursor to textualist theories of subjectivation, Abdellah Hammoudi (2009b) argues that understanding Mauss as favoring mechanistic practice is incorrect. For Hammoudi, Mauss foregrounds an experiential-phenomenological dimension of practice in which totality or perfection is an aspiration and not an achievement (2009b, 29–31).

24. Language training and language ideology make apparent the fact that Asad's (1986a) model of "discursive tradition," based on Michel Foucault's "discursive formation" (1972), emerges most naturally out of analyzing textual practices—that is writing and reading. These textual practices favor the perspective that reading texts brings about their internalization or otherwise their embodiment. Admittedly, this perspective is more successful in making visible the intentions of authoritative discourses than analyzing the unfolding of these intentions. Furthermore, in this analytical operation, the subject becomes "form and not substance" (Foucault, 1997, 290; Mahmood, 2005, 121), and the opportunity for self-reflexivity that probes the limits of the tradition (or formation) appears limited. Charles Hirschkind (2001b, 640) has sought intermediate spaces between form and substance—I refer to his use of the "sensorium" to discuss the sensory capacities that support piety—helpfully reintroducing the dynamic of "being in the world" in the analysis of piety. It is important to highlight, however, that being in the world entails extremely contradictory experiences that may halt or considerably redirect pious projects.

5. ONCE UPON A TIME, THERE WAS A HAPPY OLD BERBER COUPLE

1. The title of the unit was "*Binyat al-Qasīda al-Hadāthiyya*" (The Structure of the Modern Poem) (*al-Mumtāz fī al-Lugha al-'Arabiyya*, 76).

2. Mahmud Darwish (1941–2007), born in Birwa, experienced displacement and later confinement within Israeli territories. He is widely considered the voice of the Palestinian struggle for statehood and received numerous prizes for his poetry. In addition to his cultural contributions, he was a member of the Israeli Communist Party and served as a member of the Executive Committee of the Palestinian Liberation Organization (PLO). He drafted the "Palestinian Declaration of Independence" that the head of PLO Yasser Arafat proclaimed in 1988. In 1993, he resigned from the PLO because of his disagreement with the Oslo Accords.

3. The translation is my own.

4. The pedagogical format of the Arab Literature class is similar to that of the French class: it consists of textual analysis with comprehension questions, vocabulary clarification, and written summaries of passages.

5. Tellingly, in an interview given to the *New York Times* in December 22, 2001, Darwish singles out the poem "*Ilā Ummī*" as one that readers over-interpret by seeing the mother figure only as a metonym for the nation: "My readers expect something from me, but I write as a poet, and in my poetry a woman is a woman, a mother is a mother, and the sea is the sea" (Darwish 2002, 69).

6. We can consider the connection between poetry recitation and national sentiment as a process of structuration. By structuration, I refer to the way "abstract principles of legitimation are vested with an emotional impact, sufficient to foster action" (Hammoudi 1997, 154). Structuration does not happen in a void, but rather, as Bénéï argues, "draws upon existing and evolving structures of feeling and material constitutive of ordinary social actors' repertoires of public culture and popular knowledge" (2008, 141). Certainly, the process of structuration neither precludes critical awareness nor the possibility of partial engagement.

7. Khaïr-Eddine's interview with Bernard Pivot for the famous talk show *Apostrophes* is highly indicative of a metropolitan French articulation of difference in the 1980s. Not only does the show collapse various novelistic treatments of difference by grouping to-

gether novelists from Mali (no less than Maryse Condé), New Caledonia, China, and the United States but it also expresses its moral distance from this difference in the evocative title "Autres lieux, autres moeurs" (Other Places, Other Mores) (Khaïr-Eddine 1984a).

8. On one level, the publication aimed at reconfiguring Moroccan culture by valorizing cultural production in all of Morocco's languages (Bouanani 1966). On another level, *Souffles* was a third-worldist endeavor. It endorsed movements of liberation across the geographical spectrum that did not align with Cold War arrangements, and it adopted a Marxist-Leninist vision of social justice and economic redistribution.

9. In a televised speech that followed the suppression of student manifestations in Casablanca in 1965, the trial of 2,000 demonstrators, and the declaration of the state of emergency, King Hassan II accused public high schools of being "a space for training in contestation" (Sefriouri 2013, 56).

10. The preamble to the 1962 constitution declared, "The Kingdom of Morocco is a fully sovereign Islamic country whose language is Arabic and that partakes in the greater Maghrib region" (*al-dustūr* 1962).

11. "The Committee . . . encourages the State party to consider making the Amazigh language an official language under the Moroccan Constitution, and to provide literacy training for the Amazigh in their own language" (UN Committee on the Elimination of Racial Discrimination 2010).

12. Replacing state intentionality with historical convergence is important because it both attributes responsibility to the state for the handling of diversity and eschews easy formulations of state conspiracy, which risk undermining the active role Berbers have played in their pursuit of recognition and ignoring the global scale on which questions of liberalism, democracy, and diversity play out.

13. Sociological scholarship has often celebrated the synthesis of minority claims with a liberal vision that would portend political democratization. Earlier understandings of Berber tribal organization as egalitarian (Gellner and Micaud 1972) gave way to more recent articulations of the harmonization of the transnational Amazigh movement with Western liberal values. The shared aspiration of transnational Amazigh activism, the international community, and this scholarship was that "universal" liberal humanism would, by virtue of its detachment from Arabo-Muslim values, overcome "the formerly inviolable sanctity of a state's internal affairs" (Maddy-Weitzman 2006, 75).

14. In Algeria, the Arabization policy that accompanied the development of mass-based schooling in the 1960s and 1970s led to the shared experience of oppression by an entire generation of Berber Kabyles, who were banned from speaking and writing in their language inside pedagogical institutions. Conversely, the same schooling experience provided the intellectual means through which Berber Kabyles pressed for empowerment and representation through language advocacy (Goodman 2004). Consequently, when the police prevented intellectual and poet Mouloud Mammeri from giving a lecture on Berber poetry at Hasnaou University in Tizi-Ouzou on March 10, 1980, Kabyle demonstrators were deeply aware of how language and cultural production linked with governance in the post-independence state. The Berber Spring (*Tafsut Imazighen*) that ensued from this incident was not just a defense of the Kabyle culture and of claims to self-determination: it was a more generalized demand for a plural domain of deliberation—in short nothing less than democratization. The definition of the name *Imazighen* (free men), first adopted by Paris-based Kabyle activists, harnessed earlier tautologies between the

community and liberal modes of governance as a basis for cultural pride and political representation. The same scholars founded the *Agraw Imazighen* (Berber Academy for Cultural Exchange and Research) in 1967 (Silverstein 2004, 71).

15. Despite the fact that both the nationalist movement and the Army of Liberation against French occupation in 1955 had a strong Berber component, anxiety about the possibly Christianized and French-assimilated Berbers persisted. Notably, the *Istiqlāl*-led government physically destroyed the *Collège Berbère d'Azrou* along with most of its matriculation records (Benhlal 2005, 116).

16. Conversations about overlapping regional affiliations point to the indeterminacy of the image of Morocco. In this respect, Morocco can be no more Arabo-Muslim than it is Berber, because it emerges as a configuration of debates about community and belonging. Through an interrogation of Arab-ness and *Amazighité* as cultural politics, I advance a critique about anthropology's own regionalism, which has tended to reproduce certain categories of belonging (such as the Arab world) without problematizing their political substratum (Fardon 1990; Navaro-Yashin 2002; Guyer 2004).

17. The shutting down in 2010 of [dar.] *Nīchāne* (Straight Ahead, Directly), the arabophone equivalent of the weekly magazine *Tel Quel* (As Is), is the most publicized case. Since its founding in 2006, *Nīchāne* was the target of two lawsuits, one for publishing Moroccan popular jokes in *dārija* and one for addressing an open letter to King Mohammed VI in *dārija*. Supporters of *Nīchāne* have argued that its persecution and eventual closure, the result of the withdrawal of its advertisers, reveal that the democratic Moroccan state prohibits the dissemination of critique in the most widely spoken register in the country (see Miller 2012).

18. As we saw in earlier chapters, the Arabo-Muslim cultural narrative nourishes this authority. In 1999, a high school teacher in Casablanca translated the Qurʾan into *Tamazight*. In 2003, the translation was banned from publication. This incident received considerable publicity abroad, to the extent that *The Economist* commented, "His translation risks undermining the authority of Morocco's religious establishment and its papal potentate, King Hassan, the Commander of the Faithful" (Ben Layashi 2007, 165). The article made straightforward the connection between the de-sacralization of Arabic and the undermining of political authority.

19. UNESCO has consistently pushed this line of advocacy, as manifest in the message of Director-General Irina Bokova on the occasion of International Mother Language Day, February 21, 2011.

20. Mohammed Chafik, author of the *Berber Manifesto* (2001) and later the first rector of IRCAM, produced most of his writings about Amazigh identity in *fuṣḥā*. Despite accepting the symbolic value of the Arabic language, Chafik opposes Arabization: "The Arabic language is respected because it is associated with the Qurʾan, but at no point was it understood that Arabization was a condition of religious faith as is required by some Islamist intellectuals" (Ben Layashi 2007, 34). Moving even further from the state-sanctioned cultural narrative, , other activists have criticized the connection between Arabic and Islam, arguing that Arabic pre-dated Islam and that the tautology contradicts the universality of the religion (Rachik 2006, 35).

21. In this light, it is no wonder that the international community did not react to the abnormalities of the Moroccan state's rushed and controlled constitutional reform in June 2011 nor to the ambiguities of the new constitution that ratified some changes in decision-

making structure at the same time as it solidified monarchical control (Slyomovics 2011; Benchemsi 2012).

22. Rural berberophone students face additional challenges to academic progress because many classrooms accommodate multiple levels and students have labor obligations that cause them to miss school (Buckner 2006). Furthermore, the promotion of standardized *Tamazight* does not seem to reduce the bias that arabophone speakers show toward Berber language and culture by associating them with rurality, backwardness, and poverty (Errihani 2008).

23. The drama of celebrating some types of diversity and designating other types as repugnant plays out in contemporary Israel and Turkey, where Mizrahi Jews (Lavie 2011) and Jewish Turks (Brink-Danan 2011), respectively, develop complex choreographies of public effacement and private differentiation. These choreographies force their complicity with majority values already held as mainstream and common.

24. Prashad (2005) argues that, in the aftermath of the Civil Rights Act (1964) and its erasure of racial discrimination in legislative terms, the welfare state that would theoretically guarantee equality to heretofore second-class citizens was moving to a drastic remodeling along neoliberal lines. As the state shifted from the redistribution of tax revenue to enacting provisions that would benefit all citizens, it made achievement and integration of the diverse populations—according to color, class, region, gender—dependent on their own merit and determination. Yet for the already underprivileged, material and structural inequalities seriously impeded their participation in the competition for resources, and entrepreneurship remained an uneven upward struggle.

25. An interesting comparison can be made between Morocco and Tunisia under Ben Ali between 1987 and 2011 (Murphy 1998; Sadiki 2002).

6. DESIRES IN LANGUAGES

* This transliteration of *dārija* relates to an online writing code that I explore in this chapter. It is distinct from the transliteration style I apply to *dārija* in the rest of this book.

1. The most popular medium for cyber sociality at the time of my fieldwork in 2007–2009 was MSN, an instant messaging service by Microsoft. Gradually, *Facebook* and *Twitter* and a plethora of blogs have replaced MSN.

2. See Abu-Lughod (1993); Larkin (1997); Armbrust (1998); and Masquelier (2009). The category of youth does not assume a universal developmental phase, but rather a position of anticipation of social integration that is now prolonged because of the actualities of economic precariousness.

3. The title of this chapter, which fits well with my intention to interrogate romantic desire in relation to French speaking, also alludes to another work by Kristeva, *Desire in Language: A Semiotic Approach to Literature and Art* (1980). In addition to its enticing title, Kristeva's portrayal of the speaking self mediates my understanding of the potential of desire to disturb normativity. In this chapter, I approach desire as a fracturing, confusing, and multiplying force, not as the original *jouissance* of Freud or the unfettered bodily energy of Kristeva (Butler 1990, 93). In fact, I avoid any definition of the subject along structural or psychoanalytic lines, both of which have been foundational to postmodern, as well as postcolonial theory. Instead, I draw inspiration from the open-ended definition of subjectivity along the ethnographic lines that Biehl et al. propose: "the agonistic and practical activity of

engaging identity and fate, patterned and felt in historically contingent settings and mediated by a constellation of institutional processes and cultural forms" (2007, 5).

4. 2M was founded in 1989 by the then-largest Moroccan economic conglomerate, ONA. In 1996, the major shareholder of the station, SOREAD, sold most of its shares to the Moroccan government, which incorporated the station into the Moroccan Broadcasting Network.

5. The expression is a reworking of the Egyptian phrase *wilād al-nās* (children of the people) that originally referred to the children of the Mamluk aristocracy. This phrase came to describe the offspring of those of elevated social backgrounds as the antonym to *ibn al-balad* (son of the country), which describes the offspring of those with more populist backgrounds (Petersen 2011, 107).

6. The concepts of female shame and male honor have a long history in the literature of the Mediterranean and the Middle East, as well as in feminist scholarship more broadly. Kawtar's call for *ḥshūma* bears obvious connections to issues of gender ideology and behavior that abound in these two scholarships. I am nonetheless cautious about neatly associating this ethnographic scene with this body of work because of the tentative, shifting, and multiple dimensions of gender identity that I witnessed among the Moroccan youth I knew. Observing these dimensions brought me in agreement with certain critiques of those scholarships as veering toward the analysis of idealized and public discourses on gender (Kandiyoti 1994; Lindsfarne 1994).

7. Bakhtin uses the term "heteroglossia" to describe "a multiplicity of social voices and a wide variety of their links and their interrelationships" (1986, 263) that underpin the novel as cultural product. In this light, *Studio 2M* is hardly heteroglossic because it excludes not only certain voices, such as Berber, but it also prevents comprehension through its omission of translation between languages.

8. Moroccan filmmakers have presented other equally daring portrayals of moral transgression through feature films, such as *Ali Zaoua* (dir. Nabil Ayouch 2000) and *Casanegra* (dir. Nour-Eddine Lakhmari 2008), which dramatize the topics of street culture, criminality, drug use, pedophilia, and rape. Yet neither of these films presents sexuality and recreational drugs as enticingly as *Marock*. Also, both films feature dialogues in *dārija* in contrast to the *Marock* script that is predominantly in French. It is both for its beguiling depiction of such lifestyles and its heavy use of French that *Marock* was censored across the spectrum— Abdellillah Benkirane (then minister for the PJD party) criticized the film for religious reasons, and secretary general of the Moroccan Theater Syndicate, Mohammed Hassan El, Joundi, attacked the film for veering dangerously away from tradition (Khannous 2010, 53).

9. Abu-Lughod sees Egyptian melodramas as one of multiple state technologies "for staging interiorities" (2000, 89). She maintains that these melodramas produce, rather than reflect, images of the self in accordance with national values. Armbrust (1999) understands scenes of moral transgression on Egyptian media, usually performed by an iconic bourgeoisie, as "significant sites of social experimentation" (1999, 102). These sites, he argues, are not simply a functional space of "controlled release" (1999, 102), but are indications of the self-reflexive role that mass media have played in the exploration of Egyptian modernization.

10. Analyses of the film *Marock* as a cultural product (Edwards 2007; Babana-Hampton 2010) have sensitively explored the many levels on which the film unsettled the binaries of gender, religion, and concepts of nativeness versus foreignness. However, from the point of view of its consumption by public school youth, the film represented forms of

marginalization and transgression that overshadowed the nuanced messages *Marock* communicated.

11. A similar disjuncture caught the attention of Marwan Kraidy, who criticizes the equivalent singing contest in Lebanon in the following terms: "[It] stages an apparently fair competition whose participants count on their personal initiative, creativity and skills, and whose winners are determined by a popular vote. This reality is discordant with that of most young Arabs, who are prevented from expressing their opinions, who get their jobs because of connections and rarely because of competence, and where power is wielded arbitrarily by unelected rulers and officials" (2005, 20).

12. Many such works narrate the coming of age of Maghribian youth inside the colonial French educational system. Widely known examples across Morocco, Algeria, and Tunisia are Driss Chraibi's *Le passé simple* (Simple Past) 1952; Albert Memmi's *La statue de sel* (Pillar of Salt) 1953; Kateb Yacine's *Nedjma* (Nedjma) 1956; and Djebar's *L'amour, la fantasia* (Fantasia, an Algerian Cavalcade) 1985. What makes some of these works fascinating is that they experiment with the norms of the genres of fiction, autobiography, and essay writing. Yet it is precisely their play with genre that makes it even harder to discern when they adopt the insignia of postmodern criticism and therefore invite the reader to view them both as data and as theoretical scrutiny.

13. In his text, Derrida addresses Khatibi directly. He is shocked that Khatibi would not only qualify Arabic as his mother tongue, thereby forgetting the political dimensions of this language, but would also claim ownership of this mother tongue at the very moment of its loss: "*Il évoque une langue d'origine qui l'a peut être perdu, certes, mais qu'il n'a pas perdu. Il garde ce qui l'a perdu*" (He [Khatibi] evokes a language of origin that has perhaps lost him but that he himself has not lost. He keeps what has lost him) (1996, 64). Derrida argues that French can only very ambiguously constitute his mother tongue. As a language arriving and regulated from the metropolis, French is anything but natural (1996, 72). Therefore, French is both the language of the other and the inevitable language of the self, a predicament of double alienation that is distinct from Khatibi's double presence.

14. Arabophone Moroccan literature has engaged with extensive experimentation: this experimentation variously involved tailoring *fuṣḥā* to communicate Moroccan subjectivities, making *dārija* part of written arabophone expression, and even writing exclusively in *dārija* for wider consumption (Allen 2006; 2011). As examples of this process, I mention Abdel Majid Ben Jelloun, *Fī al-ṭufūla* (In Childhood) 2006 [1957]; Mohammed Berrada, *Luʿbāt al-nisyān* (Games of Forgetting) (1987); Ahmed al-Tawfiq, *Jārāt Abī Mūsā* (Abu Musa's Women Neighbors) (1997); and Youssouf Amine Elalamy, *Tqarqib al-nab* (Chattering Teeth) (2006)—a novel written in "literary *dārija*."

15. McClintock contends that, although the colonizer-colonized axis marginalized the particular plight of women, post-colonialism as a theoretical gesture furthered this marginalization by forgetting that "the national bourgeoisies and kleptocracies that stepped into the shoes of post-colonial progress and industrialized modernization have been dominant overwhelming and violently male" (1992, 92).

16. Algerian novelist Assia has insisted that francophonie was instrumental to her female colonial experience. Led in hand by her father to the French school in Constantine, the narrator of her novel *L'Amour, la Fantasia* (1985) defies social and cultural norms and thus separates herself from the women of her tribe. Although she often romanticizes the orality of the Algerian vernaculars (1999), Djebar wrestles with the elite social position

that language mastery gave her with regard to other Algerian women. She visualizes her distance in her documentary *La nouba des femmes du Mont Chenoua* (1977), in which she interviews rural illiterate women with whom she has trouble communicating because she does not speak Berber.

17. Using a Lacanian disruption of Saussurian linguistics, Bhabha deconstructs the linguistic "sign" as a fixed unit of signification and affirms the potential of a mobile "signifier" to multiply and individuate the production of meaning. From this foundation, Bhabha discusses conditions of "hybridity," "mimicry," and "mockery" in the writings of colonial administrators and of subaltern anglophone and francophone authors in an effort to "locate the post-colonial subject within the play of the subaltern instance of writing" (1994, 59). My contention with Bhabha is that he does not adequately recognize that, for mimicry to become at once "resemblance and menace" (1994, 86), the native has to be anglicized though remain decidedly non-English. His essay that raises the issue of language competence most succinctly is "Of Mimicry and Man; the Ambivalence of Colonial Discourse" (1994, 85–92). There, Bhabha explores the classification of competence among "natives," showing that colonial intermediaries such as teachers and translators assumed power over their monolingual fellow citizens.

18. In addition to revealing the positioned responses of an audience toward a specific staging of Moroccan society and culture, TV consumption redirects our attention to mass-mediated culture. The commercial nature of this artifact and its inability to reach an international audience due to linguistic and content constraints have made it peripheral to analyses of Third World cultural production, even of that which has claimed a place inside First World academic institutions (Jameson 1984; Ahmad 1987; Appiah 1991). Although this canon of Third World cultural production, mostly literary, has celebrated creativity in geographical settings that hitherto received little international attention, it has shown contempt for the role of mass media as key cultural institutions (Armburst 1996). Hence, this canon has largely concealed the extent to which it propagates its own set of selection criteria, criteria that have prevented a general audience from thinking of the Third World as deeply differentiated, beset with the challenges of global capitalism, and structured through hierarchies engineered nationally and transnationally.

19. I consider this sample to be the linguistic outcome of our mutual effort to communicate and not as the elucidation of the rules of the new code, which has grown exponentially in the last few years (Daoudi and Murphy 2011). I intentionally did not make grammatical or spelling corrections to emphasize that, in the context in which the discussion took place, spelling rules often go unsanctioned.

20. De Certeau focuses on the Saussurian separation of *parole* (speech) from *langue* (language), which allows him to unhinge the individual action from the institutions that have bound it. If speaking is the temporal appropriation of a linguistic code, then acting in the everyday engages in a constant redefinition of norms and rules against the horizon of power relations. Because there is no moment in time where *la langue* (structure) is not in motion, De Certeau makes the *parole* (speech) the starting point of theory. From there, culture arises from events instead of from overarching structural frameworks. My disagreement with de Certeau lies in his conviction that the act of manipulation is aware of its incapacity for cultural transformation: "The actual order of things is precisely what 'popular' tactics turn to their own ends without any illusion that it will change anytime soon" (1984, 26). At this point, structuralist and post-structuralist perspectives on creativ-

ity reach their theoretical limit and serve the students of this chapter poorly. This is because the linguistic landscape these students address is neither as integrated nor as hegemonic as the metaphor of *la langue* (metaphor for structure) would have us assume.

7. OUT OF CLASS, INTO THE STREET

1. This imbrication does not automatically reify the too neat dichotomies of colonizer-colonized within the domain of development, nor does it assume that colonialism and development have been exclusive frames of reference in people's lives. In fact, a large body of anthropological work has focused on the unexpected appropriations of development projects by their targeted "developing" populations, proving that no political agenda is able to fully control its own intentions (Taussig 1980; Manzo 1991; Pigg 1992).

2. Akin to researchers engaged in post-colonial studies, cultural historians of colonial and of post-independence Maghrib have dissected the ways in which the French colonial project of modernity informed nationalist rhetoric and decolonizing efforts (Berque 1978; Vermeren 2002; Segalla 2009). This research has helpfully singled out France's civilizational agenda as a specific genre of imperialism, which in turn enabled particular strategies of resistance. It has also foregrounded the ideological motivations behind nationalist education programs as they interacted with the fabrication of a labor force. However, this research has generally not addressed the interface between nationalist and international development initiatives or the latest transmutations of cultural policy during neoliberal reform.

3. Timothy Mitchell's (2002) trenchant critique of development expertise has pointed out that the diagnostics of international organizations shift issues of governance to managerial and technical concerns, which, in their turn, necessitate the financial involvement and expertise of these same organizations. Mitchell insightfully disentangles privatization and the free market from a common understanding of a break with the nation-state, revealing instead that the free market sustains the social and economic inequality set up by nationalist regimes. His work challenges international development not from the angle of its effectiveness, but from its own self-definition as international, showing it to be an exchange between the Egyptian state and the United States. Nonetheless, Mitchell inadvertently reifies a dominant view of development as the reorganization of economic activity, choosing the domain of rural subsistence as his space of critical exploration. It is in a different book, *Colonizing Egypt* (1988), that Mitchell traces colonial expertise within educational restructuring; this work suggests but does not explicitly address the continuities between colonial and development intervention.

4. This intellectual oscillation between order and disorder reveals more succinctly how partial or unpredictable the conservation of hierarchy can be inside and outside educational environments. James Ferguson's (1993) analysis of development projects in Lesotho provides an interesting reading of the unpredictability of hierarchy. His perspective draws on Paul Willis's (1977) seminal work on working-class youth in Manchester. The parallel between development projects and public education is significant, because it indicates that neither education nor development have fulfilled the predictions of Western enlightenment.

5. Bearing this larger role of education in mind, Bourgois states, "I never set foot inside a school or interviewed either teachers or administrators, and only very rarely encountered formally enrolled students. Nevertheless, I consider my crack dealer conversations to be a school ethnography" (1996, 251).

6. Varenne corroborates this point: "It may not be too extreme to reverse the association between cultural arbitrariness and embodiment: the deeper a cultural form may be embodied, the more likely it is that it will make itself open to deliberation as the world of experience imposes itself and reveals the gap between the form and what it seeks to deal with. It is Christians who keep reforming Christianity. And it is school people who will reform schooling" (2008, 363).

7. Amy Stambach's (2000) study of high schools in Mount Kilimanjaro defines the public school through the terms of the specific investment the community attributes to it. Taking as a starting point that schools are not inherently, as developmental positivism would have it, mechanisms for social change, Stambach defines her topic "not, in the first instance, as a picture of what schooling on Kilimanjaro is all about, but as a glimpse of some of the ways we, as human beings, variably organize social life around and through educational institutions" (2000, 5). Fida Adely's (2009) research among high school girls in North Jordan addresses a range of expected and unexpected investments in the public school that defy international development logic regarding the life trajectories of educated women. Although the girls Adely worked with appreciated and invested in their education as an entry to the public sphere and as access to the realm of ideas, they were unsure about the social potential, as well as social risks, of professional engagement: "Everyone seemed to agree with the oft-repeated phrase that, 'a diploma was a weapon in the hand of a girl'. But a weapon for what?" (2009, 115).

REFERENCES

Abdel Haleem, Muhammad A.S. 2004. *The Qur'an: A New Translation*. Oxford: Oxford University Press.

Abrams, Philip. 1988 [1977]. "Notes on the Difficulty of Studying the State." *Journal of Historical Sociology* 1 (1): 58–89.

Abu-Lughod, Lila. 1989. "Bedouins, Cassettes and Technologies of Public Culture." *Middle East Report* 159 (4): 7–11.

———. 1993. "Finding a Place for Islam: Egyptian Television Serials and the National Interest." *Public Culture* 5 (3): 493–513.

———. 2000. "Modern Subjects: Egyptian Melodrama and Postcolonial Difference." In *Questions of Modernity*, edited by Timothy Mitchell, 87–114. Minneapolis: University of Minnesota Press.

al-Achaari, Mohamed. 2010. *Al-qaws wa-l-farāsha*. Casablanca: al-markaz al-thaqāfī al-ʿarabī. Translated by Aida Bamia as *The Arch and the Butterfly*. 2011. London: Bloomsbury Qatar Foundation Publishing.

Adam, André. 1963. *Une enquête auprès de la jeunesse musulmane du Maroc* [Inquiry into Young Muslim Youth in Morocco]. Aix-En-Provence: La Pensée Universitaire.

Adely, Fida. 2009. "Educating Women for Development: The Arab Human Development Report 2005 and the Problem with Women's Choices." *International Journal of Middle East Studies* 41(1): 105–122.

———. 2012. *Gendered Paradoxes: Educating Jordanian Women in Nation, Faith, and Progress*. Chicago: University of Chicago Press.

African Development Bank. 2013. *Analyse du système de l'education et formation: Maroc* [Analysis of the Educational and Training Sector: Morocco]. Accessed September 30, 2014. http://www.afdb.org/fileadmin/uploads/afdb/Documents/Project-and-Operations/Maroc_-_Analyse_du_Syst%C3%A8me_d%E2%80%99%C3%A9ducation_et_de_formation.pdf

Ageron, Charles R. 1960. "La France a-t-elle une politique Kabyle?" [Does France Have a Kabyle Policy?] *Revue historique* 223: 311–352.

Agnaou, Fatima. 2004. *Gender, Literacy, and Empowerment in Morocco*. New York: Routledge.

Ahearn, Laura M. 2001. "Language and Agency." *Annual Review of Anthropology* 30: 109–137.

Ahmad, Aijaz. 1987. "Jameson's Rhetoric of Otherness and the 'National Allegory.'" *Social Text* 17: 3–25.

al-Aissati, Abderrahman, Suzanne Karsmakers, and Jeanne Kurvers. 2011. "'We Are All Beginners': Amazigh in Language Policy and Educational Practice in Morocco." *Compare* 41 (2): 211–227.

Akhchichine, Ahmed. 2008. *"Education: La réforme victime de la politique"* [Education: The Reform Victim to Politics], interview by Saloua Mansouri. *Challenge Hebdo*, April 26–May 2, 36–39.

al-Alawi, Mohammed al-Sadis. 2001. *"Discours prononcé par S.M le Roi Mohammed VI à Ajdir, Khénifra"* [His Royal Highness King Mohammed VI's Speech in Ajdir, Khenifra]. *Ircam.ma*, October 17. Accessed February 2, 2015. http://www.ircam.ma/fr/index.php?soc=ircam&rd=20

——. 2013. *"Khiṭāb al-malik Mohammed al-sādis bi-munāsabat al-dhikrā al-sittūn li-thawrat al-malik wa-l-shaʿb"* [King Mohamed VI's Speech on the Occasion of the 60th Anniversary from the Joint Insurrection of King and People]. *Assdae.com*, August 20. Accessed November 20, 2013. http://www.assdae.com/23943

Allen, Roger. 2006. "Lords of Misrule: History and Fiction in Two Moroccan Novels." *Middle Eastern Literatures incorporating Edebiyat* 9 (2): 199–209.

——. 2011. "Rewriting Literary History: The Case of Moroccan Fiction in Arabic." *Journal of North African Studies* 16 (3): 311–324.

Althusser, Louis. 1993 [1970]. *Essays on Ideology*. Translated by Ben Brewster. London: Verso.

Anderson, Benedict. 1983. *Imagined Communities: Reflections on the Origin and Spread of Nationalism*. London: Verso.

Anderson, Betty S. 2001. "Writing the Nation: Textbooks of the Hashemite Kingdom of Jordan." *Comparative Studies of South Asia, Africa, and the Middle East* 21 (1): 5–14.

——. 2005. *Nationalist Voices in Jordan: The Street and the State*. Austin: University of Texas Press.

Anderson, Warwick, and Hans Pols. 2012. "Scientific Patriotism: Medical Science and National Self-Fashioning in Southeast Asia." *Comparative Studies in Society and History* 54 (1): 93–113.

Anouilh, Jean. C. 1946. *Antigone*. Paris: La Table Ronde.

Aouchar, Amina. 1990 *La presse marocaine dans la lutte pour l'indépendance (1933–1956)* [The Moroccan Press in the Struggle for Independence (1933–1956)]. Casablanca: Wallada.

Aouragh, Myriem. 2012. *Palestine Online*. London: I. B. Tauris.

Appiah, Anthony K. 1991. "Is the Post- in Postmodernism and Post- in Postcolonial?" *Critical Inquiry* 17 (2): 336–357.

Armbrust, Walter. 1996. *Mass Culture and Modernism in Egypt*. Cambridge: Cambridge University Press.

——. 1998. "When the Lights Go Down in Cairo: Cinema as Secular Ritual." *Visual Anthropology* 10 (2–4): 413–442.

———. 1999. "Bourgeois Leisure and Egyptian Media Fantasies." In *New Media in the Muslim World*, edited by Dale Eickelman and Jon Anderson, 102–128. Bloomington: Indiana University Press.

Arnaud, Jacqueline. 1976. "*Le roman maghrébin en question chez Khaïr-Eddine, Boudjedra, Tahar Benjelloun.*" *Revue de l'Occident musulman et de la Méditerranée* 22 (1): 59–68.

Asad, Talal. 1986a. "The Idea of an Anthropology of Islam." Center for Contemporary Arab Studies, Occasional Paper Series. Washington, DC: Georgetown University.

———. 1986b. "The Concept of Cultural Translation in British Social Anthropology." In *Writing Culture: The Poetics and Politics of Ethnography*, edited by James and George E. Marcus, 141–164. Berkeley: University of California Press.

Ayouch, Nabil, dir. 2000. *Ali Zaoua*. 90 min. USA: Arab Film Distribution.

Babana-Hampton, Safoi. 2010. "Bringing into Focus Narrative Text and Subtext in Moroccan Film: *Marock's* Hors-Champ." *Journal of North African Studies* 15 (3): 289–303.

Badimon, Montserrat, and Koenraad Bogaert. 2014. "The State Owes Us a Future: The Framing of 'Exclusion' by the Protest Movements of the Unemployed in Morocco." In *From Silence to Protest: International Perspectives on Weakly Resourced Groups*, edited by Didier Chabanet and Frédéric Royall, 175–192. Farnham: Ashgate.

Bakhtin, Mikhail. 1986. *Speech Genres and Other Essays*, edited by Caryl Emerson and Michael Holquist, translated by Vern W. McGee. Austin: University of Texas Press.

Barthes, Roland. 1993. "Myth Today." In *A Roland Barthes Reader*, edited by Susan Sontag, translated by Annette Lavers, 93–149. London: Vintage Books.

Bauman, Richard, and Charles Briggs. 2000. "Language Philosophy as Language Ideology: John Locke and Johann Gottfried Herder." In *Regimes of Languages: Ideologies, Polities and Identities*, edited by Paul Kroskrity, 139–204. Santa Fe: School of American Research Press.

Bayat, Asef, and Linda Herrera, eds. 2010. *Being Young and Muslim: New Cultural Politics in the Global South and North*. Oxford: Oxford University Press.

Belal, Abdellaziz. 1969. "*La résistance palestinienne et le mouvement révolutionnaire mondiale*" [Palestinian Resistance and the Global Revolution Movement]. *Souffles: revue poétique et littéraire* 15:38–42.

Belbashir al-Housseini, Mohammed. 2008. "*Ḥiwarāt: taʿrīb al-taʿlīm . . . Ujhiḍa thalāth marāt bal w qubila manqūṣan li-takthīr khuṣūmihi*" [Dialogues: The Arabization of Education . . . Failed three times and got accepted despite some gaps for the multiplication of its adversaries]." *Al-Tajdīd*, January 14, 3.

Belfkih, Abdelaziz M. 2000. "*La Charte Nationale d'Éducation-Formation*" [National Charter for Education and Training]. *Revue internationale d'éducation de Sèvres* 27:77–87.

Benchemsi, Ahmed. 2012. "Morocco: Outfoxing the Opposition." *Journal of Democracy* 23 (1): 57–69.

Bénéï, Veronique. 2008. *Schooling Passions: Nation, History, and Language in Contemporary Western India*. Stanford, CA: Stanford University Press.

Benhlal, Mohammed. 2005. *Le collège d'Azrou: Une élite berbère civile et militaire au Maroc, 1927–1959* [The College of Azrou: A Berber Military and Civil Elite in Morocco 1927–1959]. Paris: Editions Karthala.

Benjamin, Walter. 1968 [1955]. "The Task of the Translator." In *Illuminations: Essays and Reflections*, edited by Hannah Arendt, translated by Harry John, 69–82. New York: Schocken Books.

Ben Jelloun, Abdel Majid. 2006 [1957]. *Fī al-ṭufūla* [In Childhood]. Rabat: dār nashr al-ma'rifa.

Ben Layashi, Samir. 2007. "Secularism in the Moroccan Amazigh Discourse." *Journal of North African Studies* 12 (2): 153–171.

Bennani-Chraïbi, Mounia. 1994. *Soumis et rebelles: les jeunes au Maroc* [Moroccan Youth: Obedient and Rebelled]. Casablanca: Éditions le Fennec.

Benrabah, Mohamed. 2007. "Language Maintenance and Spread: French in Algeria." *International Journal of Francophone Studies* 10 (1–2): 193–215.

Bensmaïa, Réda. 2009. *Experimental Nations: or, the Invention of the Maghrib*. Princeton, NJ: Princeton University Press.

Bentahila, Abdelali. 1983. "Motivations for Code-Switching among Arabic-French Bilinguals in Morocco." *Language and Communication* 3 (3): 233–243.

Benveniste, Emile. 1966. *Problèmes de linguistique générale* [Problems in General Linguistics]. Paris: Gallimard.

Benyaklef, Mustafa. 1980. *Pour une arabisation de niveau* [For an Arabization of a High Standard]. Casablanca: Graphoprint.

———.1996. *Arabisation et cheval de Troie dans l'enseignement marocain* [Arabization and a Trojan Horse in Moroccan Education]. *L'Opinion*, December 18, 1–4.

———.1997. *La francophonie déchaîne les passions* [Francophonie Unleashes Passionate Reactions]. *L'Opinion*, April 28, 1–4.

Berger, Anne-Emmanuelle, ed. 2002. *Algeria in Others' Languages*. Ithaca, NY: Cornell University Press.

Bernal, Victoria. 2005. "Eritrea On-Line: Diaspora, Cyberspace, and the Public Sphere." *American Ethnologist* 32 (4): 660–675.

Berque, Jacques. 1978. *Cultural Expression in Arab Society Today*. Translated by Robert W. Stookey. Austin: University of Texas Press.

Berrada, Mohamed. 1987. *Lu'bat al-nisyān* [The Game of Forgetting]. Rabat: dār al-amān.

Bhabha, Homi K., ed. 1990. *Nation and Narration*. London: Routledge.

———. 1994. *The Location of Culture*. London: Routledge.

Biehl, João G., Byron G. Good, and Arthur Kleinman, eds. 2007. "Introduction: Rethinking Subjectivity." In *Subjectivity: Ethnographic Investigations*, edited by João G. Biehl, Byron Good, and Arthur Kleinman, 1–23. Berkeley: University of California Press.

Blommaert, Jan. 2005. "Situating Language Rights: English and Swahili in Tanzania Revisited 1." *Journal of Sociolinguistics* 9 (3): 390–417.

Borneman, John. 2011. "Daydreaming, Intimacy, and the Inter-Subjective Third in Fieldwork Encounters in Syria." *American Ethnologist* 38 (2): 234–248.

Bouanani, Ahmed. 1966. *"Introduction à la poésie populaire marocaine"* [Introduction to Moroccan Popular Poetry]. *Souffles: revue poétique et littéraire* 3: 3–9.

Bouderbala, Négib. 2005. *Les classes moyennes comme moteur de l'ascenseur social: l'hypothèse des classes moyennes* [Middle Classes as Social Elevator: The Hypothesis about the Middle Classes]. *Prospective Maroc 2030, Actes du forum II "La société marocaine: permanences, changements et enjeux pour l'avenir."* Morocco: Haut Commissariat au Plan.

Boukous, Ahmed. 1995. *Société, langues et cultures au Maroc: enjeux symboliques* [Society, Languages, and Cultures in Morocco: Symbolic Challenges]. Rabat: Faculté des lettres et des sciences humaines.

———.2003. *"Une nouvelle vie pour l'Amazighe, un nouvel horizon pour le Maghreb"* [A New Life for Amazigh, a New Horizon for Morocco]. *Prologues: revue maghrébine du livre* 27–28: 3–9.

Boum, Aomar. 2012. "'Sacred Week': Re-Experiencing Jewish-Muslim Coexistence in Urban Moroccan Space." In *Sharing the Sacra: The Politics and Pragmatics of Intercommunal Relations around Holy Places,* edited by Glen Bowman, 139–155. New York: Berghahn Books.

———.2013. *Memories of Absence: How Muslims Remember Jews in Morocco.* Stanford, CA: Stanford University Press.

Bourdieu, Pierre. 1958. *Sociologie de l'Algérie* [The Sociology of Algeria]. Paris: Presses Universitaires de France.

———. 1962. *The Algerians.* Translated by Alan C. M. Ross. Boston: Beacon Press.

———. 1977. *Outline of a Theory of Practice.* Translated by Richard Nice. Cambridge: Cambridge University Press.

———. 1991. *Language and Symbolic Power.* Edited by John B. Thompson and translated by Gino Raymond and Mathew Adamson. Cambridge, MA: Harvard University Press.

Bourdieu, Pierre, and Jean-Claude Passeron. 1990. *Reproduction in Education, Society and Culture.* Translated by Richard Nice. London: Sage Publications.

Bourgois, Philippe.1996. "Confronting Anthropology, Education, and Inner-City Apartheid." *American Anthropologist* 98 (2): 249–258.

Bourquia Rahma, Mokhtar al-Harras, and Driss Bensaid. 1995. *Jeunesse estudiantine marocaine: valeurs et stratégies* [Moroccan University Youth, Values and Strategies]. Rabat: Faculté des lettres et sciences humaines.

Boutieri, Charis. 2012. "In Two Speeds (*À deux vitesses*): Linguistic Pluralism and Educational Anxiety in Contemporary Morocco." *International Journal of Middle East Studies* 44 (3): 443–464.

———.2013. "Inheritance, Heritage, and the Disinherited: Ambiguities of Religious Pedagogy in the Moroccan Public School." *Anthropology and Education Quarterly* 44 (4): 363–380.

———.2014. "Morocco On-Trial: De-Colonial Logic and Transformative Practice in Cyberspace." In *Wired Citizenship: Youth Learning and Activism in the Middle East,* edited by Linda Herrera and Rehab Sakr, 39–55. New York: Routledge.

Boyle, Helen N. 2004. *Qur'anic Schools: Agents of Preservation and Change.* New York: Routledge.

Brink-Danan, Marcy. 2011. "Dangerous Cosmopolitanism: Erasing Difference in Istanbul." *Anthropological Quarterly* 84 (2): 439–473.

Brouwer, Lenie. 2006. "Dutch Moroccan Websites: A Transnational Imagery?" *Journal of Ethnic and Migration Studies* 32 (7): 1153–1168.

Bryant, Rebecca. 2004. *Imagining the Modern: The Cultures of Nationalism in Cyprus.* New York: I. B. Tauris.

Buckingham, David, ed. 2008. *Youth, Identity, and Digital Media.* Cambridge, MA: MIT Press.

Buckner, Elisabeth. 2006. "Language Drama in Morocco: Another Perspective on the Problems and Prospects of Teaching Tamazight." *Journal of North African Studies* 11 (4): 421–433.

Burgat, François. 1995. *L'islamisme en face* [Face to Face with Political Islam]. Paris: la Découverte.

Burke, Edmund III. 1972. "Pan-Islam and Moroccan Resistance to French Colonial Penetration, 1900–1912." *Journal of African History* 13: 97–118.

Butler, Judith. 1990. *Gender Trouble: Feminism and the Subversion of Identity.* New York: Routledge.

Carey, James W. 2005. "Historical Pragmatism and the Internet." *New Media and Society* 7 (4): 443–455.

Caton, Steve C. 2006. "Linguistic Ideologies, Text Regulation, and the Question of Post-Structuralism." *Reviews in Anthropology* 35 (3): 221–251.

de Certeau, Michel. 1984. *The Practice of Everyday Life.* Translated by Steven Rendall. Berkeley: University of California Press.

Chafik, Mohammed. 2005. *A Brief Survey of Thirty-Three Centuries of Amazigh History.* Rabat: Institut Royal de la Culture Amazighe.

Chami, Mussa. 1987. *L'enseignement du français au Maroc* [French Instruction in Morocco]. Casablanca: al-najāh al-jadīda.

Chraïbi, Driss. 1954. *Le Passé Simple* [The Simple Past]. Paris: Denoël.

Chomsky, Noam. 1971. *Chomsky: Selected Readings.* Edited by J. P. B. Allen and Paul van Buren. Oxford: Oxford University Press.

Cohen, Shana. 2004. *Searching for a Different Future: The Rise of a Global Middle Class in Morocco.* Durham, NC: Duke University Press.

Çolak, Yilmaz. 2004. "Language Policy and Official Ideology in Early Republican Turkey." *Middle Eastern Studies* 40 (6): 67–91.

Colonna, Fanny. 1975. *Instituteurs Algériens 1883–1939* [Algerian Educators 1883–1939]. Paris: Presses de la Fondation nationale des sciences politiques.

Comaroff, Jean, and John L. Comaroff. 2000. "Millennial Capitalism: First Thoughts on a Second Coming." *Public Culture* 12 (2): 291–343.

Combs-Schilling, Elaine M. 1989. *Sacred Performances: Islam, Sexuality, and Sacrifice.* New York: Columbia University Press.

Crawford, David. 2005. "Royal Interest in Local Culture: Amazigh Identity and the Moroccan Nation." In *Nationalism and Minority Identities in Islamic Societies,* edited by Maya Shatzmiller, 164–194. Montreal: McGill-Queens University Press.

Culler, Jonathan D. 1986. *Ferdinand de Saussure.* Ithaca, NY: Cornell University Press.

Dakhlia, Jocelyne. 2004. *Trames de langues. Usages et métissages linguistiques dans l'histoire du Maghreb* [The Weaving of Languages: Linguistic Uses and Miscegenation in the History of the Maghrib]. Paris: Maisonneuve & Larose.

Damis, John J. 1970. *The Free-School Movement in Morocco 1919–1970.* Medford, MA: Fletcher School, Tufts University.

———. 1974. "The Free-School Phenomenon: The Cases of Tunisia and Algeria." *International Journal of Middle East Studies* 5 (4): 434–449.

Daoud, Mohamed. 2011. "The Sociolinguistic Situation in Tunisia: Language Rivalry or Accommodation?" *International Journal for the Sociology of Language* 211: 9–33.

Daoudi, Anissa, and Emma Murphy. 2011. "Framing New Communicative Technologies in the Arab World." *Journal of Arab and Muslim Media Research* 4 (1): 3–22.

Darwish Mahmud. 1966. *'Āshiq min filastin* [Lover from Palestine]. Haifa: maktabat al-nūr.

Davis, Douglas A., and Susan Schaefer Davis. 1995. " 'The Mosque and the Satellite': Media and Adolescence in a Moroccan Town." *Journal of Youth and Adolescence* 24 (5): 577–593.

Debraye, [M.]. 1939. "*L'enseignement des mathématiques aux collèges musulmans de Rabat et de Fès*" [Teaching Mathematics in the Muslim Colleges of Rabat and of Fes]. *Bulletin de l'enseignement public au Maroc* 165 (May): 251–253. Paris: Émile Larose.

Decock, Jean. 1970. "*L'enseignement du français en Afrique francophone*" [Teaching French in Francophone Africa]. *French Review* 44 (2): 329–340.

Derrida, Jacques. 1996. "*Le monolinguisme de l'autre ou La prothèse d'origine*," Paris: Galilée. Translated by Patrick Mensah as The *Monolingualism of the Other, or the Prosthesis of Origin*. 1998. Stanford, CA: Stanford University Press.

———.2007 [1985]. "*Des tours de Babel*" [The Towers of Babel]. In *Psyche: Inventions of the Other*, edited by Peggy Kamuf and Elisabeth Rottenberg, translated by Joseph E. Graham, 191–225. Stanford, CA: Stanford University Press.

Desrues, Thierry. 2012. "*Le mouvement du 20 Février et le régime marocain: contestation, révision constitutionnelle et elections*" [The February 20 Movement and the Moroccan Regime: Contestation, Constitutional Reform, and Elections]. *L'Année du Maghreb* 8: 359–389.

Devine, John. 1996. *Maximum Security: The Culture of Violence in Inner-City Schools*. Chicago: University of Chicago Press.

Dewey, John. 1916. *Democracy and Education: An Introduction to the Philosophy of Education*. New York: Macmillan.

Dickins, James, Sándor Hervey, and Ian Higgins. 2002. *Thinking Arabic Translation: A Course in Translation Method: Arabic to English*. Oxford: Routledge.

Dirlik, Arif. 1994. "The Postcolonial Aura: Third World Criticism in the Age of Global Capitalism." *Critical Inquiry* 20 (2): 328–356.

Djebar, Assia, dir. 1977. *La nouba des femmes du Mont-Chenoua* [The Nouba of the Women of Mount Chenoua]. 115 min. Algeria: Radio Télévision Algérienne.

———. 1985. *L'amour, la fantasia* [Love, an Algerian Cavalcade]. Paris: Edition Jean-Claude Lattès.

———. 1999. *Ces voix qui m'assiègent . . . En marge de ma francophonie* [These Voices that Besiege Me . . . On the Margins of my Francophonie]. Paris: Albin Michel.

Dodson, Michael S. 2005. "Translating Science, Translating Empire: The Power of Language in Colonial North India." *Comparative Studies in Society and History* 47 (4): 809–835.

Doumato, Eleanor Abdella, and Gregory Starrett. 2007. "Introduction: Textbook Islam, Nation Building, and the Question of Violence." In *Teaching Islam: Textbooks and Religion in the Middle East*, edited by Eleanor Abdella Doumato and Gregory Starrett, 1–26. Boulder, CO: Lynne Rienner Publishers.

Edwards, Brian T. 2007. "*Marock* in Morocco: Reading Moroccan Films in the Age of Circulation." *Journal of North African Studies* 12 (2): 287–307.

Eickelman, Dale F. 1976. *Moroccan Islam: Tradition and Society in a Pilgrimage Centre*. Austin: University of Texas Press, 1976.

———. 1978. "The Art of Memory: Islamic Education and its Social Reproduction." *Comparative Studies in Society and History* 20 (4): 485–516.

———. 2000. "Islam and the Languages of Modernity." *Daedalus* 129 (1): 119–135.

———. 2007. "Madrasas in Morocco: Their Vanishing Public Role." In *Schooling Islam: The Culture and Politics of Modern Muslim Education*, edited by Robert W. Hefner and Muhammad Q. Zaman, 131–148. Princeton, NJ: Princeton University Press.

Elalamy, Youssouf Amine. 2006. *Tqarqib al-nab* [Chattering Teeth]. Tangier: khbār bladna.

Ennaji, Moha. 2005. *Multilingualism, Cultural Identity, and Education in Morocco*. New York: Springer-Verlag.

Errihani, Mohammed. 2006. "Language Policy in Morocco: Problems and Prospects of Teaching Tamazight." *Journal of North African Studies* 11 (2): 143–154.

———. 2008. "Language Attitudes and Language use in Morocco: Effects of Attitudes on 'Berber Language Policy.'" *Journal of North African Studies* 13 (4): 411–428.

Errington, James J. 2001. "Colonial Linguistics." *Annual Review of Anthropology* 30 (1): 19–39.

Escobar, Arturo. 1988. "Power and Visibility: Development and the Invention and Management of the Third World." *Cultural Anthropology* 3 (4): 428–443.

———. 1995. *Encountering Development: The Making and Unmaking of the Third World*. Princeton, NJ: Princeton University Press.

Escobar, Arturo, David Hess, Isabel Licha, Will Sibley, Marilyn Strathern, and Judith Sutz. 1994. "Welcome to Cyberia: Notes on the Anthropology of Cyberculture (Comments and Reply)." *Current Anthropology* 35 (3): 211–231.

Fader, Ayala. 2009. *Mitzvah Girls: Bringing up the Next Generation of Hasidic Jews in Brooklyn*. Princeton, NJ: Princeton University Press.

Fardon, Richard, ed. 1990. *Localizing Strategies: Regional Traditions of Ethnographic Writing*. Edinburgh: Scottish Academic Press.

al-Fassi, Allal. 1969. *Al-naqd al-dhātī* [Self-Critique]. Beirut: dar al-lashshāt.

———. 1977. *La défense de la loi islamique* [The Defense of Islamic Law]. Translated by Charles Samara. [Casablanca?]: Commission du Patrimoine de Feu Allal al-Fassi.

al-Fassi al-Fihri, Abdelkader. 2005. *Azmat al-lugha al-ʿarabiyya fī al-maghrib bayna ikhtilālāt al-taʿddudiyya wa-taʿththurāt al-tarjama* [Arabic Language Crisis in Morocco between the Deceptions of Multilingualism and the Stumbling Blocks of Translation]. Casablanca: manshūrāt zāwiya.

Ferguson, Charles. 1959. "Diglossia." *Word*, 15:325–40.

Ferguson, James. 1993. *The Anti-Politics Machine: 'Development,' Depoliticization and Bureaucratic Power in Lesotho*. Minneapolis: University of Minnesota Press.

Fernandez-Molina, Irene. 2011. "The Monarchy vs. the 20 February Movement: Who Holds the Reins of Political Change in Morocco?" *Mediterranean Politics*, 16 (3): 435–441.

Foley, Douglas E. 1990. *Learning Capitalist Culture: Deep in the Heart of Tejas*. Philadelphia: University of Pennsylvania Press.

Fortna, Benjamin C. 2002. *Imperial Classroom: Islam, the State, and Education in the Late Ottoman Empire*. Oxford: Oxford University Press.

Foucault, Michel. 1972. *The Archaeology of Knowledge and the Discourse on Language*. Translated by Alan Mark Sheridan Smith. New York: Pantheon Books.

———. 1997. *Ethics: Subjectivity and Truth*. Vol. 1 of *Essential Works of Michel Foucault (1954–1984)*, edited by Paul Rabinow, translated by Robert Hurley et al. New York: New Press.

Freire, Paulo. 1986. *Pedagogy of the Oppressed*. Translated by M. Bergman Ramos. New York: Continuum.

Friedman, Thomas. 2010. "It's all about Schools." *New York Times*, February 9. Accessed November 2, 2014. http://www.nytimes.com/2010/02/10/opinion/10friedman.html? _r=1&

Gaonkar, Dilip Parameshwar, and Elizabeth A. Povinelli. 2003. "Technologies of Public Forms: Circulation, Transfiguration, Recognition." *Public Culture* 15 (3): 385–397.

Geertz, Clifford. 1968. *Islam Observed: Religious Development in Morocco and Indonesia.* Chicago: University of Chicago Press.

Gellner, Ernest. 1983. *Muslim Society.* Cambridge: Cambridge University Press.

Gellner, Ernest, and Charles Micaud, eds. 1972. *Arabs and Berbers: From Tribe to Nation in North Africa.* Lexington, MA: Lexington Books.

General Secretariat of the Government, Directorate of Official Printing Office. *al-dustūr* [The Constitution]. 2011. Kingdom of Morocco. Accessed April 21, 2014. http://www .sgg.gov.ma/Portals/1/lois/constitution_2011_Ar.pdf

———. 1962. *al-dustūr* [The Constitution]. 1962. Accessed April 21, 2014. http://www .righttononviolence.org/mecf/wp-content/uploads/1962/12/1962Morocco.pdf

Gilroy, Paul. 2000. *Between Camps: Nations, Cultures and the Allure of Race.* London: Penguin.

Giroux, Henry A. 2006. "Academic Freedom under Fire: The Case for Critical Pedagogy." *College Literature* 33 (4): 1–42.

Goodman, Jane E. 2002. "Writing Empire, Underwriting Nation: Discursive Histories of Kabyle Berber Oral Texts." *American Ethnologist* 29 (1): 86–122.

———. 2004. "Reinterpreting the Berber Spring: From Rite of Reversal to Site of Convergence." *Journal of North African Studies* 9 (3): 60–82.

Goody, Jack. 1986. *The Logic of Writing and the Organization of Society.* Cambridge: Cambridge University Press.

Granguillaume, Gilbert. 1983. *Arabisation et linguistique politique au Maghreb* [Arabization and Language Policy in North Africa]. Paris: Maisonneuve & Larose.

Greenhouse, Carol J. 2005. "Hegemony and Hidden Transcripts: The Discursive Arts of Neo-Liberal Legitimation." *American Anthropologist* 107 (3): 356–368.

Grillo, Ralph. 2007. "An Excess of Alterity? Debating Difference in a Multicultural Society." *Ethnic and Racial Studies* 30 (6): 979–998.

Guyer, Jane I. 2004. "Anthropology in Area Studies." *Annual Review of Anthropology* 33:499–523.

Haeri, Niloofar. 2000. "Form and Ideology: Arabic Sociolinguistics and Beyond." *Annual Review of Anthropology* 29: 61–87.

———. 2003. *Sacred Language, Ordinary People: Dilemmas of Culture and Politics in Egypt.* New York: Palgrave Macmillan.

Hall, Kathleen D. 2005. "Science, Globalization, and Educational Governance: The Political Rationalities of the New Managerialism." *Indiana Journal of Global Legal Studies* 12 (1): 153–182.

Hall, Stuart. 1996. "When Was the Post-Colonial? Thinking at the Limit." In *The Post-Colonial Question: Common Skies, Divided Horizons*, edited by Ian Chambers and Lidia Curti, 242–260. New York: Routledge.

Hamilton, Victor P. 1990. *The Book of Genesis Chapters 1–17: The New International Commentary on the Old Testament.* Grand Rapids, MI: W. B. Eerdmans.

Hammoudi, Abdellah. 1997. *Master and Disciple: The Cultural Foundations of Moroccan Authoritarianism.* Chicago: University of Chicago Press.

———. 2006. *A Season in Mecca: Narrative of a Pilgrimage.* New York: Hill and Wang.

———. 2009a. "Textualism and Anthropology: On the Ethnographic Encounter, or an Experience in the Hajj." In *The Fieldwork Encounter and the Making of Truth,* edited by John Borneman and Abdellah Hammoudi, 25–54. Berkeley: University of California Press.

———. 2009b. "Phenomenology and Ethnography: On Kabyle Habitus in the Work of Pierre Bourdieu." In *Bourdieu in Algeria: Colonial Politics, Ethnographic Practices, Theoretical Developments,* edited by Jane A. Goodman and Paul A. Silverstein, 199–254. Lincoln: University of Nebraska Press.

Harrison, Nicholas. 2003. *Postcolonial Criticism: History, Theory, and the Work of Fiction.* Cambridge, UK: Polity Press.

Harvey, David. 1990. *The Condition of Postmodernity.* Malden, MA: Blackwell.

Hefner, Robert W., and Muhammad Q. Zaman, eds. 2007. *Schooling Islam: The Culture and Politics of Modern Muslim Education.* Princeton, NJ: Princeton University Press.

Heggoy, Alf Andrew. 1973. "Education in French Algeria: An Essay on Cultural Conflict." *Comparative Education Review* 17 (2): 180–197.

Heller, Monica. 2003. "Globalization, the New Economy, and the Commodification of Language and Identity." *Journal of Sociolinguistics* 7 (4): 473–492.

Herrera, Linda, and Carlos Alberto Torres. 2006. *Cultures of Arab Schooling: Critical Ethnographies from Egypt.* New York: SUNY Press.

Herzfeld, Michael. 1986 [1982]. *Ours Once More: Folklore, Ideology, and the Making of Modern Greece.* New York: Pella.

Hibou, Béatrice. May 2011."*Le mouvement du 20 février, le makhzen et l'antipolitique. L'impensé des réformes au Maroc*" [The February 20 Movement, the Makzhen and Anti-Politics. The Unthinkable within Moroccan Reforms]. *Sciences Po-CNRS.* Accessed September 10, 2014. http://www.ceri-sciences-po.org/

Hirschkind, Charles. 2001. "Civic Virtue and Religious Reason: An Islamic Counterpublic." *Cultural Anthropology* 16 (1): 3–34.

———. 2006. *The Ethical Soundscape: Cassette Sermons and Islamic Counterpublics.* New York: Columbia University Press.

Hodgson, Marshall G. S. 1974 [1958]. *The Expansion of Islam in the Middle Periods.* Vol. 2 of *The Venture of Islam: Conscience and History in a World Civilization.* Chicago: University of Chicago Press.

Hoffman, Katherine E. 2008a. *We Share Walls: Language, Land, and Gender in Berber Morocco.* New York: John Wiley and Sons.

———. 2008b. "Purity and Contamination: Language Ideologies in French Colonial Native Policy in Morocco." *Comparative Studies in Society and History* 50 (3): 724–752.

Hoffman, Katherine E., and Susan Gilson Miller, eds. 2010. *Berbers and Others: Beyond Tribe and Nation in the Maghrib.* Bloomington: Indiana University Press.

Hoisington, William A. 1995. *Lyautey and the French Conquest of Morocco.* New York: St. Martin's Press.

Hornberger, Nancy H. 1998. "Language Policy, Language Education, Language Rights: Indigenous, Immigrant, and International Perspectives." *Language in Society* 27 (4): 439–458.

Hymes, Dell H. 1996. *Ethnography, Linguistics, Narrative Inequality: Toward an Understanding of Voice.* Bristol, PA: Taylor & Francis Group.

Ibaaquil, Larbi. 1996. *L'école marocaine et la compétition sociale: stratégies, aspirations* [The Moroccan School and Social Competition: Strategies and Aspirations]. Rabat: Babil.

International Bank for Reconstruction and Development and the World Bank. 2008. *The Road Not Traveled: Education Reform in the Middle East and North Africa.* Accessed December 20, 2014. http://siteresources.worldbank.org/INTMENA/Resources/EDU _Flagship_Full_ENG.pdf

Irvine, Judith T. 1989. "When Talk Isn't Cheap: Language and Political Economy." *American Ethnologist* 16 (2): 248–267.

Jaffé, Alexandra M. 1999. *Ideologies in Action: Language Politics on Corsica.* Berlin: Walter de Gruyter.

Jakobson, Roman. 1959. "On Linguistic Aspects of Translation." In *On Translation,* edited by Reuben A. Brower. Cambridge, MA: Harvard University Press.

Jameson, Fredric. 1984. "Postmodernism, or the Cultural Logic of Late Capitalism." *American Studies* 29 (1): 54–92.

Jeffrey, Craig. 2010. *Timepass: Youth, Class, and the Politics of Waiting in India.* Stanford, CA: Stanford University Press.

Jerad, Nabiha. 2007. "From the Maghrib to the Mediterranean: Immigration and Transnational Location." In *Places We Share: Migration, Subjectivity, and Global Mobility,* edited by Susan Ossman, 47–64. Lanham, MD: Lexington Books.

Jouad, Hassan. 1989. "Les Imdyazen, une voix de l'intellectualité rurale "[The Imdyazen, the Voice of Rural Intellectuality]. *Revue des mondes musulmans et de la Méditerranée* 51 (1): 100–110.

Kadi, Wadad, and Victor Billeh, eds. 2007. *Islam and Education: Myths and Truths.* Chicago: University of Chicago Press.

Kandiyoti, Deniz. 1994. "The Paradoxes of Masculinity." In *Dislocating Masculinity: Comparative Ethnographies,* edited by Andrea Cornwall and Nancy Lindisfarne, 196–212. New York: Routledge.

———. 2002. "Post-Colonialism Compared: Potentials and Limitations in the Middle East and Central Asia." *International Journal of Middle East Studies* 34 (2): 279–297.

Kapchan, Deborah A. 2008. "The Promise of Sonic Translation: Performing the Festive Sacred in Morocco." *American Anthropologist* 110 (4): 467–483.

Kaplan, Sam. 2005. "Religious Nationalism: A Textbook Case from Turkey." *Comparative Studies of South Asia, Africa and the Middle East* 25 (3): 665–676.

———. 2006. *The Pedagogical State: Education and the Politics of National Culture in Post-1980 Turkey.* Stanford, CA: Stanford University Press.

Keane, Webb. 2003. "Semiotics and the Social Analysis of Material Things." *Language and Communication* 23 (3): 409–425.

Khaïr-Eddine, Mohammed. 1967. *Agadir* [Agadir]. Paris: Seuil.

———. 1973. *Le déterreur* [The Human Ghoul]. Paris: Seuil.

———. 1984a. *Légende et vie d'Agounchich* [The Legend and Life of Agounchich]. Paris: Seuil.

———. 1984b. "*Autres lieux, autres moeurs*" [Other Places, Other Mores], interview by Bernard Pivot. *Apostrophes,* recording for television, June 8. Accessed February 2, 2015. http://www.ina.fr/video/CPB84053378/

———. 1998. *Le temps des refus; entretiens* [The Time of Refusals: Interviews], edited by Abdellatif Abboubi. Paris: L'Harmattan.

———. 2002. *Il était une fois un vieux couple heureux* [Once Upon a Time There Was a Happy Old Couple]. Paris: Seuil.

Khalidi, Rashid. 1991. "The Origins of Arab Nationalism: Introduction." In *The Origins of Arab Nationalism*, edited by Rashid Khalidi, Lisa Anderson, Muhammad Muslih, and Reeva S. Simon, vi–xix. New York: Columbia University Press.

Khannous, Touria. 2010. "Female Sexuality, Islam and the Global: Leila Merrakshi's Controversial Film *Marock*." *CineAction* 81: 50–56.

Khatibi, Abdelkebir. 1992 [1983]. *Amour bilingue*. Casablanca: Eddif. Translated by Richard Howard as *Love in Two Languages*. 1990. Minneapolis: University of Minnesota Press.

Kilito, Abdelfattah. 2001 [1985]. *The Author and Its Doubles: Essays on Classical Arabic Culture*. Translated by Michael Cooperson. New York: Syracuse University Press.

———. 2008. *Thou Shalt Not Speak My Language*. Translated by Wail S. Hassan. New York: Syracuse University Press.

Kinsey, David C. 1971. "Efforts for Educational Synthesis under Colonial Rule: Egypt and Tunisia." *Comparative Education Review* 15 (2): 172–187.

Kraidy, Marwan M. 2005. "Reality Television and Politics in the Arab World." *Transnational Broadcasting Studies* 1 (2): 7–28.

Kristeva, Julia. 1980. *Desire in Language: A Semiotic Approach to Literature and Art*, edited by Leon S. Roudiez, translated by Thomas Gora, Alice Jardine, and Leon S. Roudiez. New York: Columbia University Press.

———. 1989. *Language, the Unknown: An Initiation into Linguistics*. Translated by Anne M. Menke. New York: Columbia University Press.

Kroskrity, Paul V. 1993. *Language, History and Identity: Ethnolinguistic Studies of the Arizona Tewa*. Tucson: University of Arizona Press.

Laabi, Abdellatif. 1966. "*Prologue*" [Prologue]. *Souffles: revue poétique et littéraire* 1: 1–4.

Laachir, Karima. 2013. "Contemporary Moroccan Cultural Production: Between Dissent and Co-optation." *Journal of African Cultural Studies* 25 (3): 257–260.

Lakhdar-Ghazal, Ahmed. 1976. *Méthodologie générale de l'arabisation de niveau: problèmes linguistiques et graphiques, la terminologie bilingue, techniques et méthodes* [General Methodology of an Arabization of a High Standard: Linguistic and Transcription Issues, Bilingual Terminology, Techniques and Methods]. Rabat: Institut d'études et de recherches pour l'Arabisation.

Lakhmari, Nour-Eddine, dir. 2008. *Casanegra*. 124 min. Morocco: Sigma Soread 2M.

Lapidus, Ira M. 1988. *A History of Islamic Societies*. Cambridge: Cambridge University Press.

Larkin, Brian. 1997. "Indian Films and Nigerian Lovers: Media and the Creation of Parallel Modernities." *Africa* 67 (3): 406–440.

Laskier, Michael M. 1994. *North African Jewry in the Twentieth Century: The Jews of Morocco, Tunisia, and Algeria*. New York: New York University Press.

Lavie, Smadar. 2011. "Mizrahi Feminism and the Question of Palestine." *Journal of Middle East Women's Studies* 7 (2): 56–88.

Lelubre, Xavier. 2004. "*Du français à l'arabe: gestion des faits de variation en vue d'une base de données terminologiques (domaine de la physique)*" [From French to Arabic: Managing Variation in Relation to Terminological Data (Physics)]. In *Rencontres: français/arabe, arabe/français: construire ensemble dans une perspective plurilingue*. Paris: Ministère des Affaires Étrangères.

Lewis, Geoffrey. 1999. *The Turkish Language Reform: A Catastrophic Success: A Cata-strophic Success*. Oxford: Oxford University Press.

Lewis, Martin D. 1962. "One Hundred Million Frenchmen: The 'Assimilation' Theory in French Colonial Policy." *Comparative Studies in Society and History* 4 (2): 129–153.

Lindisfarne, Nancy. 1994. "Variant Masculinities, Variant Virginities: Rethinking 'Honour and Shame.'" In *Dislocating Masculinity: Comparative Ethnographies*, edited by Andrea Cornwall and Nancy Lindisfarne, 82–96. New York: Routledge.

Liu, Lydia H. 1995. *Translingual Practice: Literature, National Culture, and Translated Modernity, China, 1900–1937*. Stanford, CA: Stanford University Press.

Lorcin, Patricia, M. E. 1995. *Imperial Identities: Stereotyping, Prejudice, and Race in Colonial Algeria*. London: I. B. Tauris.

Lukose, Ritty A. 2005. "Empty Citizenship: Protesting Politics in the Era of Globalization." *Cultural Anthropology* 20 (4): 506–533.

———. 2009. *Liberalization's Children: Gender, Youth, and Consumer Citizenship in Globalizing India*. Durham, NC: Duke University Press.

Luykx, Aurolyn. 1999. *The Citizen Factory: Schooling and Cultural Production in Bolivia*. New York: SUNY Press.

Maddy-Weitzman, Bruce. 2006. "Ethno-Politics and Globalization in North Africa: The Berber Cultural Movement." *Journal of North African Studies* 11 (1): 71–84.

Mahmood, Saba. 2001. "Feminist Theory, Embodiment, and the Docile Agent: Some Reflections on the Egyptian Islamic Revival." *Cultural Anthropology* 16 (2): 202–236.

———. 2005. *Politics of Piety: The Islamic Revival and the Feminist Subject*. Princeton, NJ: Princeton University Press.

al-Mansour, Mohammed. 1994. "Salafis and Modernists in the Moroccan Nationalist Movement." In *Islamism and Secularism in North Africa*, edited by John Ruedy, 56–71. Basingstoke: MacMillan.

Manzo, Kathryn. 1991. "Modernist Discourse and the Crisis of Development Theory." *Studies in Comparative International Development* 26 (2): 3–36.

Marrakchi, Layla, dir. 2005. *Marock*. 102 minutes. France: Pan Européenne Distribution.

Masquelier, Adeline. 2009. "Lessons from Rubí: Love, Poverty, and the Educational Value of Televised Dramas in Niger." In *Love in Africa*, edited by Jennifer Coles and Lynn M. Thomas, 205–228. Chicago: University of Chicago Press.

Massialas, Byron G., and Ahmad S. Jarrar. 1991. *Arab Education in Transition: A Source Book*. New York: Garland Publishing.

Mazawi, André Elias. 2010. "Naming the Imaginary: 'Building an Arab knowledge Society' and the Contested Terrain of Educational Reforms for Development." In *Trajectories of Education in the Arab World: Legacies and Challenges*, edited by Osama Abi-Mershed, 201–225. New York: Routledge.

———. 2014. Commentary on Panel "Education and the Arab Uprisings: The End of the Social Contract?" 113th American Anthropological Annual Meeting, Washington DC, December 3–7.

Mazzarella, William. 2004. "Culture, Globalization, Mediation." *Annual Review of Anthropology* 33: 345–367.

McAlister, Melani. 2002. "A Cultural History of the War without End." *Journal of American History* 89: 439–455.

McClintock, Anne. 1992. "The Angel of Progress: Pitfalls of the Term 'Post-Colonialism,' 'Third World and Postcolonial Issues.'" *Social Text* 31–32: 84–98.

McDougall, James. 2006. *History and the Culture of Nationalism in Algeria.* Cambridge: Cambridge University Press.

———. 2011. "Dream of Exile, Promise of Home: Language, Education, and Arabism in Algeria." *International Journal of Middle East Studies* 43 (2): 251–270.

Memmi, Albert. 1953. *La statue de sel* [The Pillar of Salt]. Paris: Gallimard.

Messick, Brinkley. 1993. *The Calligraphic State: Textual Domination and History in a Muslim Society.* Berkeley: University of California Press.

Miller, Catherine. 2012. "Observations concernant la présence de l'arabe marocain dans la presse marocaine arabophone des années 2009–2010" [Observations Concerning the Presence of Moroccan Arabic in the Arabophone Moroccan Press during 2009–2010]. In *De los manuscritos medievales a internet: la presencia del arabo vernáculo en las fuentes escritas*, edited by Mohamed Meouak, Pablo Sánchez, and Angeles Vicente, 419–440. Zaragoza: Universidad de Zaragoza.

Miller, Daniel. 2010. "Anthropology in Blue Jeans." *American Ethnologist* 37 (3): 415–428.

Mitchell, Katharyne. 2003. "Educating the National Citizen in Neoliberal Times: From the Multicultural Self to the Strategic Cosmopolitan." *Transactions of the Institute of British Geographers* 28 (4): 387–403.

Mitchell, Timothy. 1988. *Colonizing Egypt.* Cambridge: Cambridge University Press.

———. 1991. "The Limits of the State: Beyond Statist Approaches and their Critics." *American Political Science Review* 85 (1): 77–96.

———. 2002. *Rule of Experts: Egypt, Techno-Politics, Modernity.* Berkeley: University of California Press.

Moatassime, Ahmed. 1992. *Arabisation et langue française au Maghreb: un aspect sociolinguistique des dilemmes du développement* [Arabization and the French Language in Morocco: A Sociolinguistic View of Development Dilemmas]. Paris: Presses Universitaires de France.

Mokhliss, Brahim, and Mohammed Zainabi. 2008. "*La faillite totale de l'enseignement au Maroc* [The Total Failure of Moroccan Education]." *Le Reporter*, April 24, 23–27.

Murphy, Emma C. 1998. "Legitimacy and Economic Reform in the Arab World." *Journal of North African Studies* 3 (3): 71–92.

Navaro-Yashin, Yael. 2002. *Faces of the State: Secularism and Public Life in Turkey.* Princeton, NJ: Princeton University Press.

Neela Das, Sonia. 2011. "Rewriting the Past and Reimagining the Future: The Social Life of a Tamil Heritage Language Industry." *American Ethnologist* 38 (4): 774–789.

Newcomb, Rachel. 2006. "Gendering the City, Gendering the Nation: Contesting Urban Space in Fes, Morocco." *City and Society* 18 (2): 288–311.

———. 2009. *Women of Fes: Ambiguities of Urban Life in Morocco.* Philadelphia: University of Pennsylvania Press.

Olender, Maurice. 1992. *The Languages of Paradise: Race, Religion, and Philology in the Nineteenth Century.* Cambridge, MA: Harvard University Press.

———. 1997. "From the Language of Adam to the Pluralism of Babel." *Mediterranean Historical Review* 12 (2): 51–59.

Ong, Aihwa. 2006. *Neoliberalism as Exception: Mutations in Citizenship and Sovereignty.* Durham, NC: Duke University Press.

Özgür, Iren. 2011. "Social and Political Reform through Religious Education in Turkey: The Ongoing Cause of Hayrettin Karaman." *Middle Eastern Studies* 47 (4): 569–585.

Ozouf, Mona. 1982. *L'École, l'Église et la République: 1871–1914* [The School, the Church and the Republic]. Paris: Editions Cana.

Özyürek, Esra. 2005. "The Politics of Cultural Unification, Secularism, and the Place of Islam in the New Europe." *American Ethnologist* 32 (4): 509–512.

Pandolfo, Stefania. 2008. "The Knot of the Soul: Postcolonial Conundrums, Madness and the Imagination." In *Postcolonial Disorders*, edited by Mary-Jo Del Vecchio Good, Sandra T. Hyde, Sarah Pinto, and Byron J. Good, 329–358. Berkeley: University of California Press.

Peterson, Mark Allen. 2011. *Connected in Cairo: Growing up Cosmopolitan in the Modern Middle East.* Bloomington: Indiana University Press.

Pigg, Stacey L. 1992. "Investing Social Categories through Place: Social Representations and Development in Nepal." *Comparative Studies in Society and History* 34 (3): 491–513.

Povinelli, Elizabeth A. 2002. *The Cunning of Recognition: Indigenous Alterities and the Making of Australian Multiculturalism.* Durham, NC: Duke University Press.

Prashad, Vijya. 2005. "Second-Hand Dreams." *Social Analysis* 49 (2): 191–198.

Qattab, Tarik. 2008. "Le Remède de Cheval d'Ahmed Akchichine" [The Sledgehammer Reform of Ahmed Akchichine]. *Le Soir*, April 17, 3.

Rachik, Hassan, ed. 2006. *Usages de l'identité amazighe au Maroc* [The Usages of the Amazigh Identity in Morocco]. Casablanca: Al-najāh al-jadīda.

Ramaswamy, Sumathi. 1997. *Passions of the Tongue: Language Devotion in Tamil India, 1891–1970.* Berkeley: University of California Press.

al-Rasheed, Madawi. 1996. "God, the King and the Nation: Political Rhetoric in Saudi Arabia in the 1990s." *Middle East Journal* 50 (3): 359–371.

Rausch, Margaret. 2006. "Ishelhin Women Transmitters of Islamic Knowledge and Culture in Southwestern Morocco." *Journal of North African Studies* 11 (2): 173–192.

Rawls, John. 1993. *Political Liberalism.* New York: Columbia University Press.

Reynolds, Dwight F., and Kristen Brustad. 2001. *Interpreting the Self: Autobiography in the Arabic Literary Tradition.* Berkeley: University of California Press.

Robinson, Francis. 1993. "Technology and Religious Change: Islam and the Impact of Print." *Modern Asian Studies* 27 (1): 229–251.

Rose, Martin. 2014. "Education in North Africa." *The Hammamet Conference 2014: The Leadership Challenge.* UK: British Council.

Rosen, Lawrence. 1984. *Bargaining for Reality: The Construction of Social Relations in a Muslim Community.* Chicago: University of Chicago Press.

———. 2004. *The Culture of Islam: Changing Aspects of Contemporary Muslim Life.* Chicago: University of Chicago Press.

———. 2008. *Varieties of Muslim Experience: Encounters with Arab Political and Cultural Life.* Chicago: University of Chicago Press.

Rousseau, Jean-Jacques, and Johann G. Herder. 1986. *On the Origin of Language.* Edited and translated by Alexander Gode. Chicago: University of Chicago Press.

Sadiki, Larbi. 2002. "Ben Ali's Tunisia: Democracy by Non-Democratic Means." *British Journal of Middle Eastern Studies* 29 (1): 57–78.

Said, Edward. 1978. *Orientalism: Western Conceptions of the Orient.* London: Penguin Books.

Sawaie, Mohammed. 2006. "Language Academies." *Encyclopedia of Arabic Language and Linguistics Online,* edited by Lutz Edzard and Rudolf de Jong. Accessed February 8, 2015. http://referenceworks.brillonline.com/entries/encyclopedia-of-arabic-language -and-linguistics/language-academies-EALL_COM_vol2_0082

Sbaiti, Nadya. 2010. "'If the Devil Taught French': Strategies of Language Learning in French Mandate Beirut." In *Trajectories of Education in the Arab World: Legacies and Challenges,* edited by Osama Abi-Mershed, 59–83. New York: Routledge.

Schielke, Samuli. 2009. "Being Good in Ramadan: Ambivalence, Fragmentation, and the Moral Self in the Lives of Young Egyptians." *Journal of the Royal Anthropological Institute* 15 (s1): 24–40.

Sefrioui, Ahmed. 1954. *La boîte à merveilles* [The Wonderbox]. Paris: Éditions du Seuil.

Sefriouri, Kenza. 2013. *La revue Souffles: Espoirs de révolution culturelle au Maroc (1966–1973)* [The Journal Souffles: Hopes for a Cultural Revolution in Morocco (1966–1973). Casablanca: Sirocco.

Segalla, Spencer. 2009. *The Moroccan Soul: French Education, Colonial Ethnology, and Muslim Resistance, 1912–1956.* Lincoln: University of Nebraska Press.

Shatz, Adam. 2002. "A Love Story between an Arab Poet and His Land. Interview with Mahmud Darwish." *Journal of Palestine Studies* 31 (3): 67–78.

Shepard, Todd. 2006. *The Invention of Decolonization: The Algerian War and the Remaking of France.* Ithaca, NY: Cornell University Press.

Shohat, Ella. 1992. "Notes on the 'Post-Colonial.'" *Social Text* 31–32: 99–113.

Silverstein, Paul A. 2004. *Algeria in France: Transpolitics, Race, and Nation.* Bloomington: Indiana University Press.

———. 2007. "Islam, Laïcité, and Amazigh Activism in France and North Africa." In *North African Mosaic: A Cultural Reappraisal of Ethnic and Religious Minorities,* edited by Nabil Boudraa, Joseph Krause, and David L. Crawford, 104–118. Cambridge: Cambridge Scholars Publishing.

———. 2012. "In the Name of Culture: Berber Activism and the Material Politics of 'Popular Islam' in Southeastern Morocco." *Material Religion: The Journal of Objects, Art and Belief* 8 (3): 330–353.

Silverstein, Paul A., and David Crawford. 2004. "Amazigh Activism and the Moroccan State." *Middle East Report* 233: 44–48.

Slyomovics, Susan. 2005. *The Performance of Human Rights in Morocco.* Philadelphia: University of Pennsylvania Press.

———. 2011. "100 Days of the 2011 Moroccan Constitution." *Jadaliyya.com,* June 30. Accessed July 5, 2012. http://www.jadaliyya.com/pages/index/2023/100-days-of-the-2011 -moroccan-constitution/

Sobhy, Hania. 2012. "The de facto Privatization of Secondary Education in Egypt: A Study of Private Tutoring in Technical and General Schools." *Compare: A Journal of Comparative and International Education* 42 (1): 47–67.

Sontag, Susan. 1993. "Writing Itself: On Roland Barthes." In *A Roland Barthes Reader,* edited Susan Sontag, vii–xxxviii. London: Vintage Books.

Spitulnik, Deborah. 1993. "Anthropology and Mass Media." *Annual Review of Anthropology* 22: 293–315.

Spivak, Gayatri C. 1988. "Can the Subaltern Speak?" In *Marxism and the Interpretation of Culture*, edited by Cary Nelson and Lawrence Grossberg, 271–313. Chicago: University of Illinois Press.

Sraieb, Noureddine. 1993. "L'idéologie de l'école en Tunisie coloniale (1881–1945)" [The Ideology of Schooling in Colonial Tunisia (1881–1945)]. *Revue des mondes musulmans et de la Méditerranée* 68 (1): 239–254.

Stambach, Amy. 2000. *Lessons from Mount Kilimanjaro: Schooling, Community, and Gender in East Africa*. New York: Routledge.

Suleiman, Yasir, ed. 1994. *Arabic Sociolinguistics: Issues and Perspectives*. Oxford: Routledge.

——. 1996. *Language and Identity in the Middle East and North Africa*. London: Curzon.

Starrett, Gregory. 1998. *Putting Islam to Work: Education, Politics, and Religious Transformation in Egypt*. Berkeley: University of California Press.

——. 2007. "Textbook Meanings and the Power of Interpretation." In *Teaching Islam: Textbooks and Religion in the Middle East*, edited by Eleanor Abdella Doumato and Gregory Starrett, 215–231. Boulder, CO: Lynne Rienner Publishers.

Steiner, George. 1998 [1975]. "The Hermeneutic Motion." In *After Babel: Aspects of Language and Translation*, 312–435. Oxford: Oxford University Press.

Stetkevych, Jaroslav. 2006. *The Modern Arabic Literary Language: Lexical and Stylistic Developments*. Washington, DC: Georgetown University Press.

Stock-Morton, Phyllis. 1988. *Moral Education for a Secular Society: The Development of Morale Laïque in Nineteenth Century France*. New York: SUNY Press.

Taleb Ibrahimi, Khaoula. 1995. "Algérie: l'Arabisation, lieu de conflits multiples" [Algeria: Arabization, Site of Multiple Conflicts]. *Monde arabe, maghreb-machrek* 150: 57–71.

Taussig, Michael T. 1980. *The Devil and Commodity Fetishism in South America*. Chapel Hill: University of North Carolina Press.

al-Tawfiq, Ahmed. 1997. *Jārāt Abī Mūsā* [Abu Musa's Female Neighbors]. Casablanca: Dār al-qubba al-zarqāʾ.

Taylor, Charles. 1994. *Multiculturalism: Examining the Politics of Recognition*. Princeton, NJ: Princeton University Press.

Théry, Gabriel. 1941. "*Philosophie musulmane et culture française*" [Muslim Philosophy and French Culture]. *Bulletin de l'enseignement public au Maroc* 170 (October–December): 287–316. Paris: Émile Larose.

Touaf, Larbi. 2012. "The Sense and Non-Sense of Cultural Identity in Mohammed Khaïr-Eddine's Fiction." *Alif: Journal of Comparative Poetics* 32: 151–166.

Tozy, Mohammed. 1999. *Monarchie et islam politique au Maroc* [The Monarchy and Political Islam in Morocco]. Paris: Presses de la Fondation nationale des sciences politiques.

——. 2008. "Islamists, Technocrats, and the Palace." *Journal of Democracy* 19 (1): 34–41.

Trouillot, Michel R. 2001. "The Anthropology of the State in the Age of Globalization 1: Close Encounters of the Deceptive Kind." *Current Anthropology* 42 (1): 125–138.

Tsing, Anna L. 1993. *In the Realm of the Diamond Queen: Marginality in an Out-of-the-Way Place*. Princeton, NJ: Princeton University Press.

——. 2000. "The Global Situation." *Cultural Anthropology* 15 (3): 327–360.

United Nations Committee on the Elimination of Racial Discrimination. 2010. *Concluding Observations of the Committee on the Elimination of Racial Discrimination: Morocco* (CERD/C/MAR/CO/17-18). September 13. Accessed January 28, 2015. http://www .refworld.org/docid/4d2c5f112.html

United Nations Development Programme and the Regional Bureau for Arab States. 2004. *Arab Human Development Report: Towards Freedom in the Arab World.* Accessed January 20, 2015. http://www.arab-hdr.org/publications/other/ahdr/ahdr2004e.pdf

United Nations Development Programme, the Regional Bureau for Arab States, and the Mohammed bin Rashid al Maktoum Foundation. 2009. *Arab Knowledge Report: Towards Productive Intercommunication for Knowledge.* Accessed January 20, 2015. http:// www.arab-hdr.org/akr/AKR2009/English/AKR2009-Eng-Full-Report.pdf

United Nations Educational, Scientific and Cultural Organization. 2011. "Message of the UNESCO Director-General, Irina Bokova on the Occasion of International Mother Language Day." February 21. Accessed February 3, 2015. http://unesdoc.unesco.org /images/0019/001910/191071e.pdf

Urciuoli, Bonnie. 2008. "Skills and Selves in the New Workplace." *American Ethnologist* 35 (2): 211–228.

Van Gennep, Arnold. 2004 [1960]. *The Rites of Passage.* London: Routledge.

Varenne, Hervé. 2008. "Culture, Education, Anthropology." *Anthropology and Education Quarterly* 39 (4): 356–368.

Venuti, Lawrence, ed. 2000. *The Translation Studies Reader.* New York: Routledge.

Vermeren, Pierre. 2002. *École, élite, pouvoir au Maroc et en Tunisie au 20ème siècle* [School, Elite, and Power in Morocco and Tunisia in the 20th Century]. Rabat: Alizés.

Versteegh, Kees. 1997. *The Arabic Language.* Edinburgh: Edinburgh University Press.

Wagner, Daniel. 1993. *Literacy, Culture, and Development: Becoming Literate in Morocco.* New York: Cambridge University Press.

Wagner, Daniel, and Abdelhamid Lotfi. 1980. "Traditional Islamic Education in Morocco: Socio-Historical and Psychological Perspectives." *Comparative Education Review* 24 (2): 238–251.

Waterbury, John. 1970. *The Commander of the Faithful: The Moroccan Political Elite, a Study in Segmented Politics.* London: Weidenfeld & Nicolson.

Watson, David R. 1960. "The Politics of Educational Reform in France during the Third Republic 1900–1940." *Past and Present* 34: 81–99.

Wedeen, Lisa. 1999. *Ambiguities of Domination: Politics, Rhetoric and Symbols in Contemporary Syria.* Chicago: University of Chicago Press.

Wien, Peter. 2011. "Preface: Relocating Arab Nationalism." *International Journal of Middle East Studies* 43 (2): 203–204.

Willis, Michael J. 2012. *Politics and Power in the Maghrib: Algeria, Tunisia and Morocco from Independence to the Arab Spring.* London: Hurst Publishers.

Willis, Paul E. 1977. *Learning to Labor: How Working Class Kids Get Working Class Jobs.* Farnborough, UK: Saxon House.

Wizārat al-tarbiya al-waṭaniyya wa-l-takwīn al-mihnī [Ministry of National Education and Professional Training]. 2006/2007. *Mudhakira raqm 43: tanẓīm al-dirāsa bi-l-taʿlīm al-thānawī* [Memo 43: The Organization of Education in Secondary School]. Kingdom of Morocco.

Wizārat al-tarbiya al-waṭaniyya wa-l-takwīn al-mihnī [Ministry of National Education and Professional Training]. 2008. *Malaf shāmil li-mashārīʿ al-barnāmaj al-istiʿjālī 2009–2012* [Executive Summary of Projects for the Emergency Program 2009–2011]. Kingdom of Morocco. Accessed September 10, 2011. http://portail.men.gov.ma/Prog _urgence_ar/default.aspx

Woolard, Katherine A., and Bambi B. Schieffelin. 1994. "Language Ideology." *Annual Review of Anthropology* 23: 55–82.

World Bank. 2013. "Maintaining Momentum on Educational Reform in Morocco." September 11. Accessed January 22, 2015. http://www.worldbank.org/en/news/feature /2013/09/11/maintaining-momentum-on-education-reform-in-morocco

Wyrtzen, Jonathan. 2011. "Colonial State-Building and the Negotiation of Arab and Berber Identity in Protectorate Morocco." *International Journal of Middle East Studies* 43 (2): 227–249.

Yacine, Kateb. 1959. *Nedjma*. Paris: Seuil.

Zeghal, Malika. 1999. "Religion and Politics in Egypt: The ʿUlamaʾ of al-Azhar, Radical Islam, and the State 1952–94." *International Journal of Middle East Studies* 31(3): 371–399.

Zejly, Btissame, and Samir Achehbar. 2014. *"France: un ami qui nous veut du bien?"* [A Friend Who Wishes You Well?] *Tel Quel*, June 22. Accessed July 16, 2014. http://telquel .ma/2014/06/22/france-ami-veut-du-bien_139855

Zeldin, Theodore, ed. 1970. *Conflicts in French Society: Anticlericalism, Education and Morals in the Nineteenth Century*. London: Allen and Unwin.

Zougarri, Ahmed. 2006. *"Le système d'enseignement sous le protectorat Français et Espagnol"* [The Educational System under the French and Spanish Protectorates]. In *50 Ans de Développement Humain & Perspectives 2025*. Morocco: Haut Commissariat au Plan.

TEXTBOOKS

* The following student textbooks for the Baccalaureate cycle were in use in public high schools during the period 2007–2009. They were all approved by the *Wizārat al-tarbiya al-waṭaniyya wa-l taʿlīm al-ʿalī wa-l-takwīn al-aṭār wa-l-baḥth al-ʿilmī, qiṭaʿ al-tarbiya al-waṭaniyya* [Ministry of National Education, Higher Education, the Training of Executives, and Scientific Research, Section for National Education].

al-Arar, Mohammed, and Mohamed Sakhi. 2007/2008. *Parcours de traduction* [Course of Translation]. *2ème année du cycle du baccalauréat. Sciences Expérimentales et Sciences Mathématiques* [Second Year of the Baccalaureate Cycle. Experimental and Mathematical Sciences Tracks]. Rabat: al-massar.

Dekkan, Ahmed et al. 2006. *Manuel de traduction* [Translation Manual]. *1ère année du cycle du baccalauréat. Sciences Expérimentales et Sciences Mathématiques.* [First Year of the Baccalaureate Cycle. Experimental and Mathematical Sciences Tracks]. Rabat: Librairie al-maarif.

Hamoud, Mohamed et al. 2007. *Al-lugha al-ʿarabiyya* [The Arabic Language]. *Al-sana al-thāniyya min silk al-bakālūryā. Masālik al-ʿUlūm al-Tajrībiyya, al-ʿUlūm al-Riāḍiyya* [Second Year of the Baccalaureate Cycle. Experimental and Mathematical Sciences Tracks]. Casablanca: Top Edition.

Wahabi, Mohamed et al. 2007. *Al-mumtāz fi-l-lugha al-ʿarabiyya* [Excellence in the Arabic Language]. *Al-sana al-thāniyya min silk al-bakālūryā. Masālik al-Adab wa-l-ʿUlūm al-insāniyya* [Second Year of the Baccalaureate Cycle. Literature and Humanities Tracks]. Casablanca: Maktabat al-umma li-l-nashr w-l-tawziyaʿ.

Sibawi, Abdel Nasser. 2010. *al-Tarbiya al-islāmiyya* [Islamic Education]. *Al-sana al-ūla min silk al-bakālūryā*. [First Year of the Baccalaureate Cycle]. Casablanca: Top Edition.

Sibawi, Abdel Nasser et al. 2010. *al-Tarbiya al-islāmiyya* [Islamic Education]. *Al-sana al-thāniyya min silk al-bakālūryā* [Second Year of the Baccalaureate Cycle]. Casablanca: Top Edition.

INDEX

CHARIS BOUTIERI

is Assistant Professor in the Social Anthropology of the Middle East at King's College London.